This book is due on the last date stamped below.
Failure to return books on the date due may
result in assessment of overdue fees.

NATIVE AMERICANS

IN THE TWENTIETH CENTURY

James S. Olson and Raymond Wilson

University of Illinois Press

Urbana and Chicago

To Judy Olson and Sharon Wilson

Contents

Preface

Throughout the course of United States history, few issues of public policy have been as complex, controversial, intractable, or painful as the status of Native Americans in the larger society of descendants of European settlers. From the moment the first colonists from Europe confronted members of the Powhatan Confederacy in the seventeenth century, ignorance and ethnic rivalry clouded the perceptions of both peoples, crippling most attempts at understanding and accommodation. Caught between the greed of land developers, the misguided paternalism of "reformers," and their own tribal loyalties and intertribal competitions, Native Americans have had an especially difficult time in protecting their resources and cultural values. Even today, after more than 370 years of dealing with the problem, Americans are no closer than ever to working out the questions of poverty, discrimination, sovereignty, and cultural survival. Our only hope for the future is understanding and knowledge, a shared appreciation for the several cultures involved, and a willingness on the part of Native Americans and non–Native Americans to accept the reality of ethnic pluralism.

From experience gained from teaching courses in Native American history and American ethnic history for several years, we have come to the realization that problems of Native Americans in the twentieth century have generally been slighted. Most historians, when writing Native American history, devote the bulk of their time to pre-twentieth-century themes, usually ignoring or giving only cursory attention to Native Americans after 1900. In his book *God Is Red,* Vine Deloria, Jr., has stated:

For generations it has been traditional that all historical literature on Indians be a recital of tribal histories from the pre-Discovery culture through the first encounter with the white man to about the year 1890. At that point the tribe seems to fade gently into history, with its famous war chief riding down the canyon into the sunset.*

---

*Vine Deloria, Jr., *God Is Red* (New York: Grosset and Dunlap, 1973), 41.

In *Native Americans in the Twentieth Century,* we provide a history of Native Americans since that mythical chief rode down into the sunset.

Like Gerald D. Nash's *The American West in the Twentieth Century: A Short History of an Urban Oasis,* ours is a "little book about a big subject."* We have not attempted to include all the detail of a subject of such scope in one volume. Rather, we offer a synthesis of what in our opinion are the most significant elements of Native American history designed for the general reader and for undergraduate students taking courses in Native American studies. In this regard, since it is impossible to discuss Native American history without understanding the pre-1900 period, we first address the nature of tribal ethnicity and government policies as far back as the 1880s, as political and bureaucratic pressures beginning at that time exerted themselves well into this century.

Native Americans in the twentieth century are no longer a "vanishing race" or a silent minority. They have survived centuries of cultural genocide inflicted on them by non–Native Americans—both the well-meaning and the self-seeking—and their values remain intact today. Indeed, the recognition of being "Indian" is stronger than ever, and non–Native America is increasingly coming to realize the valuable contributions that Native Americans have made and are making to American culture. Here, we hope, is a readable text surveying Native American affairs in the twentieth century—one that shows how this group of people has resisted the destruction of traditional ways by a technologically superior culture but that also demonstrates how complex the future will be as Native Americans try to maintain their cultural independence and achieve new forms of political sovereignty.

This book is based on the research and writings of many scholars. Readers desiring more information on a particular subject are encouraged to consult the suggested readings after each chapter. Special acknowledgment is given to the works of Vine Deloria, Jr., Margaret Connell Szasz, Lawrence C. Kelly, Kenneth R. Philp, Graham D. Taylor, Angie Debo, Arrell Morgan Gibson, and Alvin M. Josephy, Jr.

We are grateful for and hereby acknowledge the financial support of the American Philosophical Society for research on this book.

Finally, we are aware that there is disagreement regarding what to call the native peoples of the United States. We have chosen to use Native Americans because it represents to us, and we hope to others, that they were the first to inhabit this land. We wish no disrespect to those who find the term offensive.

---

*Gerald D. Nash, *The American West in the Twentieth Century: A Short History of an Urban Oasis* (1973; reprint, Albuquerque: University of New Mexico Press, 1977), ix.

Chapter One

The World
of Native Americans

In September of 1953, several of us left our second-grade class for morning recess and discovered a strange commotion out on the playground. Children were milling about in small groups, buzzing with excitement about the "Indian"—a real Indian—who was going to our school—Hollydale Elementary in South Gate, California. Jerry Pete was a Navajo, and as he rocked back and forth on the playground swing he seemed a bit surprised about and perhaps suspicious of all the attention. I still remember thinking as I watched him that he was rather ordinary for a real Indian; he was not doing anything spectacular, at least not compared to television images of screaming warriors killing innocent pioneers. Jerry Pete rode my bus home that afternoon, disembarked at my stop, and ran into the neighbor's house. A real Indian was living next door, right in the middle of a white working-class suburb.

Our neighbors were Mormons who, through a church program, had entered into an arrangement with Jerry's parents whereby he would spend the school year with that family in California and return each summer to his home on the Navajo Reservation in Arizona. Jerry Pete, a Navajo, and I, a grandson of Norwegian and Swedish immigrants, became fast friends. We played baseball, basketball, flag football, Monopoly, crazy-eights, and over-the-line together; went to cub scouts and boy scouts; watched situation comedies and game shows on hot summer afternoons; and rode our bicycles through the streets and paved riverbeds of south Los Angeles. During two summers I was a guest in his home in Arizona. We swam in the Colorado River, slept at night in an old hogan, hunted rabbits and snakes, and wandered daily through the Navajo community. Once I watched in total fascination as an old man worked on an elaborate sand painting. On graduation night Jerry and I went to the all-night party in the high school gymnasium and then went to Laguna Beach to bodysurf at the "wedge." The next afternoon, Jerry Pete packed his bags and returned to the reservation. He still lives there.

His decision to trade life in the city suburbs for what I considered the quaint but abject poverty of an Arizona reservation shocked me terribly—perhaps even angered me, as if in some way he had passed

judgment on my way of life. What had happened? Had he encountered some discrimination? Had someone been thoughtless or ugly?
Perhaps the Mormon family had tired of him? But none of these was
true. I insisted on looking for what had "pushed" Jerry back to the
reservation, some visible crisis driving or expelling him from the prosperity of my world. Years later, as I came to appreciate Native
American history, I realized that Jerry had been pulled, not pushed.
Celsa Apapas, a Cupeño woman from California, eloquently described her feelings in 1965:

You asked us to think what place we like next best to this place, where we
always lived. You see that graveyard out there? There are our fathers and our
grandfathers. You see that Eagle-nest Mountain and that Rabbit-hole
Mountain? When God made them, He gave us this place. We have always
been here. We do not care for any other place. . . . If you give us the best place
in the world, it is not so good for us as this. This is our home. . . . If we cannot
live here, we want to go into the mountain and die. We do not want any other
home.*

With hindsight, I remembered that Jerry Pete had always seemed a
little shy around European Americans. He was rarely excited about
our ambitions and curiously quiet about his own—as much an observ-
er of my childhood as he was a participant. On the reservation, around
his own people, Jerry was always more relaxed and animated, as if invisible restraints on his feelings had disappeared. And on the reservation, despite gracious hospitality, I often felt like an outsider—a so-
journer—which is exactly what I was. Despite ten years of
companionship, I never really made the cultural jump from my world
to his. A barrier existed between the two societies, and neither one of
us was ever able to cross it, despite the innocence of boyhood friendship. It was not a question of either self-righteousness or self-
consciousness, but simply a set of different expectations buried deep in
our psyches. In this sense, I was symbolic of American history, for most
European Americans never crossed that cultural barrier either; rather,
they spent hundreds of years viewing Native American society from a
very distorted perspective. Ever since 1607, when the English colonists
first settled along the James River in Virginia, a profound veil divided
the two peoples; and more than three centuries later, after countless
contacts and confrontations, the veil is still intact, still preventing
much understanding.

In the 1960s and 1970s curiosity about Native Americans increased
dramatically, becoming almost a fascination born of guilt about the
past and a nostalgia for earlier times. Bestselling books such as Vine

---

*Quoted in Shirley Hill Witt and Stan Steiner, eds., *The Way: An Anthology
of American Indian Literature* (New York: Alfred A. Knopf, 1972), 60.

Deloria's *Custer Died for Your Sins,* Dee Brown's *Bury My Heart at Wounded Knee,* and Ruth Beebe Hill's *Hanta Yo,* and movies such as *Little Big Man* and *A Man Called Horse* symbolized the growing interest, as did the increased popularity of such Native American writers as N. Scott Momaday, Simon Ortiz, and James Welch. For the first time people were beginning to discard a few of their traditional stereotypes, and they were just beginning to sense the distinctiveness of Native American culture—its holistic independence from the assumptions of Western civilization. Jerry Pete, of course, along with hundreds of thousands of other Native Americans, had realized this all along; but it has taken all of United States history for non–Native Americans even to approach the same idea. In the process, Native Americans have suffered.

A recent television commercial illustrates not only a Native American vision of contemporary America but the consuming interest Americans of European descent have in Native American values today. Produced by the Advertising Council, the commercial pictures Iron Eyes Cody, a lone and proud Native American astride a horse, looking out over a freeway somewhere in the United States. Cody is painfully reviewing the blacktop, traffic jams, heat, noise, litter, pollution, blinking lights, crowding, and mounting frustration—the more debilitating consequences of a modern technological society. In the closing scene, the camera pans back and focuses on Cody again, particularly on the tear he is shedding for the condition of his country. Native Americans had developed a special relationship with their environment. They believed in the kinship of all living things and practiced a form of reciprocity with nature, giving something back for something taken. But only four centuries of European civilization seemingly had changed the country forever. The traditional faith in "Manifest Destiny," with its emphasis on expansion, progress, unbridled growth, as well as racial superiority, had a new generation of critics in the 1960s and 1970s. As modern society began to choke on its own materialism, and as Americans suffered through inflation, unemployment, pollution, and chronic energy shortages, the world of Native Americans suddenly took on a new meaning; to some it even became an appealing alternative to the endless series of crises. Perhaps the Native Americans had been right all along in their approach to life, death, and change. Even then, of course, most non–Native Americans had no appreciation for the structure and complexity of Native American values; but they did, for the first time, realize that Native Americans were indeed different (but not necessarily different in the sense of being inferior), that their vision of living and dying was not at all like that of Europeans, and (perhaps most important) that they were not likely to change easily or quickly.

When Columbus waded through the surf at San Salvador on October 12, 1492, he looked upon the natives with curious delight, a euphoria based on relief and a sense of fulfillment after a long and sometimes difficult voyage. Convinced that he had reached the East Indies, that he was close to Japan and China, Columbus named the natives Indians, a historical misnomer born of geographical ignorance which stuck. Years later, as Europeans came to realize that they had not reached Asia but had accidentally discovered a "new world," they began to wonder about the "Indians." If not Asians, then who were these strange people? And where did they come from? Few other questions so obsessed European explorers or intrigued generations of American folklorists. Some Europeans argued that the "Indians" were long-lost descendants of ancient Celtic, Nordic, Phoenician, Carthaginian, or Chinese travelers, while others believed them to be a remnant of the ten tribes of Israel or of the mysterious city of Atlantis. Millions of Mormons believe that Native Americans are descendants of three separate migrations from the Middle East between 2000 and 400 B.C. Some people have even held to an independent creation idea—that is, that God engaged in co-creations of man in the Old World and in the New World. Among scholars, the consensus is that most Native Americans migrated to the New World from Siberia during the last two ice ages.

There was a time, almost forty thousand years ago, when the New World really was a vast island, empty of human beings and completely isolated from Europe and Asia. Exchanges of plants and animals had not occurred since before the great continental drifts. But then, slowly and almost imperceptibly, the native migrations commenced. As strange as it seems, these journeys of prehistoric people were unplanned and unconscious, not at all like the usual movement of immigrants. The wandering hunters never decided, once and for all, to leave for America, nor did they ever understand the significance of their migration—that they had traveled to a new continent. Indeed, the migrations were generational and not individual; only over the course of hundreds of generations and thousands of years can they be considered as migrations at all. Of the nomadic hunters leaving Siberia on the trail of bison, musk ox, mammoth, moose, and caribou, no single individual, family, or even group ever completed the entire journey; the immigrants were ignorant of their own migration.

According to most New World archaeologists and anthropologists, the first Americans left Siberia sometime between forty and twenty-five thousand years ago. Sometime around 40,000 B.C., the onset of an ice age depressed general temperature levels around the world. Huge glaciers gradually covered all of Canada and the northern United States, freezing up millions of cubic miles of ocean water. The sea level dropped hundreds of feet as ocean water was absorbed into glacial ice, and the continental shelves around the world surfaced. Land masses became much more extensive. The shallow Bering Sea, North Pacific Ocean, and Arctic Ocean floors appeared, and a land bridge, known now as Beringia, connected Siberia with Alaska. The stage was set for the journey of the Siberian hunters.

At an evolutionary pace, vegetation slowly rooted and thrived in Beringia; and as the big game headed east from Siberia, small game such as foxes and woodchucks headed west from Alaska. Each season the temporary villages of Siberian families and tribes moved farther east in the eternal quest for big game until, after thousands of years, the Asians had reached Alaska. And as thousands more years passed, the hunters slowly moved down through the Yukon and Mackenzie river valleys and the slopes of the Rocky Mountains. Around 13,000 B.C. the Ice Age ended, the great glaciers slowly melted back into the oceans, and Beringia submerged again under three hundred feet of water. Unknowingly, the Siberians had now become Americans.

For the next fifteen thousand years the Native American hunters settled throughout the New World, from the Arctic in North America to Tierra del Fuego in South America and from the Atlantic to the Pacific. The diaspora across the two New World continents was another unplanned journey of extended families splitting off from one another every generation. The passage of time and the need to adjust to new environment resulted in a kaleidoscope of cultures in America. When the European explorers first arrived in the 1490s, those wandering bands of Siberian hunters had become hundreds of separate ethnic groups, as independent from one another as they were distinct from the European invaders to come.

But Europeans were blind to that diversity and insisted on viewing Native American culture through a single lens, as if all Native Americans could somehow be understood in terms of a few monolithic assumptions. Social life in colonial and frontier America was terribly complex—a cauldron of competing racial, religious, and linguistic groups—and settlers saw Native Americans as just one more group among many. The Europeans should have known better. They were divided too—Sephardic, German, and Ashkenazi Jews; Baptist, Methodist, Congregational, Presbyterian, Pietistic, Lutheran, and Reformed Protestants; Roman and Uniate Catholics; Russian, Greek, Bulgarian, Syrian, Armenian, and Rumanian Orthodox; and Anglo-Saxon, German, Scandinavian, Magyar, Italian, Celtic, and Slavic ethnics. It is an irony that probably *because* of their own diversity, Europeans were unable to see Native Americans as anything more than a single group. Unlike black Africans, who came from diverse tribal backgrounds but were forced into a single, highly integrated African American slave culture, Native Americans were divided tribally by economic organization, language, religion, and political loyalty.

As the earliest hunters spread across the two continents, they adapted their lives to the land. Whether the environment included arctic
ice, frozen tundra, mountains, oceans, forests, deserts, or jungles, they
were remarkably successful in adjusting to it. A subsistence people in a
rich and varied land, they developed hundreds of separate economic
styles and technologies, and economic life became uniquely important
to tribal identities. At first, they were big-game hunters, and until perhaps 9000 B.C. they organized life around the bison, caribou, mammoth, moose, or musk ox. Long before agriculture developed or foraging became important, they spent the spring and summer killing the
game, drying the meat, and making clothes and stone tools. Then,
during the late fall and winter, they retreated into protective valleys to
wait out the harsh northern cold. For thousands of years this remained
the predominant life-style.

Many Native Americans were still living as big-game hunters when
the Europeans arrived and even centuries later. Along the edges of the
Arctic Ocean and in the northern tundra, Eskimo hunters went after
whales, walruses, sea lions, seals, and polar bears. Living in igloo ice
houses, venturing out on the ocean in umiak canoes, or hunting in the
tundra with ivory goggles and harpoons, they adapted successfully to
one of the world's most inhospitable regions. Farther south, the Chip-
ewyans followed the caribou. Caribou meat and fat fed them, caribou
skins clothed and housed them, and caribou bones provided their tools.
On the Great Plains, tribes such as the Comanches, Arapahos, Cheyennes,
and Sioux hunted the buffalo. Always on the move with portable tipis
and horses, the Plains tribes pursued the buffalo with a passion. The
buffalo served them as the caribou served the Chipewyan: buffalo meat,
fat, skin, and bones supplied their material world. From the buffalo
carcass they took fresh meat and dried the rest into jerky. Buffalo skins
gave them their blankets, moccasins, clothes, and covering for their
tipi homes. Buffalo hair and tendons became thread and strings for
their bows. Buffalo horns were used as cups and spoons, and they even
turned buffalo tongues into hairbrushes and buffalo fat into hair oil.
The buffalo hunt was central to the tribal identity.

As most Native Americans scattered out over the continent and
learned more about the nature of their surroundings, they began to
rely less on big game and more on a wider variety of exploitable resources. Wood, ground stone, and chipped stone provided axes, drills,
scrapers, spears, fishhooks, and harpoons. When the Great Lakes tribes
invented the lightweight birchbark canoe, which was ideal for navi-
gating shallow streams and easy portaging, their range and mobility
increased enormously. For some tribes the end of the big-game hunts
relieved them of their nomadism; they could establish semipermanent
villages as long as the supply of fish, small animals, and plants held
out. When, after a while, these resources became more scarce, tribes

simply relocated their villages. The big-game hunters had always re-
lied to an extent on plants and small animals, primarily as dietary
supplements; but by 4000 B.C. most Native Americans (the Plains
tribes being the major exception) had completed the transition to a
new economy in which foraging for small game, fish, and plants filled
all material needs.

There was a great deal of variety to the foraging economies. Coastal
tribes in California, like the Costanoans south of San Francisco, lived
off sea snails, shrimp, mussels, oysters, crabs, and abalone. Because of
the abundant oak trees, many California tribes used the acorn as a
dietary staple. They gathered, shelled, and pounded the acorns into
flour and were able to store grain surpluses for long periods of time. To
collect and carry the acorns and flour, they developed elaborate techniques of basketmaking. Along the Northwest Coast, from Oregon
through British Columbia, the richest foraging economies appeared.
Forests abounded in bear, deer, elk, and moose, while the mountains
were full of mountain sheep and goats. The sea delivered whales, dol-
phins, seals, salmon, halibut, sturgeon, smelt, and grunion, as well as
crabs, oysters, and clams, to the Yurok, Coo, Umpqua, Chinook,
Chehalis, and Makah tribes. And other tribes such as the Klamaths,
Cayuse, Yakimas, and Walla Wallas occupied the major rivers and
streams in the spring and summer, organizing economic life around
the giant salmon, returned from the sea, which they speared, hooked,
netted, or trapped and then dried for the future. In the Great Basin—
the arid, hot, and economically austere deserts of Nevada, Utah, and
eastern California—such tribes as the Utes, Paiutes, Paviotsos, and
Shoshones lived a marginal existence, perpetually hunting for rabbits,
snakes, insects, roots, berries, seeds, nuts, and green leaves. Starvation
was often close at hand, although these people developed a splendid
desert lore. And throughout the upper Midwest, Native Americans
traveled in their canoes along the rivers and streams, catching lake
trout, pike, and pickerel and hunting small game. For all these various
tribes, the foraging process created a distinct form of economic life
which shaped their outlook on the world.

Finally, beginning more than five thousand years ago, many Native
Americans, especially the tribes east of the Mississippi River and in
the southwestern deserts, made the transition to agriculture. It was a
small move at first: simply a collective discovery at different times and
in different places of how to plant and harvest the wild beans, squash,
and corn they had been gathering for thousands of years. The tribes
still hunted and foraged for food, but at least part of their nutritional
needs were now filled by farming. Gradually, over the course of hundreds of years, farming techniques grew more sophisticated as the
Native Americans discovered the best times to plant and harvest, how
to rotate crops, how to fertilize the land with animal wastes or dead

fish, and how to irrigate the land. When they learned how to preserve crops through the winter and spring, they were able to settle into permanent villages and then cities, and farming became the basis of their entire economy. Hunting and foraging became purely supplementary in importance, providing additions to their diet rather than the foundation.

Beans, squash, and corn became staple crops for all Native American agricultural societies, but the conditions for farming varied according to region. Among the early Hohokam people of southern Arizona, where rainfall was limited and often confined to summer thunderstorms, irrigation was essential. They constructed small dams and ditches to trap rainfall or tilled their gardens on hillsides where the runoff from melting snow would water the plants. Later tribes adopted and further developed Hohokam techniques for irrigating crops. The Havasupais, whose home was the Grand Canyon in northwestern Arizona, constructed large irrigation ditches to water their fields. On the Gila and Salt rivers in Arizona, the Pimas built elaborate canal systems to trap flood water for irrigating their plants. In the Eastern Woodlands, because of the discovery of agriculture, the now-famous Moundbuilder societies appeared more than a thousand years ago. Native Americans there lived in cities with substantial, permanent housing, religious temples, community centers, communal fields, and unique burial grounds. Later, such northeastern tribes as the Mohawks, Senecas, Menominees, and Sacs and Foxes lived in settled agricultural villages, cultivating corn, beans, and squash in communal gardens. Their wigwams or bark houses were separated by streets and surrounded by protective stockades. In the Southeast, the Five Civilized Tribes (Cherokees, Choctaws, Chickasaws, Creeks, and Seminoles) lived in similarly well-developed farming villages. Their way of life was completely different from the wandering nomadism of the big-game hunters. Perhaps the most striking example of the early agricultural society is that of the several Pueblo tribes, whose unique multistory rock-and-stucco villages are still in use after as long as a thousand years.

Today, the values associated with work, education, status, and class create powerful group identities; out of those identities, as well as self-perceptions based on language, national origins, race, and religion, emerges ethnicity. A steelworker living in a working-class suburb in Youngstown, Ohio, identifies closely with other blue-collar workers rather than with a wealthy physician living in a well-to-do suburb of Long Island, New York. Or a wheat farmer in the Texas Panhandle would likely feel more comfortable with other farmers than with a group of Greenwich Village artists. Economic identities were similarly important to Native Americans. With such vast differences between the hunting, fishing, and farming economies, as well as between the different technologies of different regions, it is no wonder that economic organization became an important part of Native American ethnicity. Identity is closely related to the way people feed and clothe themselves, so ethnic loyalties naturally cluster around those feelings.

But technology and economic organization are only part of ethnicity. Indeed, compared to Native American linguistic differences, the varieties of tribal economic life seem relatively minor, at least as far as ethnicity is concerned. Because the New World was settled by several waves of migrating people who spread across two enormous land-masses over the course of perhaps four hundred centuries, linguistic development was amazingly diverse, a "Tower of Babel" in its own right. When two tribal languages were completely different, mutually unintelligible to one another, it is clear that the two tribal groups were totally unrelated or related only in the very distant past. And, of course, when two tribes spoke similar languages, their common histories in the Americas were more recent and their origins in time and space more common.

European languages are classified into such major groups as Romance, Germanic, Slavic, and Uralo-Altaic, and each of these groups is then subdivided into specific languages. The Romance languages, for example, consist of Spanish, Portuguese, French, Italian, Latin, and Rumanian, while Russian, Czech, Polish, Slovakian, Serbo-Croatian, Slovenian, Bulgarian, Rusin, and Ukrainian are Slavic languages. Individual languages, then, can be subdivided again into dialects, remnants of different origins. Although most people in the United States speak English, there are immediately recognizable differences between a southern "drawl," a New England "brogue," or "Brooklynese." Ethnic loyalties group around languages as well as dialects. Native American languages were similarly diverse and complex, and tribal identities were closely related to them.

Although historians, anthropologists, and linguists are still debating the structure of Native American languages, many now agree that there were thirteen major native language groups in what is now the United States: Eskimo-Aleut, Na-Dene, Algonquian-Ritwan-Kutenai, Iroquois-Caddoan, Gulf, Siouan-Yuchi, Utaztecan-Tanoan, Mosan, Penutian, Yukian, Hokaltecan, Keres, and Zuñi. Except for the Yukian and Zuñi groups, each of these can be divided into many different languages. Yukian is one language and one language group spoken only by the Yuki tribe of California, as is the Zuñi group, spoken by the Zuñis of the Southwest. But the Iroquois-Caddoan group, on the other hand, is divided into the Iroquois group of languages and the Caddoan group. The Iroquois group consists of the Erie, Huron, Iroquois, Neutral, Susquehannock, and Tionontati languages, spoken by the northeastern tribes, and the Cherokee, Nottoway, and Tuscarora languages in the Carolinas. Caddo, Kichai, Tawakoni,

Waco, and Wichita are Caddo languages spoken on the southeastern plains, as are the Arikara and Pawnee languages on the eastern plains. The Algonquian-Ritwan-Kutenai language group was even more complex, indicating the vast tribal migrations that had once occurred in North America. The Algonquian group consisted of the Cree, Montagnais, and Naskapi languages in the subarctic regions of North America; the Abnaki, Chickahominy, Delaware, Lumbee, Malecite, Massachuset, Mattapony, Micmac, Mohegan, Nanticoke, Narraganset, Nipmuc, Pamlico, Pamunkey, Pennacook, Passamaquoddy, Penobscot, Pequot, Powhatan, Shawnee, Wampanoag, and Wappinger languages in the Eastern Woodlands; the Illinois, Kickapoo, Menominee, Miami, Ojibwa, Ottawa, Peoria, Potawatomi, Sac, and Fox languages in the Midwest; and the Arapaho, Atsina, Blackfoot, Cheyenne, and Plains Cree languages on the Great Plains. The related Ritwan group languages consisted of the Wiyot and Yurok languages in northern California, and the Kutenai group consisted of the Kutenai language in northern Montana and Idaho. At one time, thousands of years ago, all of these tribes were a closely related people, and only over the course of hundreds of generations did they scatter across the continent and develop into dozens of independent groups. In all there were more than two hundred separate languages spoken by the Native Americans of what is now the United States when the European settlers began arriving in the seventeenth century.

In many cases, these languages contained different dialects. The Santee, Teton, and Yankton Sioux all spoke slightly different versions of their language, and the Blood, Piegan, and Siksika Blackfeet spoke different versions of the Blackfoot language. All of this made for an enormous linguistic diversity. In a stretch of only three hundred miles along the Pacific Coast between northern California and Washington, dozens of languages were spoken, including Bella Coola, Chehalis, Coast Salish, Tillamook, Makah, Wiyot, Haida, Hupa, and Mattole, as well as several dialects of each. It was the same in southern Alaska, where Native Americans spoke nineteen versions of the Athapascan language. Sometimes small groups lived next to one another without being able to communicate except through interpreters or sign language. For example, the Tañoans and Keresans, who lived side by side in the Rio Grande Valley, could only communicate by sign language (and, later, Spanish). Although identity and dialect are close kin, if only because communication and problem resolution depend so directly on linguistic tools, language of the early migrants diversified to reach a state of bewildering variety in America, as complex as anywhere on earth.

Beyond economic organization and language, for most societies the marrow of ethnicity is religion, and Native American cultures were certainly no exception. But like the economies and the languages, Native American religions were hardly monolithic; instead, they were characterized by a rich variety of theological assumptions and ceremonial rituals. The theologies provided them with a common tribal perspective on the purpose of life and the operation of the cosmos, and the ceremonial rituals became forms of symbolic association in which members of the tribes expressed and acknowledged a common heritage and a common future. Out of common faiths and symbolic associations emerged the religious dimension of Native American ethnicity.

Still, there were some major religious characteristics common to many tribal groups. Most indigents of North America were polytheistic, believing in many gods and many levels of deity. At the basis of most Native American beliefs in the supernatural was a profound conviction that an invisible force, a powerful spirit, permeated the entire universe and ordered the cycles of birth and death for all living things. The Iroquois called this spirit the *Orenda,* the Algonquins *Manitu,* the Cayuse *Honeawoat,* the Ojibwa *Gitchimanidu,* and the Sioux *Wakan Tanka.* European Christians and Jews incorrectly tried to equate this "Great Spirit" with the God of their own religious views. But for Native Americans the *Orenda* or *Manitu* or *Wakan Tanka* or *Honeawoat* was more pantheistic—a fusion of matter, spirit, time, and life, a divine energy unifying all of the universe. It was not at all a personal being presiding omnipotently over the salvation or damnation of individual people.

Beyond this belief in a universal spirit, most Native Americans attached supernatural qualities to animals, heavenly bodies, the seasons, dead ancestors, the elements, and geologic formations. In short, their world was infused with the divine.

Common characteristics essentially ended there. Most other beliefs and practices were amazingly and colorfully diverse. The Pawnees, for example, believed that the wind, sun, and stars were all divine spirits but that they were ruled by an even higher god called *Tirawahat,* "The Expanse of the Heavens." Eskimo and Aleut tribes worshipped *Sedna,* the sea goddess who directed their hunts, as well as the "Mother of the Caribou" and the "Moon Man." The Pomos of California believed in the coyote god. Paiutes in the Great Basin had various plant spirits they tried to please, and the Yumans accepted predestination at face value. The Navajos had well-developed fears of witches dressed like wolves. Each tribe also had unique views of the creation and their own origins. The Cayuses in Oregon and Washington believed they sprang originally from the heart of a giant beaver trapped in the Palouse River. Tribal legend had the Kiowas emerging eons ago from a hollow cottonwood log at the command of a supernatural being, while the Navajos believed mankind slowly evolved from four underworlds beneath the surface of the earth. Or among the California Luiseños, "the people" came from two supernatural parents, floating in the sky, who united and created all the "thoughts" of what was to come in the world. So each Native American tribe possessed its own pantheon of deities and theologies.

The abundance of divinities, however, was nothing compared to the array of ceremonial rituals designed to propitiate them. In their ceremonialism Native Americans were even more diverse, and that diversity was linked directly to economic organization and population. Among the Native Americans of the northwestern plateau and the Great Basin, ceremonialism was limited, often being confined to simple individual rites. Among the Pueblos of the Southwest, on the other hand, where people lived settled, agrarian lives in urban concentrations, ceremonial rituals were far more elaborate, sometimes consuming more than a hundred days each year. Among many of the California tribes also ceremonialism was very elaborate because they had the time necessary for such devotions; food was plentiful and economic survival almost guaranteed. Hunting and foraging societies prayed for good hunts and abundant food supplies. The Tlingits performed salmon rites to guarantee the return of the salmon each year, while the Mandans on the Great Plains performed the Okipa ceremony to guarantee successful buffalo hunts. Farming societies, on the other hand, prayed for benign weather conditions to bring good harvests. The Pomos, for example, believed the Kuksu Dance would bring rain. The Iroquois tribes of New York had maple syrup, wild strawberry, corn, bean, and harvest ceremonies, and the Choctaws of the Southeast performed the Green Corn Dance.

Native American religious ceremonies also revolved around the relationship between the individual, the community, and the cosmos; mystical rituals were performed to reveal universal truth; sharpen individual understanding; and acknowledge birth, puberty, marriage, and death. The Yuroks of northern California had "World Renewal" ceremonies each year involving the Jumping Dance and the Deerskin Dance, both designed to preserve harmony in nature. In southern California, the Luiseños held the Toloache Ceremony every few years. Men would consume a narcotic drink from the Jimsonweed to induce visions of life and the world. It was also an initiation rite into manhood for young boys, who had to fast, take the narcotic, and endure several minutes lying on top of a red ant bed. The Pueblos performed curing and cleansing rituals, initiation into secret societies, and prayer vigils in underground kivas. Once a year, for example, the Hopis initiated young men and women into the Katcina Cult, symbolic of adulthood. On the Great Plains, Native Americans went on "vision quests" through dancing, prayer, fasting, and even self-mutilation to establish contact with the invisible power of the universe. Many tribes, such as the Arapahos and Cheyennes, sought their vision through the Sun Dance ceremony. Although the Sun Dance varied from tribe to tribe, it usually took place in the summer and lasted for seven days. Tribesmen erected a central pole, danced around it, and stared at it in trancelike concentration for hours on end. In some tribes, a young man would cut the skin of his chest, insert leather strips through the wounds, secure the strips to the pole, and then dance until the strips tore through his skin—all this acted as a measure of his sincerity and dedication. In the 1880s the Ghost Dance spread to the Great Plains; it was a "vision quest" too, in which the participants, wearing what they considered to be protective garments, danced in anticipation of the transformation of the earth, the disappearance of white people, and the return of all the dead buffalo and dead Native Americans. To all tribes, such rituals were of great importance; even the fierce Chiricahua Apaches, though in their last years of freedom perpetually at war with Mexicans and Americans alike, would risk death or capture to observe Ceremonials for the Maidens when one of the girls reached maturity. So throughout Native America, religious rituals were as much an ingredient of ethnic identity as language and economic organization, and they were diverse enough to divide Native Americans into hundreds of religious communities.

Finally, Native American culture in the United States involved complex forms of political authority and loyalty, some very parochial in scope and others quite broad and inclusive. Political organizations helped guarantee internal order and govern external relations; and even though some Native Americans might have shared economic organization and technology, language, and religion, they could still have been divided by conflicting political loyalties. In areas such as the Great Basin, where food was scarce and population dispersed, political loyalty often did not transcend small groups of extended families. The Paiutes wandered the Great Basin in small bands of perhaps one hundred people and met just once a year with other Paiute bands to hunt antelope and arrange marriages. For Paiutes, political loyalty did not extend beyond the band. Tribal authority, on the other hand, was more extensive and usually involved more people, often including many bands or clans. On the Great Plains, the Comanches and the Cheyennes hunted buffalo in bands, but governing warrior societies or councils had members from all the bands. Political loyalty here transcended the clan or band to include the entire tribe. And in a few instances, political loyalty even transcended the tribe. The Senecas, Cayugas, Onondagas, Oneidas, Mohawks, and, later, Tuscaroras were members of the Iroquois League, a political confederation formed to resolve disputes and promote peace between the tribes.

In addition to different levels of political loyalty, Native American society was characterized by different forms of political sovereignty, with the source of political power flowing from a number of individuals or groups. Most bands were quite egalitarian, with several heads of families making most decisions. Many small California tribes functioned without central leadership at all. Other Native American groups were quite the opposite. The Natchez of the Southeast were ruled by a powerful chief called the "Great Sun." In Virginia, Powhatan was the great leader of several tribes when the English colonists established Jamestown in 1607. Where political power was centralized, the tribal chief shared power with war chiefs and religious chiefs, shamans, and priests. The Cheyennes had a council of forty-four men who advised the chief, and the Iroquois League chiefs worked with a council of fifty other men. Political sovereignty was as diverse as political loyalty, varying from tribe to tribe and ranging from the nearly pure democracy of nomadic foraging bands to the centralized autocracy of the Natchez.

Before and many centuries after the arrival of Europeans, Native America was actually hundreds of Native Americas, a kaleidoscope of ethnic groups, each unique because of its combination of economic organization and technology, language, religion, and political values. It is almost impossible to describe with any meaningful accuracy this ethnic diversity. In California, for example, there were nearly three hundred separate tribes, each with a distinct identity. The Sioux on the Great Plains were actually from many different tribes. The Western Sioux were nomadic hunters and consisted of the Brulé, Hunkpapa, Two Kettles, Blackfeet Sioux, Sans Arcs, Miniconjou, and Oglala tribes. The Yankton and Yanktonai Sioux lived in eastern South Dakota, and the Santee Sioux of Minnesota consisted of the Sisseton, Wahpeton, Mdewakanton, and Wahpekute tribes. In the Southwest, the Apaches consisted of the Jicarillas of northeastern New Mexico, the Mescaleros of southern New Mexico, the Chiricahuas of southeastern Arizona, the Western Apaches of eastern Arizona, and the Lipans and Kiowa-Apaches of the Great Plains. And there were, for example, the River Crow and the Mountain Crow; the Northern Cheyenne and the Southern Cheyenne; the Siksika, Piegan, and Blood Blackfeet; the Northern Paiutes and the Southern Paiutes in the Great Basin; and in California the Pit River Achomawais and the Pit River Atsugewis. The list could go on and on, but the reality is quite clear: Native American society was neither monolithic nor highly integrated, contrary to what many non–Native Americans have believed. It was, instead, hundreds of ethnic groups, each characterized by a high degree of independence and cultural integrity as well as a highly developed sense of tribal loyalty.

Not surprisingly, it is difficult, even intellectually dangerous, to generalize about Native American culture. Few, if any, descriptions of "Native American values" apply to all North American tribal groups.

There was simply too much diversity. But in a number of ways, most Native American tribes interpreted life from a certain common perspective, employing a set of values sharply at odds with the assumptions of European civilization. When compared to one another, the tribes are highly diverse; but when all of them are compared to European society, a Native American culture becomes discernible— one that revolved around Native American visions of life, time, community, and the environment. Because most of these values contrasted sharply with European assumptions, nearly four hundred years of intense controversy between Americans of European extraction and Native Americans has resulted—a struggle which today is not at all ready to end.

During the fifteenth and sixteenth centuries in Europe, when religious faith and science were still closely fused, scholars neatly classified all of existence into a "great chain of being," a hierarchical order of life placing God and angels at the top, human beings just below the angels, and all other forms of life in a descending priority of importance, from the great apes to the tiniest insects. Poor people were not equal to rich people, nor were animals equal to any people at all; a divinely imposed hierarchy fixed the ranks of life according to natural, inflexible inequalities. The grace of God extended only to the higher forms of life: human beings and angels. To the European, humanity unquestionably represented the highest form of life, as humans were the only beings on earth possessing immortal souls with the prospects of eternal existence and thus the only forms of life deserving serious ethical consideration. And even then, some groups of people were more deserving of ethical consideration than others, particularly white Europeans when compared to the black and brown peoples in other parts of the world. God looked upon white people, they assumed, with special favor.

But while Europeans placed all things into this fixed, eternal hierarchy of categories, most Native Americans were just as certain that all of creation—animals, plants, insects, lakes, mountains, rivers, oceans, stars, the sun, the moon, and the wind—had souls of their own of some spiritual essence imparted from the source of all life. Man was not unique and transcendent but only part of a larger, eternal whole. The human place in the scheme of things had no special, predestined significance. Indeed, man was usually no better or worse than anything else; he was merely different, as all things were unique and different. Not only did all things have spirits which gave them life, but all spirit was basically of the same essence, different only in degree and not in kind; and through discipline, observation, and personal tranquility, individuals could learn from the world and make contact with the soul of the universe or any of its creations. There was no "great chain of being" relegating most forms of life to eternal insignificance.

For most Native Americans there was a unity to the universe which European society little appreciated.

For example, while Europeans respected animals only for their size and ferocity—bears, wolves, and mountain lions, for instance—Native Americans generally felt that every animal had a special gift which humans could cultivate by imitation. Vultures, though repulsive to Europeans, were admired by Native Americans for their keen sight and ability to live their entire lives without ever directly consuming water. Native Americans respected such a gift. Mountain lions, just before a kill, exhibited extraordinary stealth and patience, talents which people could use as well. Beavers were industrious, otters play-ful, salmon relentless, wolves cooperative, and dogs loyal. All living things were useful and necessary—for food, information, and worship. And all living things deserved respect and ethical consideration. Many tribes even required ceremonial apologies to game animals about to be killed—an expression of sorrow for terminating their stay on earth. Every form of life was equal in its divinely appointed sphere and fitted perfectly into the natural whole.

Because of this pantheism, most Native American tribes felt com-fortable with the environment, close to the moods and rhythms of na-ture, in tune with the living planet. Europeans were quite different, viewing the earth itself as lifeless and inorganic, subject to any kind of manipulation or alteration. Europeans tended to be alienated from nature and came to the New World to use the wilderness, to conquer and exploit its natural wealth for private gain. Theirs was an aggres-sive, acquisitive culture set on converting nature into money, proper-ty, and security. For most of them, the environment was not sacred and the earth had no transcendent meaning in itself. Even the Christian heaven, with its gold-paved streets and perpetual rest, was distant and otherworldly, as if for heaven to be heaven it had to be far away.

But for Native Americans, the environment was sacred, possessing a cosmic significance equal to its material riches. The earth was sacred— a haven for all forms of life—and it had to be protected, nourished, and even worshipped. For the Plains Indians, the cottonwood tree was spe-cial. Even the slightest breeze set the cottonwood branches and leaves in motion, so they felt that the cottonwood was especially close to the spirit of the universe, a barometer of the "Great Spirit." They burned logs from the cottonwood tree only in religious ceremonies. Because of their belief that the earth in spring was pregnant and ready to issue forth new life, the Taos of New Mexico removed hard shoes from their horses and walked about barefoot or in soft moccasins themselves, hesitant to disturb the "mother" of everything. Chief Smohalla of the Wanapun tribe illustrated Native American reverence for the earth when he said in 1885:

God said he was the father and earth was the mother of mankind; that nature was the law; that the animals, and fish, and plants obeyed nature, and that man only was sinful.

You ask me to plow the ground! Shall I take a knife and tear my mother's bosom? Then when I die she will not take me to her bosom to rest.

You ask me to dig for stone! Shall I dig under her skin for her bones? Then when I die I cannot enter her body to be born again.

You ask me to cut grass and make hay and sell it, and be rich like white men! But how dare I cut off my mother's hair?*

Many Native Americans had a compelling, religious loyalty to place—the space from which man and spirit flowed. For the Taos, Blue Lake in northwest New Mexico was an ancient holy place, a religious shrine, the source of life and a manifestation of the great spirit of the universe. Economically and spiritually, Blue Lake was the center of their lives. For the Shoshone in eastern California, Coso Hot Springs was a sacred place of healing and worship, a living well to which they talked, sang, and prayed. For the Sioux tribes, the Black Hills of South Dakota were sacred as the home of Wakan Tanka, the burial ground of the dead, and the place where "vision quests" took place. In their simple economies and reverence for land and space, Native Americans lived tens of thousands of years in a symbiotic relationship with the earth, using resources without exhausting them, prospering without destroying. Celsa Apapas, therefore, could have been speaking for Native Americans of many tribes throughout the land.

The Native Americans' approach to individual time, as well as their attachment to space, set them apart from Europeans, creating a cultural gap which four centuries have still not bridged. People of European background viewed time in linear terms as a consecutive, sequential commodity against which the individual measured a life. "Life" for them was inextricably linked to "time," a series of goals between birth and death—childhood, adolescence, young adulthood, middle age, and old age as well as schooling, career, and retirement. All these were "passages," different stages of "times" of life people experienced before death. Death too, then, was linked with time. Early death seemed especially tragic to them because of what the deceased had *not* been able to achieve and what "passages" of life had been missed. Time was precious and fleeting, something not to be wasted—like health and money. Time was a commodity, an economic good for sale or rent; most of European society was dedicated to its full employment.

Except in their sense of childhood, most Native Americans had little sense of such "passages." Adulthood itself implied fulfillment, and

---

Fourteenth Annual Report of the Bureau of American Ethnology (Washington, D.C.: U.S. Government Printing Office, 1896), Part 2, 720–21.

there was no feeling of wasting life, of not having done or experienced enough, of having dissipated time. Nor did they think of "having their whole lives ahead of them." The past and the future, for individuals at least, were vague concepts, and Native Americans usually functioned in what might more properly be called an "expanded present." In the Hopi language there was no word for "time," no vehicle for expressing a concept the Hopis did not possess. Time was not a commodity occurring between two fixed points, not a tangible product that could be measured and manipulated. Above all else, time was intangible, a natural process in which all living things fulfilled the promise of their creation—the stages of the moon, the rising and setting of the sun, the seasons of the year, the blooming and withering of flowers, the greening and browning of grasses, the hibernation of bears, the hatching of doves, and the births and deaths of people. Theirs was a life without clocks, deadlines, or rigid schedules. Time was not an enemy.

The individual relationship to the community among Native Americans was just as unique as their view of the cosmos and time, at least when compared to European values. Ever since the Reformation, English intellectuals and philosophers had separated individuals from society, lifting them out of a community context. The more traditional, corporate assumption that individual goals were subordinate to community needs—the collective view of the medieval world—was replaced by a competitive individualism, the view that community needs were best served by the aggressive assertion of individual self-interest. Only in individual, worldly success, the Puritans claimed, could people assure themselves of divine approbation; and success was interpreted as the accumulation of material wealth, especially when compared to the wealth of friends and peers. The almighty God, in other words, revealed his will through the successes and failures of individual people. Europeans were capitalists, and the true measure of a person—temporal as well as spiritual—was economic, a function of monetary status.

In a way, most Native Americans maintained a corporate view of society, even though the intricacies of that perspective made it quite different from the concept in European medieval thought. Native Americans managed, at once, to encourage individuality without worshipping individualism. Many tribes tried to avoid competitive, self-centered attitudes in children. With little or no sense of time in individual terms, parents did not pressure children into weaning, bowel or bladder control, walking, or talking before they were ready. Society offered no particular status or reward for such early childhood development, and trying to hasten it along would have been considered as ludicrous as making an egg hatch or a flower blossom early. Parents were rather permissive, content to let children learn and grow at a natural, individual pace. The ultimate values to be given children were self-confidence, tranquility, and emotional security, not a compulsive need to be materially richer than the neighbors. Most tribal cultures also encouraged people to seek an individual accommodation with the universe, a personal bond of trust with the earth and all living things. Individuality—not necessarily individual success—was the measure of social status in Native America.

The result was a culture which venerated individuality while nurturing community needs. Native Americans expected human society to function harmoniously, just as nature did; and even though occasional shocks might upset the natural balance, stability would always return. Even nature rebelled into tornadoes, hurricanes, earthquakes, floods, and droughts, only to revert quickly to its usual predictability. While the European settlers needed lawyers to resolve disputes in court, Native Americans expected earlier settlement of disputes, long before they disrupted tribal harmony. A complex web of intellectual, economic, and social networks bound individuals into a morally integrated society, one which venerated community and group survival.

Intellectually, Native Americans were carefully bound into communities by history as well as by the oral traditions conveying the past to each new generation. If Native Americans possessed only vague notions of time in individual terms, they were more conscious of historical time, at least as it affected their own community. Major events of the past—a tribal move to new territory, a natural disaster, a military defeat or victory—were all remembered; it was the practice of passing on these and other traditions to young people through oral history which sustained Native American communalism. In the written world of Europeans, where knowledge was visual through the printed page, the individual could independently acquaint himself with the community in the solitude of a library. Indeed, learning could be a solitary experience, simply absorbing knowledge from inanimate books. But in nonliterate societies, history and its conveyance were of necessity a community experience in which the storyteller created mental images or "pictures" of the past, intelligible to all, and passed them on to members of the tribe during ceremonial rituals. Generation after generation, the same "pictures" were handed down with remarkable consistency to young people, each time explaining the origins and history of the tribe. To begin their tribal history, for example, many of the Sioux went back to the beginning of time when Wakan Tanka was walking through the Black Hills of South Dakota. Surveying the fruits of his creations, he was pleased. He gloried in the gifts he had given to the animals: strength to the bear, swiftness to the hawk, grace to the deer, perseverance to the turtle, and majesty to the eagle. He had but one more gift to impart, and that was love; so Wakan Tanka joined with the Earth Mother and created the first man, right there in the Black Hills. This story was the very fabric of Sioux life. In the visual, literate world of the Europeans, where authors and publishers printed words and distributed books, people interpreted them on their own, according to their own prejudices, and there was rarely agreement on the meaning or significance of history. But in the oral traditions of such Native American societies as the Sioux, where group interaction with the storyteller occurred constantly and where individuals were forced to interpret the storyteller's message immediately and in the presence of the group, history became a community constant, a source of unanimity, security, and agreement. Unlike Europeans, the Sioux and many other Native Americans enjoyed a communality of knowledge binding the tribes into tightly knit groups.

Native American economic life in most instances served to melt individual interests into those of the larger community. Despite vast differences in organization and technology, Native American economic life operated on a subsistence level, with most people engaged directly in the pursuit of food, whether hunting, foraging, or farming. Until the Industrial Revolution and the commercialization of agriculture, the peasant and small farming economies of Europe and America had been much the same. But by 1800 more and more people were able to live off the agricultural production of relatively few, and each year tens of thousands of people were released for industrial or service occupations. It is not coincidental that the rise of liberal individualism accompanied the Industrial Revolution, for the economic activities of most people became indirectly related to the production of living necessities. For most Native Americans, however, where a subsistence economy prevailed, divisions of labor were minimal and accumulation of surpluses problematical; the cooperation of everyone in the community was a prerequisite to survival. Individual economic independence is a function of prosperity, of guaranteed material security. Most Native Americans, too close to the potential disasters of nature, never enjoyed such a luxury, at least in the United States. Whether in the buffalo hunts on the Great Plains, the communal corn gardens of the Southeast, or the irrigation projects of the Southwest, survival demanded community cooperation, a submersion of individualistic compulsions to group necessities. Most Native Americans maintained an overpowering concern for community welfare, for the economic survival of everyone. The gap between the rich and the poor was far less pronounced than among Europeans; the capriciousness of subsistence living generated a moral dynamic to assist neighbors. The willingness to share, to part with material security, was often considered a personal asset, a sure sign of status and nobility. Christianity, of course, preached a similar message but ran up against the pressures of competitive, entrepreneurial individualism. Most Native American societies proved far more successful in implementing those values.

Finally, the Native American social structure helped create an atmosphere in which individual interests fused with those of the larger community. The building blocks of all Native American societies were kinship groups, even though family authority could be patrilineal or matrilineal and genealogies real or imagined. Among the Hopis, for example, men joined their wives' households after marriage, supporting them economically but maintaining very passive roles in terms of authority and discipline. From the nuclear or small extended families of the most primitive Great Basin tribes to the elaborate clans and clan alliances of the Iroquois tribes, Native Americans tended to view authority in family or clan terms; and different positions within a family implied different roles. In a patrilineal family, for example, "grandfather" offered wisdom to everyone; "father" offered authority and responsibility; "uncle" offered assistance; "children" offered obedience; and "brother" offered equality. Since everyone understood the behavior associated with these roles, and most people occupied several roles simultaneously, family values actually governed society, providing direct moral restraints on individual deviancy. The pull of family loyalty, perhaps the most powerful governing force in human society, was overwhelming in Native America, guaranteeing reciprocal devotions among individuals and the group.

Native American views of life, earth, individuality, and community all merged in their approach to land ownership, and it was this issue which lay at the heart of the Native American–European conflict in the United States, directly precipitating most of the violent confrontations. From 1607, when the English colonists first arrived, right through the controversies ongoing in the 1980s, the issue has always been land, with European and American settlers seizing it throughout United States history and Native Americans fighting to keep it from individual ownership historically and wanting it back today. Europeans wanted the land—all the land—and were never satisfied as long as Native Americans possessed any of it that was worthwhile. This was because they were frustrated by the subsistence economies of Native Americans, considering their land-use methods inefficient and incapable of extracting the most from the soil. The Native Americans were not concerned with extracting everything from the soil, but only enough for them to live in the present. That fact alone, some settlers believed, justified taking the land, peacefully if possible (whether by fair trading or trickery), but violently if necessary. Year after year they moved Native Americans to worthless land, promising them permanent control of it, only to move them again once better reconnaissance, technology, and/or population expansion had rendered the land valuable.

Convinced that the land there was useless, the Virginia settlers pushed the Powhatan Indians north of the York River after 1644 but had to move them again after settlers began pouring into the area a few years later. President Andrew Jackson was sure that much of the land west of the Mississippi River would forever be useless for agriculture, so he signed the Indian Removal Act of 1830, pushing the eastern tribes onto the Great Plains, erroneously called the "Great American Desert." By the 1850s settlers were pouring into Kansas and Nebraska. The federal government relocated the Five Civilized Tribes to Indian Territory, now Oklahoma, only to violate their land titles and civil rights again when "sooners" and then oil speculators settled there. Allotment, termination, and relocation, major policies toward Native Americans in the twentieth century, all had as their rationale the "protection" of Native Americans from encroaching civilization by moving them off land they had inhabited for as far back as tribal memory extended.

The most fundamental question involved ownership of land. The idea of private property—in which one man or one group possessed eternal, exclusive control of a piece of land—was foreign and confusing to most Native Americans, who had long ago adopted communal land systems. Giving one person exclusive, perpetual control of land was as inconceivable as distributing the sky. Like time, land was not a commodity—not a tangible, lifeless item to be measured and sold. It was, instead, a living thing in its own right, imbued with a soul and held in trust by all the living for their use and the use of their children. The Reverend John Heckewelder, a Moravian minister, recalled a Native American's reaction to his complaint about the Native American's horses eating grass on his land:

My friend, it seems you lay claim to the grass my horses have eaten, because you had enclosed it with a fence: now tell me, who caused the grass to grow? Can you make the grass grow? I think not, and no body can except the great Manni-to. He it is who causes it to grow for both my horses and for yours! See, friend! The grass which grows out of the earth is common to all; the game in the woods is common to all. Say, did you never eat venison and bear's meat? . . . Well, and did you ever hear me or any other Indian complain about that? No; then be not disturbed at my horses having eaten only once, of what you call your grass, though the grass my horses did eat, in like manner as the meat you did eat, was given to the Indians by the Great Spirit. Besides, if you will but consider, you will find that my horses did not eat all your grass.*

Private property seemed ridiculous, insanely selfish, even sacrilegious to most Native Americans. Throughout the history of the United

---

*John Heckewelder, *Account of the History, Manners, and Customs of the Indian Nations, Who Once Inhabited Pennsylvania and the Neighboring States* (Philadelphia: A. Small, 1819), 281.

States, they could not understand or accept the European approach to the land; and out of this conflicting perspective came centuries of violence.

But questions of private property were only part of the larger cultural autonomy common to most Native American societies. Europeans failed to understand the dynamics of those cultures, seeing them as nothing more than a pathology, a deviant life-style badly in need of reform. Europeans were dangerously ethnocentric—self-righteously convinced of their own religious, political, and economic superiority. They approached Native America from two different but equally damaging perspectives. Some Europeans denied even the humanity of Native Americans and created powerful negative stereotypes about them, justifying the conflict necessary to drive them off the land. If Indians really were bloodthirsty savages, society was better off without them. The notion that "the only good Indian is a dead Indian," begun by Puritan colonials, peaked late in the nineteenth century with a nearly genocidal assault on Native American civilization.

The other perspective seemed more humane, superficially, and grew out of a combination of liberal guilt and missionary zeal. Dismayed about the violence inflicted upon Native Americans, these Europeans wanted to protect them, to insulate them from the more aggressive, less morally restrained settlers. But beyond these feelings of guilt, they also wanted to change the Native Americans. They accepted their humanity—as well as their cultural inferiority—but instead of annihilating them to clear the land, liberals and missionaries sought to assimilate them into the European culture. That is, they sought to remake the Native Americans' society, transforming them into "law-abiding" farmers who believed in property and Jesus Christ. The irony is that although the methods of the assimilationists were far more benign than the genocidal ravages of Indian haters, the results were the same: the virtual elimination of much of Native American civilization. The land would be cleared of Native American society after all.

The debate between the Indian haters and the liberal assimilationists persisted throughout United States history, shaping Native American policy at every turn and governing all relations between the European and Native American cultures; but the debate exposed the moral shortcomings of European expectations. To most Native Americans, the assimilationists were little better than the genocidal maniacs; for, although they did not hate individual Native Americans, they did hate their culture and were committed to tearing individuals from their cultural moorings. Indeed, they may have been more destructive than the Indian haters, for at least Native Americans always knew where their more overt enemies stood on the issues. Assimilationists always blanketed their ideas in the rhetoric of love, peace, and harmony, making it easy for Native Americans to take them at their word. Off their guard temporarily, Native Americans lost time after time, especially when Indian haters joined forces with the assimilationists, as they did with the Indian Removal Act of 1830 and the Dawes Severalty Act of 1887. Liberals saw in both instances an opportunity to protect Native Americans, while Indian haters saw a clear opportunity to clear Native Americans off valuable land. This unique coalition of liberals and reactionaries proved to be one of the great political ironies of the nineteenth century. United States Native American policy, therefore, was basically an incestuous political struggle among non–Native Americans, with each side promoting a set of ideas out of touch with Native American values but commonly dedicated, consciously and unconsciously, to the destruction of their culture.

In the twentieth century the trumpets of genocide stopped sounding, as did the "cant of conquest," but the assimilationist refrain became louder than ever. Most non–Native Americans, ignorant of Native American needs, applauded the triumph, seeing real progress each time in the allotment program of the Dawes Severalty Act of 1887, the Indian Citizenship Act of 1924, the modified tribalism of the Indian Reorganization Act of 1934, the termination and relocation policies of the 1950s, the antipoverty programs of the 1960s, and the self-determination policies of the 1970s and 1980s. Although some of these programs were better than others—or, at least, less destructive— the federal government still failed to come to grips with Native American culture.

The allotment programs—institutionalized in the Dawes Act of 1887, the Curtis Act of 1898, the Dead Indian Land Act of 1902, and the Burke Act of 1906—succeeded in taking over ninety million acres of land from Native Americans by 1932, all to eliminate "retarded" tribal loyalties and to transform individual Native Americans into family farmers. The allotment program was formally criticized as recently as 1981, when a U.S. District Court decision branded it as "probably one of the best-intended grievous errors in the history of American policy-making."* In the end, most Native Americans did not become successful commercial farmers and still lost their land. The Indian Citizenship Act of 1924, designed as a reward for the loyal service of thousands of Native Americans in World War I and as an attempt to integrate them legally into the polity, did nothing to ameliorate their economic problems or restore tribal sovereignty and culture. The Indian Reorganization Act of 1934, ending allotment and presumably restoring tribal authority, only replaced direct Bureau of Indian Affairs supervision of the tribes with indirect BIA supervision

---

*Ute Indian Tribe v. Utah, C75-408 (D. Utah 1981).

of all tribal decisions through tribal councils. Also, by providing for election of tribal leaders and majority rule in tribal decisions, the Indian Reorganization Act undermined the hereditary rule and consensus politics common to many Native American tribes. In some ways, the act actually insulated BIA officials from Native American criticism by redirecting their anger toward the tribal officials implementing federal policies. Native Americans still did not really enjoy self-determination.

After World War II Congress resurrected earlier attempts to clear Native Americans off the land. Once again assimilationists triumphed, sending thousands to live in the cities and trying to end federal supervision of the tribes altogether, all with the intention of incorporating individual Native American families into the larger United States population. Termination and relocation were not much different from the allotment programs, being merely a twentieth-century version of them. During the 1960s federal antipoverty programs trained Native Americans for jobs in an industrial economy—as welders, auto and diesel mechanics, machinists, construction workers, secretaries, and heavy equipment operators. But to make full use of these skills, Native Americans would have had to relocate to the cities where most of the jobs existed. The result of many antipoverty programs was thousands of culturally alienated Native Americans living in the cities and thousands of unemployed, skilled Native American workers living on the reservations. High-minded liberals in the Department of Justice promoted the civil rights movement, often assuming that Native Americans wanted integration as much as blacks did. They were bewildered and sometimes angry when tribal leaders scoffed at the whole idea of integration, preferring the isolation of their people from "white" values. Even the Indian Self-Determination Act of 1975, designed to shift more authority to tribal councils, left the Bureau of Indian Affairs in a position to approve all tribal decisions, an arrangement Native American activists greatly resented. After more than 350 years of contact, the political relationship between Native Americans and non–Native Americans was still a tenuous one, marked by mutual suspicion and enormous cultural differences.

Suggested Readings

Alexander, Hartley Burr. *The World's Rim: Great Mysteries of the North American Indian.* Lincoln: University of Nebraska Press, 1953.

Chamberlain, J. E. *The Harrowing of Eden: White Attitudes toward North American Natives.* New York: Seabury Press, 1975.

Claiborne, Robert, and the editors of Time-Life Books. *The First Americans.* New York: Time-Life, 1973.

Debo, Angie. *A History of the Indians of the United States.* Norman: University of Oklahoma Press, 1977.

Denevan, William, ed. *The Native Population of the Americas in 1492.* Madison: University of Wisconsin Press, 1976.

Driver, Harold E. *Indians of North America.* Chicago: University of Chicago Press, 1969.

Farb, Peter. *Man's Rise to Civilization: The Cultural Ascent of the Indians of North America.* New York: Dutton, 1978.

Fourteenth Annual Report of the Bureau of American Ethnology. Washington, D.C.: U.S. Government Printing Office, 1886.

Gibson, Arrell Morgan. *The American Indian: Prehistory to the Present.* Lexington, Mass.: D. C. Heath, 1980.

Gill, Sam D. *Sacred Words: A Study of Navajo Religion and Prayer.* Westport, Conn.: Greenwood Press, 1981.

Heizer, Robert F., and Albert B. Elsasser. *The Natural World of the California Indians.* Berkeley: University of California Press, 1980.

Josephy, Alvin M., Jr. *The Indian Heritage of America.* New York: Alfred A. Knopf, 1970.

Linden, George. "Dakota Philosophy." *American Studies* 18 (Fall 1977).

Marriott, Alice, and Carol K. Rachlin. *American Epic: The Story of the American Indian.* New York: Thomas Crowell, 1969.

Martin, Paul S., George Quimby, and Donald Collier. *Indians before Columbus: Twenty Thousand Years of North American History Revealed by Archaeology.* Chicago: University of Chicago Press, 1947.

Mathur, Mary E. Fleming. "The Body Polity: Iroquois Village." *Indian Historian* 8 (Spring 1975).

Oliver, Symmes C. *Ecology and Cultural Continuity as Contributing Factors in the Social Organization of the Plains Indians.* Berkeley: University of California Press, 1962.

Oswalt, Wendell H. *This Land Was Theirs: A Study of the North American Indian.* New York: John Wiley, 1966.

Parks, Douglas R. "The Northern Caddoan Languages: Their Subgrouping and Time Depths." *Nebraska History* 60 (Summer 1979).

Pearce, Roy Harvey. *Savagism and Civilization: A Study of the Indian and the American Mind.* Baltimore: Johns Hopkins Press, 1965.

Russell, Howard S. *Indian New England before the Mayflower.* Hanover, N.H.: University Press of New England, 1980.

Sanders, William T., and Joseph P. Marino. *New World Prehistory: Archaeology of the American Indian.* Englewood Cliffs, N.J.: Prentice-Hall, 1970.

Spencer, Robert F., et al. *The Native Americans: Ethnology and Backgrounds of the North American Indians.* New York: Harper and Row, 1977.

Underhill, Ruth M. *Red Man's America: A History of Indians in the United States.* Chicago: University of Chicago Press, 1971.

Washburn, Wilcomb E. *The Indian in America.* New York: Harper and Row, 1975.

Wax, Murray L., and Rosalie H. Wax. "Religion among American Indians." *Annals of the American Academy of Political and Social Science,* 436 (March 1978).

Weltfish, Gene. *The Lost Universe.* New York: Basic Books, 1965.

Wise, Jennings C. *The Red Man in the New World Drama: A Politico-Legal Study with a Pageantry of American Indian History.* New York: Macmillan, 1971.

Wissler, Clark. *Indians of the United States.* Garden City, N.Y.: Doubleday, 1940.

Witt, Shirley Hill, and Stan Steiner, eds. *The Way: An Anthology of American Indian Literature.* New York: Alfred A. Knopf, 1972.

Chapter Two

The Conquest
of Native America

The rediscovery and subsequent colonization of the New World by Europeans spelled doom for the traditional ways of Native Americans. Besides losing most of their land, they were decimated by diseases, liquor, and warfare, and they were threatened with the loss of tribal values. Possessing superior technological skills, Europeans were able to subjugate tribe after tribe, exploiting tribal differences and rivalries by employing other Native Americans as allies and auxiliaries. Coveting the advanced technology of the European invaders, Native Americans in time became dependent on the knives, guns, and horses which made economic life so much easier. But the price they paid was dear and the consequences ironic. Alone, the technology could have improved Native American economies without threatening their cultures; but, paradoxically, Native Americans could not have the superior trade items without the destructive influence of the European intruders as well. In the wake of European technology, inevitably, came European values.

Estimates vary considerably on the exact number of Native Americans living in what would become the continental United States; most historians and anthropologists put the figure at approximately one million on the eve of contact, although other estimates by reputable scholars put the number considerably higher. Reports on these "inferior" but ingenious people in the New World inspired most Europeans, filling them with feelings of intense curiosity and religious enthusiasm. Indeed, on October 12, 1492, after landing on the island he called San Salvador and meeting several natives whom he called "Indians," Christopher Columbus noted in his journal:

They should be good servants and of quick intelligence, since I see that they very soon say all that is said to them, and I believe that they would easily be made Christians, for it appeared to me that they had no creed.*

Thus blinded by severe ethnocentrism, Columbus and most other Europeans who followed him viewed Native Americans as savages and

---

*Wilcomb E. Washburn, ed., *The Indian and the White Man* (Garden City, N.Y.: Doubleday, 1964), 5.

pagans, people in desperate need of religious conversion and economic acculturation. Spain, France, and England, the three major colonizers of the New World, all sent missionaries to the different tribes. Sincere but usually shortsighted, these zealous carriers of European civilization hoped to transform Native Americans into Christian farmers who would till their own land, harvest and sell their own crops, and attend church services on Sunday. Well into the twentieth century the United States government pursued a similar set of policies.

Much has been written on Spanish, French, English, and United States policy toward Native Americans. In general, each nation recognized Native American rights of occupancy. Still, these Europeans thought they owned the land by right of discovery or subsequent conquest and perceived the tribes as independent, albeit inferior, nations. Naively confident, the Europeans expected Native Americans, through negotiations, to surrender their usufruct rights and eventually become functioning members of the dominant society. When the Native Americans resisted, the Europeans felt perfectly justified in taking the land by any means available.

Visions of "glory, gold, and God" inspired the Spanish conquest of the New World. The conquistadores, and their financial supporters back in Europe, were "rainbow seekers" searching for precious metals, and they were often accompanied by friars and priests looking for converts. The great discoveries of rich civilizations in Mexico and Peru only whetted their appetites and led to further expeditions into what would become the United States. Although they found very little monetary wealth, explorers such as Hernando de Soto and Francisco Vásquez de Coronado did bring back valuable knowledge about the native peoples of North America. Eventually, Spain came to see "her Indians" as cheap laborers working on ranches or in the mines, and as tributaries channeling taxes into the national treasury. The missionaries were also vehicles for attacking Native American culture. Although Spanish missionaries protected Native Americans from other tribes and violence-prone Europeans, the mission system was far from humane. Often the missions resembled concentration camps, with bells signaling hourly duties and missionaries employing various means, from instruction to torture, to convert their wards to Roman Catholicism. The lash was frequently and freely used to punish backsliders.

Outraged by Spain's mistreatment of Native Americans, especially at the hands of civil authorities, some individuals urged the Crown to enact laws guaranteeing them certain legal rights. Bartolomé de Las Casas of the Dominican Order was in the vanguard of the reform movement. Although he was successful, by the middle of the sixteenth century, in convincing the Spanish government to pass laws protecting Native Americans from enslavement, the legislation did not prevent the blatant mistreatment and subsequent deaths of hundreds of thousands of them. Ironically, Las Casas was responsible for "The Black Legend"—the attempt to embarrass Spain into treating Native Americans better by citing the cruelties inflicted upon them by Spanish conquistadores and others. The Black Legend perpetuated the myth that Spanish policy toward Native Americans was inherently more barbaric than the programs practiced by France, England, and the United States.

Because the French constructed their New World empire on the fur trade, historians have usually singled them out as having the most benevolent policy. Native Americans were valuable junior partners in the fur trade, and the French took time to learn some of their customs and cultivate their friendship. The system of trading post colonies established by the French scattered the European population so widely that Native Americans did not feel the inexorable settlement pressures on land and hunting grounds. However, when French settlers established permanent colonies in Louisiana and eastern Canada, these pressures became more overt, and the all-too-common conflicts and wars of extermination began to occur there too. Still, because France did not pursue an aggressive policy of densely settled agricultural colonies in Canada, the political relationship between the French and Native Americans there was more peaceful and harmonious.

In the English colonies, on the other hand, the settlers were primarily farmers interested in acquiring land of their own. Assimilation programs received a good deal of rhetoric and concerned religious discussion, but most colonists viewed Native Americans as obstacles that had to be removed. Unlike the Spanish and French attitudes toward the mingling of races, the English frowned upon interracial marriages and miscegenation. For hundreds of years, the Spanish and French had had contact in the Mediterranean with "colored" peoples of North Africa. Interracial sexual contact, if not common, was at least understood; and both Spanish and French society had become accustomed to such contact. But England, isolated in the North Sea and the North Atlantic, had experienced very little contact with different races. At the same time, the Spanish and French migrations to the New World differed in an important way, especially as far as social history is concerned. Relatively few families made the journey to New Spain and New France; consequently, sexual contact between white men and Native American women there was common. However, in most cases large numbers of English women settled with their husbands in the Atlantic colonies, and sexual contacts between these immigrants and the Native Americans were far more limited. In New Spain the blending of the races produced a new ethnic group: the mestizo. No such interracial culture appeared in the English colonies.

The colonial period of American history was filled with suspicion, resentment, and calamitous wars between Native Americans and the English. At first the Native Americans generally welcomed the English, showing them survival techniques in the new land. In Virginia the powerful Powhatan ruled several tidewater tribes. To cement relations between these tribes and the English, John Rolfe married Pocahontas, the daughter of Powhatan, in 1614. A mock and humorous coronation was also held to recognize Powhatan's leadership and, according to the English perspective, to place the chief under the lordship of King James I. There was peaceful coexistence until Powhatan's death in 1618. Opechancanough, a relative of Powhatan, then emerged as the leader of the confederacy, but he was considerably less patient and more aggressive than his predecessor.

Angry over minor incidents between his people and the English settlers, as well as the growing number of colonists and the expanding tobacco plantations, Opechancanough decided to attack and destroy the intruders. Otherwise, he feared, they would soon drive his people far into the northwest. His devastating assault in March 1622 resulted in the deaths of 350 of the approximately 1,200 settlers and destroyed several communities. The colonists fought back in kind, justifying their genocidal rage on the grounds that the Native Americans were incapable of salvation. Regularly throughout the 1620s and early 1630s the Virginia militia methodically attacked native villages, destroying people, homes, and food supplies. Not until the mid-1630s did peace return. The aged Opechancanough then struck again in 1644, his warriors killing nearly 500 of the 8,000 Virginia settlers. With superior numbers and technology, the English quickly crushed the rebellion, capturing and killing Opechancanough and destroying the Native American confederacy.

In 1646 the English colonists and Virginia natives agreed to end hostilities in a treaty that was to become typical of future such transactions between Native Americans and non–Native Americans in the United States. For a variety of reasons, the colonists wanted to move the Native Americans to distant lands so that the two communities would be permanently separated. Some colonists supported such a plan because it would liberate native lands for development, while others saw it as a way to protect both native Americans and European settlers from future violence. The treaty moved the tidewater tribes north of the York River and promised them permanent tenure on their new land. They were to be protected by Virginia courts and were expected to serve in the colonial militia. The reservation system in American history had begun.

But the hoped-for peace was only temporary. During the 1670s European pressures to settle all of the Virginia Piedmont mounted, as did Native American anxiety about the land. Settlers along the

Virginia and Maryland frontier moved against the Susquehannas and the remnants of the Powhatan confederacy. When Governor William Berkeley of Virginia attempted to protect the Native Americans, he precipitated Bacon's Rebellion in 1676. Nathaniel Bacon and a host of western settlers wanted nothing less than extermination of the Virginia tribes, and his attacks on even peaceful tribes intensified Native American resentment. Bacon's Rebellion was soon crushed; but by the late 1670s, Native American resistance in Virginia had been eliminated, and only one thousand of an original thirty thousand Native Americans still lived there. The rest were either dead or had moved, voluntarily and involuntarily, into the western forests.

In the other southern colonies, a similar pattern of tribal resentment at the proliferation of English settlements occurred. Unlike Virginia, there were no powerful Native American confederacies in Maryland, and coastal tribes living along the southern seaboard were defeated and driven away in the seventeenth century. Not so in the Carolinas. In 1711 the Tuscaroras in North Carolina finally rebelled after years of exploitation at the hands of fraudulent traders and slave raiding parties, as well as the inexorable expansion of English settlement. After two years of bitter fighting, a colonial militia finally crushed Tuscarora resistance, killing hundreds of Native Americans and enslaving hundreds more. Those fortunate enough to escape death or enslavement moved north and eventually joined the tribes of the Iroquois Confederacy. The Yamasees of South Carolina rebelled in 1715. Once friendly allies with the English, the Yamasees were outraged when English traders cheated them and seized and sexually exploited their wives and daughters, and when English settlers presumptuously seized tribal lands. In their uprising, they gained the support of several other tribes, including the Creeks and Catawbas, and inflicted heavy casualties on the colonists, at one point threatening the very future of the South Carolina colony. With the assistance of the Cherokees, the colonial militia finally ended the rebellion by a nearly genocidal assault on the Yamasees which virtually eliminated them from South Carolina. Relations with the Creeks later improved after the founding of Georgia in 1733. James Oglethorpe's relationship with a mixed-blood named Mary, a close relative of a Creek chief, helped alleviate tensions between the Creeks and the English.

In New England the all-too-familiar pattern of encroachment, ethnic conflict, and savage warfare was repeated. On initial contact, friendly Native Americans such as Squanto, Samoset, and Massasoit extended peaceful assistance to the Pilgrims who founded the Plymouth colony. Yet, the Pilgrims and the Puritans of Massachusetts Bay were all Calvinists, convinced of the predestined will of God. They were certain that God had elected them to salvation and to the establishment of a model community to be emulated by the rest of the world. They expected the Native Americans to conform, to fit into that larger scheme of things. When they refused to cooperate, the Puritans branded them as disciples of the devil. After a major small-pox epidemic struck in 1633 and 1634, for example, the Puritans ap-plauded the deaths of thousands of Native Americans as the will of God.

The strict Puritan cosmology and the insatiable appetite for more land eventually caused two major uprisings in New England during the seventeenth century. The first involved the Pequots, a tribe which had migrated into Connecticut during the last half of the sixteenth century. Surrounding tribes resented the arrival of the Pequots almost as much as they resented the presence of European settlers. When the Pequots killed several unscrupulous English traders in 1636, the Puritan magistrates retaliated in vengeance. Employing the Narraganset tribe as an ally, the Puritan army surrounded the main village of the Pequots on the Mystic River, set it afire, then brutally slaughtered the more than four hundred unprotected inhabitants (most of their braves were in a war party elsewhere) as they attempted to escape the flames. The Puritans then pursued survivors mercilessly, hunting them down and either killing them or selling them into slav-ery. The Pequots as a people were essentially extinct in 1638, what few survivors there were having joined the Mohegans. In describing the attack on the Pequot village at Mystic, Governor William Bradford of the Plymouth colony illustrated the fervent union of religious zeal, racism, and cosmic certainty so characteristic of the Puritan mind:

Those that escaped the fire were slain with the sword, some hewed to pieces, others run through with their rapiers, so as they were quickly dispatched and very few escaped. It was conceived they thus destroyed about 400 at this time. It was a fearful sight to see them thus frying in the fire and the streams of blood quenching the same, and horrible was the stink and scent thereof; but the victory seemed a sweet sacrifice, and they [the Puritans] gave the praise thereof to God, who had wrought so wonderfully for them, thus to enclose their enemies in their hands and give them so speedy a victory.*

In the years immediately following the Pequot War, the Puritans also tried to deal with their "Indian problem" through creation of a reservation system. Amid the violence and exploitation, there were some sympathetic voices demanding justice for Native Americans. The most well known and influential sympathizers were John Eliot and Roger Williams. Both of them approached Native Americans with benign intentions. The missionary Eliot translated the Bible into

---

*William Bradford, *History of Plymouth Plantation,* ed. Charles Deane (Bos-ton: privately printed, 1856), 114.

native languages and established several "praying towns"—settlements of Christianized Native Americans. Roger Williams, on the other hand, openly denounced Puritan policy, claiming that Native Americans had valid titles to the land and that Puritans had no fore-ordained right to it. Incensed Puritan magistrates banished him from Massachusetts in 1635, in large measure because of his stand on the Native American issue. So Puritan values reflected both economic and religious motives, with some interested only in clearing valuable land of Native American occupants and others dedicated to converting Native Americans to Christianity by concentrating them on reservations and teaching them the gospel. In 1638 New Haven officials created a twelve-hundred-acre reservation for the Quinnipiac tribe, and the Massachusetts General Court set aside eight thousand acres for the Nonantums at Natick. By 1675 thousands of Native Americans were living on Puritan-supervised reservations in New England.

But the Puritan experiment in conversion came to a devastating conclusion in 1675 with the uprising of King Philip, son of the Wampanoag leader Massasoit. Disgusted by the strict and harsh rules imposed upon Native Americans by the Puritans and by the constant pressures of colonial governments to take tribal lands, Philip went to war in July 1675. Later joined by several other tribes, most notably the Narragansets and the Nipmucks, his followers killed over six hundred settlers and destroyed dozens of towns, which losses for a time seriously threatened the economic existence of New England. At the Great Swamp Fight in December 1675, however, the English prevailed. Philip later died at the hands of a Native American avenging Philip's alleged murder of his brother, and the Puritans gleefully displayed Philip's head at Plymouth. They then sold his friends and family into slavery. Native American power in New England never recovered.

In the middle colonies, the Dutch and the Swedes had nearly eliminated the Native American threat in southern New York and New Jersey by the time of the English takeover in 1664, but in Pennsylvania the situation was different. A persecuted people dedicated to nonviolence and the belief that all men and women were children of God, the Quakers and their leader William Penn wanted a colony in which everyone could live in harmony. They respected the right of the Delawares to the land and purchased it from them only after careful negotiations. Word spread, and in the 1690s and early 1700s the Tuscaroras, Shawnees, and Miamis all migrated to Pennsylvania. Eventually, as Scots-Irish Presbyterians, German Lutherans, and more English Protestants pushed west in Pennsylvania and squatted on tribal land, tensions increased; and when the colonial rivalry for control of the Ohio Valley erupted during the 1750s between the English and the French, open warfare commenced between Native Americans and the European settlers, despite the enlightened Quaker legacy.

As the British empire expanded west and the French empire in Canada expanded south, their rivalry increased dramatically and both colonial powers tried to collect as many tribes as possible as their allies. Generally, the French were more successful. Most tribes gravitated to the French during the four colonial wars: King William's War (1689–97), Queen Anne's War (1702–13), King George's War (1740–48), and the French and Indian War (1754–63). Although the powerful Iroquois Confederacy generally favored the English in these wars, they frequently assumed the balance-of-power role, playing off the English against the French. Alarmed at the success of the French in acquiring Native American allies, the English government developed a new policy in 1755. Colonial control over Native American affairs was diminished. Two superintendents of Native American affairs, one for the northern colonies and another for the southern colonies, took over all negotiations between the Native Americans and the colonists. Sir William Johnson became the superintendent in the north, while Edmond Atkin (replaced by John Stuart in 1762) assumed the position in the south. England's new policy, coupled with a more vigorous war effort against the French, ultimately resulted in victory and the French surrender of its possessions in North America in 1763.

Native Americans could no longer play off the French against the English. With the expulsion of the French, hundreds of English settlers hoped to reap the spoils of war: rich lands west of the Appalachian Mountains. Their encroachment into that area—as well as the end of gift giving, a diplomatic device for coaxing tribes to trade exclusively with one side by using attractive gifts—caused another major war. Pontiac, an Ottawa chief, led his people (as well as the Shawnees, Delawares, Miamis, and Kickapoos) against the English settlements in 1763. Although several forts were captured, one by one Pontiac's allies came to terms with the English, and by April 1765 Pontiac had also negotiated a peace treaty.

Meanwhile, the English government tried to improve relations with recalcitrant tribes by returning to gift giving—and by the Proclamation of 1763, which established a temporary boundary west of the Appalachian Mountains, separating Native American from settler-claimed land. All settlers west of the line had to leave. Deeply resented by the colonists, the Proclamation established an important precedent by creating the concept of "Indian country," an area reserved for Native Americans.

Colonists ignored the Proclamation of 1763, and continued migration soon forced the British government to accelerate already-developed plans for colonial expansion into the "Northwest Territory." The Iroquois signed the Treaty of Fort Stanwix in 1768, giving up their claims to land south of the Ohio and Susquehanna rivers. But other tribes still lived there. The Shawnees, Delawares, Wyandots, and others repudiated the treaty, declaring that the Iroquois had no right to surrender the land. Land speculators and settlers poured into Kentucky, the inevitable conflict grew, and open war once again erupted in 1774. Known as Lord Dunmore's War, the conflict pitted the Virginia militia against the Shawnees and Mingos. The militia prevailed and the Native Americans sued for peace, although no terms were set as that episode was swallowed by the onset of the Revolution.

During the American Revolution both England and the United States vied for Native American support. The Continental Congress formed a Committee on Indian Affairs in 1775, and commissioners went to different tribes either to win their support or to convince them to remain neutral during the conflict. Most tribes, however, joined the English cause. When the war ended in 1783, England recognized the independence of the United States but neglected to have any provisions put into the treaty protecting their former Native American allies. Under the Articles of Confederation, the central government of the United States was too weak to control Native American affairs effectively, especially since the states had supreme authority to handle political, social, and economic policy within their boundaries. When the Confederation government passed the Northwest Ordinance of 1787, establishing steps by which an area could achieve statehood, it included a clause urging the fair and just treatment of Native Americans. But again, land speculators and settlers, now resentful about the Native American role during the Revolution, continued to ignore Native American rights.

For a brief period after the American Revolution, the United States adopted a policy toward Native Americans known as the "conquest" theory. Having defeated the English, Americans believed they had also defeated their Native American allies. Although many tribes remained unconvinced, the government dictated rather than negotiated several treaties. In the Treaty of Fort Stanwix of 1784, for example, the Iroquois had to cede lands in western New York and Pennsylvania. Those Iroquois living in the United States (many had gone to Canada where the English gave them refuge) rapidly degenerated as a nation during the last decades of the eighteenth century, losing most of their remaining lands and much of their ability to cope. Witnessing the decline of the Iroquois Confederacy, tribes such as the Shawnees, Miamis, Delawares, Ottawas, Wyandots, and Potawatomis formed their own confederacy and informed the United States that the Ohio River was the boundary between their lands and those of the settlers. It was only a matter of time before further hostilities ensued.

By 1790 the tens of thousands of settlers living in Kentucky and the Ohio Valley demanded that the United States send expeditions against the Native Americans who were attacking their settlements. In 1790 and again in 1792, American expeditionary forces were defeated in their attempts to subdue the confederacy. Finally, in August 1794, General "Mad" Anthony Wayne defeated the confederacy's warriors at Fallen Timbers. Their resistance broken, they signed the Treaty of Greenville in 1795, thereby surrendering to the United States most of present-day Ohio and some of Indiana. However, the defeated Native Americans received annuity payments in both goods and cash for ceding these lands. The United States thus adopted a more liberal approach to making treaties with Native Americans, abandoning the sole use of the conquest theory and reverting to the need to recognize and pay Native Americans for their legitimate land claims.

The demise of the conquest theory was part of a much larger shift in policy during the 1790s and early 1800s. Directing Native American affairs under the new federal government, Secretary of War Henry Knox began recommending establishment of assimilation programs among Native Americans. Thomas Jefferson and many other prominent European Americans supported such programs, believing that if Native Americans could be re-created in their image, the bitter conflicts between the two cultures would end. This was simply a more contemporary version of the early Puritan attempts to convert Native Americans and settle them in "praying towns." Knox, Jefferson, and the other assimilationists went beyond the Puritans' almost exclusive emphasis on religion to envision the transformation of Native Americans into individualistic, success-oriented Christian farmers anxious to participate in a democratic society. Congress allocated some federal funds to educate Native Americans toward the values of a Christian, materialistic society, and many missionaries responded to the call to teach. They too were convinced that, as Christian farmers, Native Americans would fulfill their destiny. Not surprisingly, Native Americans were seldom consulted about decisions affecting their lives, and many of them stubbornly resisted the assault on their traditional ways.

By the first decade of the nineteenth century there were approximately 875,000 settlers in Ohio, Kentucky, Tennessee, Indiana, Illinois, and Missouri. Tecumseh and his brother, The Prophet, alarmed at the rising tide of settlement, set about forming an alliance of the several tribes remaining in the area as well as in the South (especially the Creeks), with the purpose of presenting a united front against American encroachment. Tecumseh also hoped to win English support, since relations between the United States and England were reaching the breaking point. His visions of a grand military alliance never developed, however; tribal unity was not easily accomplished among Native American groups who had contended with each other for centuries. Disunity, a problem to which Native Americans have been generally susceptible throughout the history of their relations with non–Native Americans, may have fatally flawed what turned out to be the last real attempt to retain control of the Old Northwest.

Responding to the threat of Tecumseh, in 1811 Governor William Henry Harrison of Indiana Territory led a strong militia force into the field, repulsed an attack by a multitribe force at Tippecanoe Creek (while Tecumseh was away attempting to recruit support from the southern tribes), then assaulted and destroyed Tecumseh's primary camp at Prophetstown. Harrison's discovery of English weapons there stimulated widespread anger in the United States, contributing indirectly to the outbreak of the War of 1812. During the war, Harrison's forces met and defeated Tecumseh at the Battle of the Thames in October 1813. Tecumseh was killed and Native American resistance crumbled. His death, as well as the loss of English support when the War of 1812 ended, forced many tribes to move further west. Another era in Native American history was coming to an end.

But American settlers still confronted more than one hundred thousand Native Americans living east of the Mississippi River, and the idea of removing them gained popularity. West of the Mississippi lay vast amounts of unoccupied land; by pushing the eastern Native Americans beyond the river, settlers would be free to fill all of Ohio, Indiana, Illinois, Kentucky, Tennessee, and the southern states. Such a plan was not a new idea that emerged following the War of 1812. President Thomas Jefferson had supported such a scheme, and the establishment of an "Indian country" beyond the Mississippi River was one reason for the Louisiana Purchase in 1803.

"Removal" was more than another assault on Native American land titles. Insatiable greed for land remained a primary consideration, but many people now believed that the removal policy was the only way of saving Native Americans from extermination. As long as Native Americans remained on land that settlers coveted, their lives were in danger, the argument went; and as long as Native Americans even lived in close proximity to non–Native American communities, they would be decimated by disease, alcohol, and poverty. Removal would also serve to promote assimilation, albeit assimilation by separation. Such a paradox did not seem to bother the humanitarians. Before they could be incorporated into European American society, Native Americans would have to acquire the civility necessary to facilitate assimilation; but that would have to be accomplished apart from European American society in order to avoid its evil aspects.

The federal government negotiated several removal treaties before President Andrew Jackson signed the Indian Removal Act in 1830. Some tribes, particularly the remnants of the Iroquois Confederacy and other northeastern tribes, were not removed. Hit hardest by removal, of course, were those still living in freedom in the Old

Northwest and in the South. Tribes such as the Shawnees, Delawares, Ottawas, Potawatomis, Wyandots, Miamis, Kickapoos, Peorias, and Winnebagos signed removal treaties. The Sacs and Foxes had accepted the policy of removal in 1804 but were allowed to remain on their lands until the advancement of settlements dictated otherwise. As removal commenced in earnest after 1830, many Sacs and Foxes renounced the 1804 treaty, and in 1831 a large party returned to lands they had previously evacuated. A war bearing the name of their leader—Black Hawk—ensued in 1832. But Black Hawk's forces were thoroughly defeated and further land cessions were extracted from his people.

The infamous removal of the Five Civilized Tribes—the Choctaws, Creeks, Chickasaws, Cherokees, and Seminoles—is a dismal page in United States history. The states of Alabama, Georgia, and Mississippi put enough pressure on the Choctaws, Creeks, and Chickasaws that they had to accept removal or face extermination. The Cherokees, a tribe which had by the 1820s established a written constitution modeled after the United States Constitution, a newspaper, schools, and industries in their settlements, resisted removal. They appealed to the United States Supreme Court, and in 1831 Chief Justice John Marshall handed down an opinion in *Cherokee Nation v. Georgia* declaring that the Cherokees were a "domestic dependent nation." The following year, in *Worcester v. Georgia,* Marshall ruled that the federal government had exclusive jurisdiction over the Cherokees. President Andrew Jackson and Georgia officials refused to accept these rulings, and federal troops evicted the Cherokees in 1838. Approximately four thousand Cherokees died during the removal process because of poor planning by the United States government. Cherokees still refer to the exodus to Indian Territory as the "Trail of Tears," an experience which descendants of those migrating Cherokees sorrowfully remember.

The Seminoles resisted removal by escaping to the Everglades in Florida. The government fought them from 1835 to 1842, spending more than $50 million and losing nearly fifteen hundred soldiers before breaking Seminole resistance by seizing the Seminole chief Osceola while under a flag of truce. Most Seminoles were removed in 1843. Some, however, remained in the Everglades and their descendants continue to live there today.

Nearly one hundred thousand Native Americans eventually crossed the Mississippi River under the authority of the Indian Removal Act. Life in the West was very hard for them. The land and the climate were vastly different, and their economic expectations had to be adjusted accordingly. Additionally, Native Americans who had long occupied the lands west of the Mississippi River resented these newcomers and often made life miserable for them. Comanches, Pawnees,

Osages, and other western tribes, taking advantage of the failure of the government to provide protection as promised, raided their camps and drove off their livestock. Poverty, suffering, bitterness, and despair were common.

Placing the tribes on land in the West which most settlers found undesirable permitted Native Americans to live in peace for a while at least. But the idea of removal soon gave way to the policy of "concentration." The fever of Manifest Destiny swept the nation in the 1840s, and the penetration of the "Great American Desert" meant that Native Americans would have to give up their lands in exchange for smaller, concentrated areas. By the 1850s settlers were pouring into the Far West and into land west of the Mississippi River that had been reserved "forever" for the Native Americans. The mining frontier in California and the Intermountain West and glowing reports of good farming land served as magnets attracting hundreds of thousands of settlers into the western territories. Whenever they established settlements, the all-too-familiar pattern of conflict surfaced in a cyclical pattern of frustration and violence.

In the Pacific Northwest, most of the tribes had been friendly toward the first incoming waves of farmers. As pressure for land increased, however, several tribes unsuccessfully resisted. By the end of the 1850s, Governor Isaac I. Stevens of Washington Territory had negotiated treaties, frequently by devious means, with such tribes as the Cayuse, Yakima, Spokane, Walla Walla, and Nez Perce. They ceded millions of acres of land and "accepted" reservations. As with most other treaties negotiated with Native Americans, the questions of who represented the tribes and of what both sides were actually agreeing to laid the foundation for many subsequent problems.

In California, the gold rush brought an influx of tens of thousands of miners who soon decimated the Native Americans, since many tribes there did not have the organization or means to offer even token resistance. Between 1849 and 1860, the Native American population of California declined from over one hundred thousand to about thirty thousand people. In the Southwest, acquired from Mexico through the Treaty of Guadalupe Hidalgo in 1848, the United States inherited the intense hostility between Europeans and the Apaches and Navajos, hostility that had been ongoing since the sixteenth century. The Pueblos, however, remained relatively docile after the Mexican War.

During the Civil War, many western tribes naively believed that the American soldiers had left their lands for good to fight each other in the East. Some tribes, including the Cherokees and others of the Five Civilized Tribes, made the tragic choice of joining the Confederate side. After the war ended, they were treated as the conquered foe and were forced to give up even more of the lands granted them in present-day Oklahoma. Also during the Civil War, in 1862, the Santee Sioux in Minnesota staged a major rebellion in large part due to the deplorable conditions on their reservations and the insensitivity and unresponsiveness of the government officials. The uprising was one of the bloodiest in American history (estimates vary between 450 and 800 settlers and soldiers killed), but the Sioux were defeated within a few months. As partial punishment they lost their annuity payments from the government and had to move from Minnesota to reservations in Dakota Territory.

The Homestead Act of 1862, which granted 160 acres of land to settlers for a small filing fee, and the efforts to provide adequate transportation between the East and the West (five transcontinental railroads were completed between 1869 and 1893) put additional pressures on the western tribes. Not only their lands but their economic source of existence—the buffalo—were threatened by the influx of settlers. The mass slaughter of the buffalo made it easier to convince Native Americans to move to reservations in order to become assimilated. Reservation life was anything but pleasant. Although some Native Americans tried to become farmers, lands unsuitable for agriculture and corrupt government officials hampered and discouraged their efforts. Most Native Americans resented this paternalism and refused to accept assimilation programs.

Under President Ulysses S. Grant the government attempted to improve relations between Native Americans and non–Native Americans. The United States had previously created a Bureau of Indian Affairs in 1824 and the office of Commissioner of Indian Affairs in 1832. In 1849 the Bureau of Indian Affairs was transferred from the War Department to the Department of the Interior, but military versus civilian control of Native American affairs remained a bureaucratic problem throughout the nineteenth century. During the 1870s, in order to eliminate corrupt officials, the government allowed religious groups to recommend men for BIA positions. The program became known as the "Quaker Policy," since the Quakers were the first to participate in the selection process. At the same time, President Grant implemented the "Peace Policy", placing all Native Americans on reservations, peaceably or forcibly, in order to "protect" them and to speed up the policy of assimilation. Non–Native Americans interested in Native American land supported the "Peace Policy" enthusiastically. In 1869 Congress created the Board of Indian Commissioners consisting of ten unpaid humanitarians who served as a watchdog on the operations of the Bureau of Indian Affairs and who could recommend policy changes.

But despite all these "reforms," incessant Indian wars erupted through the 1860s, 1870s, and 1880s. One by one the Native American tribes accepted reservation life after several major confrontations with

American soldiers and settlers. In eastern Colorado, the Cheyennes and Arapahos did not get along well with the incoming settlers. Several skirmishes had occurred early in the 1860s, and many Coloradans adopted the philosophy of a militia officer (and Methodist minister) named John M. Chivington. To Chivington, Native Americans were all vermin that should be exterminated. In November 1864 a militia force under his command attacked a village at Sand Creek, killing and mutilating the bodies of men, women, and children. The Cheyenne leader, Black Kettle, tried in vain to ward off the attack by waving a white flag and an American flag, but Chivington's militia had gone into a mindless orgy of violence. Black Kettle and a few other survivors fled, and a general Native American uprising ensued for several years. Black Kettle ultimately fell victim to another surprise attack (led by Lieutenant Colonel George A. Custer) at the Washita River in November 1868. By the 1870s the Cheyennes, Arapahos, Kiowas, Comanches, and others had signed treaties accepting reservations in the Indian Territory of Oklahoma.

The tribes in the Pacific Northwest and California were also defeated in wars and forced to accept reservations either in Indian Territory or, if more fortunate, closer to their homelands. The Modocs were beaten in the lava beds of northern California and removed to Indian Territory in 1874. In 1877 Chief Joseph and the Nez Perces made a valiant attempt to escape reservation life by fleeing to Canada. They were captured within fifty miles of the border and sent to Indian Territory as well. Both the Modocs and the Nez Perces were later allowed to return to reservations in the Northwest, after several years of suffering in Indian Territory.

In the Southwest, Kit Carson led an expedition against the Navajos in 1864, defeating them in Canyon de Chelly. They were herded to a bleak reservation (more like a concentration camp) at Bosque Redondo in eastern New Mexico to live with Mescalero Apaches who had also been forcibly removed there in 1863. Bosque Redondo was a terrible experience, owing to a combination of corrupt and ill-planned government administration and a smallpox epidemic that killed more than a fourth of all the approximately eight thousand people detained there. The Mescalero Apaches slipped away one night in November 1865, and the Navajos were allowed to return to a fraction of their lands in Arizona in 1868. The "Long Walk" and the horrible years at Bosque Redondo remain as clear in the minds of the Navajos (and Mescalero Apaches) as the "Trail of Tears" in the minds of the Cherokees.

The Sioux Wars of the 1860s and 1870s were just as devastating. Red Cloud, an Oglala Sioux, had successfully driven settlers out of the Powder River country by 1868 and by treaty that same year the

Sioux and Northern Cheyennes accepted a larger reservation, including the western half of present-day South Dakota with the Powder River country of eastern Wyoming added as a hunting reserve. When gold was discovered in the Black Hills in 1874, the United States tried to convince the Sioux to sell the land. The Sioux refused. Ineffective in keeping miners out of the area, the United States allowed them to enter the reservation at their own risk, a violation of the 1868 treaty. The Sioux declared the treaty void, and many bolted the reservation, joining Sitting Bull and Crazy Horse in the Yellowstone River country of eastern Montana. In 1876 large army forces converged on that area from three directions and several major battles ensued, including the Battle of the Little Big Horn in which Lieutenant Colonel George A. Custer and 207 of his men were trapped and annihilated in a foolhardy assault on their enemy's main camp. Encounters continued into 1877, when Sitting Bull, determining that further resistance was futile, led remnants of the Sioux nation into exile in Canada.

In the Southwest, Apache resistance to the United States began in the 1860s and lasted over two decades. No longer able to tolerate mistreatment and incursions of increasing numbers of American miners and settlers, Mangas Coloradas and Cochise led Mimbreño and Chiricahua Apaches into battle. Vicious warfare resulted, with carnage committed by both sides. Although the Apache bands finally agreed to accept reservations, their traditional custom of raiding into Mexico continued. Leading the Apache raiders were Victorio, Nana, Juh, and Geronimo. Geronimo finally surrendered to American troops (aided by Apache scouts) in September 1886, whereupon all the Chiricahua Apaches, including those residing peaceably near Fort Apache and the Apache scouts employed by the army, were taken into custody and sent to the old Spanish fort at St. Augustine, Florida. The Chiricahuas were to remain in captivity (as prisoners of war) for the next twenty-eight years.

The last major bloody encounter, however, was in December 1890, at the Pine Ridge Reservation (Sioux), when an inept government agent panicked and called in troops to suppress the Ghost Dance religion. Suspecting Sitting Bull of leading the agitation, the federal government decided to arrest him; but he was killed by Native American police sent to escort him into the agency. At nearby Wounded Knee Creek, another band of Sioux were forced to surrender. When United States troops tried to disarm them, the Sioux, angry about reservation conditions and the death of Sitting Bull, fought back. United States soldiers, armed with rapid-fire Hotchkiss guns, opened fire on the assembled Native Americans, indiscriminately killing more than 150 men, women, and children. Although Wounded Knee essentially ended the era of open violence, the cultural assault on Native American values continued in earnest.

Suggested Readings

Andrist, Ralph K. *The Long Death: The Last Days of the Plains Indians.* New York: Macmillan, 1964.

Berkhofer, Robert F., Jr. *The White Man's Indian: Images of the American Indian from Columbus to the Present.* New York: Vintage Books, 1978.

Berthrong, Donald J. *The Southern Cheyennes.* Norman: University of Oklahoma Press, 1963.

Bradford, William. *History of Plymouth Plantation.* Ed. Charles Deane. Boston: privately printed, 1856.

Chamberlain, J. E. *The Harrowing of Eden: White Attitudes toward North American Natives.* New York: Seabury Press, 1975.

Cook, Sherburne F. *The Conflict between the California Indians and White Civilization.* Berkeley: University of California Press, 1976.

Cotterill, R. S. *The Southern Indians: The Story of the Civilized Tribes before Removal.* Norman: University of Oklahoma Press, 1954.

Craven, Wesley Frank. *White, Red, and Black: The Seventeenth Century Virginian.* Charlottesville: University Press of Virginia, 1971.

Dale, Edward Everett. *The Indians of the Southwest: A Century of Development under the United States.* Norman: University of Oklahoma Press, 1949.

DeRosier, Arthur H., Jr. *The Removal of the Choctaw Indians.* Knoxville: University of Tennessee Press, 1970.

Downes, Randolph C. *Council Fires on the Upper Ohio: A Narrative of Indian Affairs in the Upper Ohio Valley until 1795.* Pittsburgh: University of Pittsburgh Press, 1940.

Drinnon, Richard. *Facing West: The Metaphysics of Indian-Hating and Empire Building.* Minneapolis: University of Minnesota Press, 1980.

Edmunds, R. David, ed. *American Indian Leaders: Studies in Diversity.* Lincoln: University of Nebraska Press, 1980.

Fehrenbach, T. R. *Comanches: The Destruction of a People.* New York: Alfred A. Knopf, 1974.

Forbes, Jack D. *Apache, Navajo, and Spaniard.* Norman: University of Oklahoma Press, 1960.

Foreman, Grant. *Indian Removal: The Emigration of the Five Civilized Tribes of Indians.* Norman: University of Oklahoma Press, 1932.

Heckewelder, John. *Account of the History, Manners, and Customs of the Indian Nations, Who Once Inhabited Pennsylvania and the Neighboring States.* Philadelphia: A. Small, 1819.

Jacobs, Wilbur R. *Dispossessing the American Indian: Indians and Whites on the Colonial Frontier.* New York: Charles Scribner's Sons, 1972.

———. *Wilderness Politics and Indian Gifts: The Northern Colonial Frontier, 1748–1763.* Lincoln: University of Nebraska Press, 1966.

Jennings, Francis. *The Invasion of America: Indians, Colonialism, and the Cant of Conquest.* Chapel Hill: University of North Carolina Press, 1975.

Josephy, Alvin M., Jr. *The Nez Perce Indians and the Opening of the North-west.* New Haven, Conn.: Yale University Press, 1971.

————. *The Patriot Chiefs: A Chronicle of American Indian Leadership.* New York: Viking Press, 1961.

Kupperman, Karen Ordahl. *Settling with the Indians: The Meeting of English and Indian Cultures in America, 1580–1640.* Totowa, N.J.: Rowman and Littlefield, 1980.

Leach, Douglas Edward. *Flintlock and Tomahawk: New England in King Philip's War.* New York: W. W. Norton, 1958.

Meyer, Roy W. *History of the Santee Sioux: United States Indian Policy on Trial.* Lincoln: University of Nebraska Press, 1967.

Miner, H. Craig, and William E. Unrau. *The End of Indian Kansas: A Study of Cultural Revolution, 1854–1871.* Lawrence: Regents Press of Kansas, 1978.

Nash, Gary B. *Red, White, and Black: The Peoples of Early America.* Englewood Cliffs, N.J.: Prentice-Hall, 1974.

Peckham, Howard, and Charles Gibson, eds. *Attitudes of Colonial Powers toward the American Indian.* Salt Lake City: University of Utah Press, 1969.

Priest, Loring Benson. *Uncle Sam's Stepchildren: The Reformation of United States Indian Policy, 1865–1887.* New Brunswick, N.J.: Rutgers University Press, 1942.

Prucha, Francis Paul. *American Indian Policy in Crisis: Christian Reformers and the Indian, 1865–1900.* Norman: University of Oklahoma Press, 1976.

————. *American Indian Policy in the Formative Years: The Indian Trade and Intercourse Acts, 1790–1834.* Cambridge, Mass.: Harvard University Press, 1962.

Rogin, Michael Paul. *Fathers and Children: Andrew Jackson and the Subjugation of the American Indian.* New York: Vintage Books, 1975.

Sandoz, Mari. *Crazy Horse: The Strange Man of the Oglalas.* New York: Alfred A. Knopf, 1942.

Satz, Ronald N. *American Indian Policy in the Jacksonian Era.* Lincoln: University of Nebraska Press, 1975.

Segal, Charles M., and David C. Stineback. *Puritans, Indians, and Manifest Destiny.* New York: Putnam, 1977.

Sheehan, Bernard W. *Savagism and Civility: Indians and Englishmen in Colonial Virginia.* Cambridge, Eng.: Cambridge University Press, 1980.

————. *Seeds of Extinction: Jeffersonian Philanthropy and the American Indian.* Chapel Hill: University of North Carolina Press, 1973.

Slotkin, Richard, and James K. Folsom, eds. *So Dreadful a Judgment: Puritan Responses to King Philip's War, 1676–1677.* Middletown, Conn.: Wesleyan University Press, 1978.

Spicer, Edward H. *Cycles of Conquest: The Impact of Spain, Mexico, and the United States on the Indians of the Southwest, 1533–1960.* Tucson: University of Arizona Press, 1962.

Stuart, Paul. *The Indian Office: Growth and Development of an American Institution, 1865–1900.* Ann Arbor, Mich.: UMI Research Press, 1979.

Thrapp, Dan L. *The Conquest of Apacheria.* Norman: University of Oklahoma Press, 1967.

Trennert, Robert A., Jr. *Alternative to Extinction: Federal Indian Policy and the Beginnings of the Reservation System, 1846–1851.* Philadelphia: Temple University Press, 1975.

Tucker, Glenn. *Tecumseh: Vision of Glory.* Indianapolis: Bobbs-Merrill, 1956.

Tyler, S. Lyman. *A History of Indian Policy.* Washington, D.C.: U.S. Government Printing Office, 1973.

Utley, Robert M. *The Last Days of the Sioux Nation.* New Haven, Conn.: Yale University Press, 1963.

Vaughan, Alden T. *New England Frontier: Puritans and Indians, 1620–1675.* Boston: Little, Brown, 1965.

Vestal, Stanley. *Sitting Bull, Champion of the Sioux: A Biography.* Boston: Houghton Mifflin, 1932.

Wallace, Anthony F. C. *The Death and Rebirth of the Seneca.* New York: Vintage Books, 1969.

Washburn, Wilcomb E., ed. *The Indian and the White Man.* Garden City, N.Y.: Doubleday, 1964.

———. *Red Man's Land/White Man's Law: A Study of the Past and Present Status of the American Indian.* New York: Charles Scribner's Sons, 1971.

Chapter Three

The Assault on
Native American Tribalism

In the 1880s, with the great buffalo herds gone and the trans-continental railroads finally constructed, Native Americans rapidly approached a watershed in their history. Non–Native American set-tlers were everywhere. After thousands of years of economic and politi-cal independence, the Native Americans faced the final onslaught of European civilization. Confined to carefully measured reservations, surrounded and smothered by the material artifacts of the dominant society, and dependent economically on the federal government, Native Americans looked back nostalgically to the past and looked for-ward apprehensively if not bitterly to the future. Unlike ever before, they had to deal culturally with a profound sense of impotence—a col-lective inability to control their own environment and contain the ex-pansion of European values. For the next century, from the Ghost Dance spiritualism of the 1880s to the demands for self-determination in the 1970s, Native American history would revolve around a quest for power. The quest, of course, was as complex and diverse as Native American culture, but no longer did Native Americans harbor much hope for a military triumph. Instead, they wanted to carve out a se-cure place in American society where their customs and values could flourish.

Given the course of political and economic development in the United States, their struggle would be an extraordinarily difficult one. In 1880 the Native American population had fallen to less than three hundred thousand people, down dramatically from the million or more who had once lived in what is now the United States. Reduced to virtual impotence, Native Americans reluctantly surrendered to the enormous non–Native American population—and their farms, ranches, towns, cities, machines, and diseases. Some tribes, like the Iroquois in New York or the Pueblos in New Mexico, still occupied tracts of their original homelands, but most Native Americans lived on government reservations, in most cases in locations distant from their homelands, where poverty and disease plagued them. Smallpox, measles, mumps, cholera, and syphilis ravaged the reservations, and another national tragedy was in the making.

But reservation life was much more than a temporal crisis; it was a spiritual trauma as well, a great moral threat to Native American culture. For hundreds of years, despite intense hostility and misunderstanding, European Americans and Native Americans had confronted one another equally, psychologically at least, and Native Americans had successfully sustained a sense of honor, pride, and cultural integrity. All that began to change on the reservations. Politically, economically, and socially, the reservations transformed relations between Native Americans and Americans of European descent and strained the interpretive mechanisms of Native American culture.

Throughout their history Native Americans considered their tribes to be independent nations, but on the reservations tribal leaders lost much of their former power. Although some tribes ferociously maintained their sense of political integrity—such as the Iroquois Nation, which declared war on Germany in 1917—most tribes had to acquiesce to the federal government. Instead of deferring to traditional tribal chieftains, most Native Americans found themselves subject to the authority of non–Native American agents from the Bureau of Indian Affairs. Older ideas about power, authority, and responsibility decayed; and decisions about law and community conflict, once left to tribal leaders seeking consensus and unanimity, were now left up to agents who all too often made their decisions arbitrarily, reflecting personal whim, the needs of assimilated mixed-bloods, or the pressures of various non–Native American interest groups. Former tribal leaders found themselves in untenable positions, caught between the fiat of government directives and the needs and expectations of their people. On the reservations of the late nineteenth century, Native American political power seemed destined for extinction.

Economic life on the reservations was no better. Native Americans had always enjoyed the natural independence of subsistence peoples, all simply but subtly tuned to the local environment. Whether they were buffalo hunters on the Great Plains, fishermen on the coasts and salmon tributaries, food gatherers in California and the Great Basin, or agriculturists in the Southwest and Eastern Woodlands, they meshed perfectly into their economic surroundings and were dependent only upon themselves for survival. That intimate relationship with the environment had even assumed a spiritual dimension supplying many tribes with the cosmic rationale for their existence. But on the reservations Native Americans were wards of the federal government, dependent not upon their own resources but upon regular shipments of food and clothing from the dominant culture. They were the first recipients of "welfare" in United States history, occupying "ghettos in the wilderness." Surrendering the hunter-warrior ideal, Native American men lost part of their identity and had to deal with the paralyzing realization of economic uselessness. With neither political power nor the resources to support their families, Native Americans looked out from the reservations on a world that did not need them.

Reservation life also presented Native Americans with a cultural crisis. For years prominent non–Native Americans had reflected endlessly on the "Indian problem"—how to protect Native Americans from the ravages of European American society, how to bridge the vast differences between the two cultures, and how to reconcile Native American subsistence economies with European development. The removal policies of the 1830s and the 1840s, and then the reservation policies of the 1860s and 1870s, seemed ideal solutions at the time: by concentrating the Native Americans on relatively worthless reserves, the federal government had separated them from non–Native Americans, opened original tribal homelands for commercial development, and made Native American families more accessible to liberal reformers bent on transforming their culture. The ultimate solution to the "Indian problem," the reformers believed, was to divest Native Americans of their cultural heritage by introducing them to Christianity, teaching them English, and preparing them to function in an industrial-agrarian economy. Once they had accepted Jesus Christ, learned to read and write, and decided to "succeed" economically, hostility against them would rapidly disappear. So, with missionaries and government agents on reservations condemning Native American customs and promoting European values, Native Americans experienced a good deal of cultural pressure and sometimes even personal guilt about feeling loyal to older ways.

Centuries of tribal autonomy, freedom of movement, and environmental harmony were coming to an end. With their tribal land taken, their game gone, their population dwindling rapidly, and their values under siege, Native Americans were at a loss to deal with their new situation. Arapaho dancers in the 1880s sang a plaintive refrain on the reservation:

> My Father, have pity on me!
> I have nothing to eat,
> I am dying of thirst—
> Everything is gone.*

Dependent and bewildered, thousands of Native Americans sought new ways of handling reservation life by turning to the Ghost Dance, alcohol, peyotism, the Sun Dance, and the Dream Dance. Here, in new cultural adaptations, they sought tools for interpreting their predicament.

---

*Quoted in Ralph K. Andrist, *The Long Death: The Last Days of the Plains Indians* (New York: Macmillan, 1964), 338.

In 1869 or 1870 a Paiute prophet named Wodziwob initiated the original Ghost Dance religion. The Ghost Dance religion of the 1870s spread from Nevada to tribes in California and Oregon. Within a few years the movement died. But it had a resurgence in 1889 when another Paiute prophet, Wovoka, began preaching essentially the same doctrine after he received a special revelation from the Great Spirit:

When the sun died, I went up to heaven and saw God and all the people who had died a long time ago. God told me to come back and tell my people they must be good and love one another, and not fight, or steal, or lie. He gave me this dance to give to my people.*

Wovoka's teachings spread rapidly throughout the plateau, the Great Basin, and onto the Great Plains. The ceremony consisted of five straight days of physically exhausting dances and other rituals, and the religion offered a spiritual explanation for the Native American dilemma and a prognosis for the future. As one of the Paiutes explained it:

All Indians must dance, everywhere, keep on dancing. Pretty soon in next spring Big Man [Great Spirit] come. He bring back all game of every kind. The game be thick everywhere. All dead Indians come back and live again. They all be strong just like young men, be young again. Old blind Indians see again and get young and have fine time. When Old Man [God] comes this way, then all the Indians go to mountains, high up away from whites. . . . Then while Indians way up high, big flood comes like water and all white people die. . . . Nobody but Indians everywhere and game all kinds thick.†

A burst of supernaturalism transcending narrow tribal loyalties, the Ghost Dance theology explained that God had punished the Native Americans for their sins by sending invaders to overrun the land and slaughter the people and animals. Soon, however, with repentance complete and the sins atoned for, God would destroy all the invaders, resurrect all the Native American dead, and restore the great buffalo herds. Although details varied from tribe to tribe, all adherents to the Ghost Dance religion looked for the day when the promises would come true; in the meantime, Native Americans wore sacred undergarments to protect themselves from danger. Otherworldly and essentially escapist, promising a great purifying cataclysm, the Ghost Dance offered hope to warriors unable to divine their future. Sadly, this exercise of hope was dashed in the slaughter at Wounded Knee.

The exaggerated use of alcohol was another way of escaping from reality on the reservation and resisting the assimilation demands of

---

*Quoted in James Mooney, *The Ghost-Dance Religion and the Sioux Outbreak of 1890* (Chicago: University of Chicago Press, 1965), 2.
†Ibid., 26.

reformers. Alcohol had played a conspicuous role in relations between Native Americans and European Americans ever since the seventeenth century. At first, when they had met on fairly equal political terms, alcohol was a diplomatic tool, a device used frequently to facilitate the negotiating process. Native Americans adopted alcohol from settlers just as they had adopted the horse, rifle, and metal tools; it became part of their social life, not as a transformer of native culture or as a pathological deviance but simply as a way to relax and celebrate. Alcohol was at first just one among many artifacts of European culture which Native Americans found useful.

But as the political relationship between European Americans and Native Americans deteriorated from one of equality to one of dominance and subservience in the nineteenth century, Native American uses of alcohol changed too. Because reservation life so often stimulated feelings of rejection and lack of purpose, some turned to alcohol as an escape from reality, a means of temporarily reaching back into the past to dream of freedom and independence. Alcoholism and crimes related to the abuse of alcohol were more common on the reservations of hunting and gathering tribes formerly conditioned to loose social organization and freedom of movement. Among the White River Apaches, Chippewas, or Utes, for example, reservation life had a numbing effect on them and they had very high rates of alcoholism and alcohol-related crimes. Among tightly organized agricultural tribes more accustomed to sedentary life, alcohol-related social problems were not as pronounced.

Although drunkenness was an escape from reality, there was another dimension to the widespread use of alcohol by many reservation Native Americans. People of European extraction viewed public inebriation either as a gross sin or as a pathological, and pathetic, response to social and cultural stress; those who looked on it as a sin tried to eliminate it through temperance movements, while others explained it as a vicarious attempt to regain lost glory. In either case, European Americans developed a powerful stereotype of the "drunken Indian"—a pitiful creature unable to resist the bottle and incapable of controlling the emotional effects of drinking. The increasingly widespread use of alcohol on the reservations in the 1880s only confirmed the stereotype for most reformers.

From the Native American perspective, however, there was much more to drinking than sin or escapism. In so many ways reservation life restricted the expression of Native American culture. Tribal political and economic power had given way to dependence on the federal government, and tribal customs were under assault by liberal reformers dedicated to cultural genocide. On the reservations, opportunities for asserting "Indianness"—positive public confirmations of personal identity—were vanishing in the 1880s, and some Native

Americans institutionalized drunkenness as a form of protest against the dominant society. Among loosely organized tribes occupying unfamiliar reservations, public drunkenness was more common. The Standing Rock Sioux, for example, tolerated alcoholics and imposed no social sanctions on tribal members for public intoxication. Consciously and unconsciously, some Native Americans used public intoxication as a tool to demonstrate their identity to non–Native Americans. By becoming publicly drunk, they purposefully fulfilled the stereotype, confirming to themselves and to others that they really were Native Americans and were not ashamed of it. For many Native Americans, the use of alcohol was as much a form of cultural rebellion as an escape from reality.

While some were using alcohol to protest or escape from their situations, others turned to peyote, a stimulant drug taken from mescal. Peyote found ready acceptance in the reservations of Indian Territory, especially among Native Americans familiar with religious vision quests, because it gave its users spectacular dreams and a heightened sense of personal value. The peyote cult came from Mexico to the Mescalero Apaches, who passed it on to the Kiowas, Caddos, and Comanches. Quanah Parker, the mixed-blood child of a Comanche chief father and a European American mother, resisted settlement until his surrender in 1875 and then resisted assimilation by becoming a leader of the peyote cult. Parker gained great influence over reservation Native Americans; and the use of peyote, like that of alcohol, became an effective means of dealing with the new world. Indeed, the exaggerated use of alcohol was less pronounced among tribes such as the Arapaho who had adopted peyotism. In the 1880s peyotism had spread to the Cheyennes, Shawnees, and Arapahos, and in the early 1890s to the Pawnees, Delawares, Osages, and Winnebagos. Like the Ghost Dance religion and the public use of alcohol, the peyote cult offered Native Americans on reservations another means of interpreting their environment and asserting their fundamental differences with European American culture.

A new version of an older Native American religion called the Sun Dance also appeared. Before the European American conquest the Sun Dance had been one of the most elaborate ceremonies among the Plains tribes. Although the particular ceremony varied from tribe to tribe, all of the Sun Dance ceremonies involved dancing, thirsting, fasting, and self-mutilation. Men sometimes sliced open the skin of their chests, passed rawhide skewers through the cuts, tied the rawhide to poles, and stepped back forcefully until the skewers ripped through the skin. The purposes of the Sun Dance also varied from tribe to tribe but usually included a quest for bountiful hunts, good health, personal courage, and victory over enemies—in short, to bring about peace with the Great Spirit and prosperity in the world. But as the buffalo disappeared and the Plains tribes moved to government reservations, the Sun Dance ceremony vanished, only to be revived later among the Utes, Shoshones, and Gosiutes of the Great Basin. They adapted the ceremony to a redemptive, individual religion, one that helped accommodate the collective ethic of Native American society to the Protestant culture imposed by non–Native Americans on the reservations. For them the Sun Dance ceremony, by belittling European American society and imposing obligations of temperance, sexual fidelity, and community service, guaranteed a supernaturally transformed individual personality enabling them to maintain their identity amid the vast cultural pressures of government reservations. Where the Ghost Dance promised changes in reality, the Sun Dance promised only the possibility of individual virility and understanding, a oneness with the universe that non–Native Americans could never achieve.

Finally, the Dream Dance emerged in the 1870s from the vision quests and spiritual experiences of a Santee Sioux woman named Wananikwe. Her visions of the future struck a responsive chord in the upper Midwest, where political impotence and military inferiority were driving Native Americans to desperation. The Potawatomis and Ojibwas of Wisconsin first adopted the new faith, and the Dream Dance spread throughout the Algonquian-speaking communities of Wisconsin, Michigan, Iowa, and Kansas in the 1880s. Like the Sun Dance, the Dream Dance condemned alcoholism, adultery, individual violence, and gambling, but like the Ghost Dance it also promised a restoration of the old tribal world. Missionary disciples of the Dream Dance traveled widely, hoping to create harmony within individual tribes by restoring the emphasis on consensus which European American values were destroying and to stimulate the development of a pan-Indian unity among all of the tribes so that the traditional conflicts of the past that prevented Native Americans from uniting against non–Native Americans could be resolved. With that unity and harmony, the Dream Dance guaranteed the day when

a great drum will tap in heaven, and at that time all the whites and Catholic Indians will be paralyzed, when all they [Native Americans] have got to do is to walk forth and tap them on the head—and take possession of the land.*

Like the Sun Dance, the Dream Dance too was a major transformative movement in the Midwest.

Expecting a rapid acculturation of Native Americans to European American values, reformers were surprised at the tenacity of tribal

---

*Quoted in James A. Clifton, *The Prairie People: Continuity and Change in Potawatomi Indian Culture, 1665–1965* (Lawrence: Regents Press of Kansas, 1977), 383.

cultures; and the rapid appearances of the Ghost Dance, alcohol "abuse," peyotism, the Sun Dance, and the Dream Dance frightened them. Not only were Native Americans passively resisting the efforts of missionaries, but they were even turning to bizarre "deviations" from their own cultures. Frustrated missionaries and government agents then redoubled their efforts to stamp out Native American customs by teaching Christianity, English, and industrial and farming skills. Once again, Native Americans were to be remade in the image of European Americans. Urging Native Americans to become commercial farmers, the Department of the Interior sent agriculture teachers, farm implements, and instruction books to the reservations, all in a great program to destroy the reliance on subsistence values. Only by raising a surplus and selling it on the open market could Native Americans be fully integrated into a money economy and function like people of European ancestry. Reformers in the federal government and various Protestant churches also decided to prohibit even the *expression* of Native American culture. In a nation where freedom of religion was the most sacred of all individual rights, in 1884 Congress authorized government agents on the reservations to cooperate with local missionaries in suppressing Native American religions. They outlawed the Ghost Dance on the Sioux reservations and the Sun Dance on the Ute and Shoshone reservations. In New Mexico the Pueblos could not continue their centuries-old initiation rites for the young, nor could the Luiseños in California. In Wyoming the Arapahos had to give up their vision quests and funeral ceremonies. In Montana the Blackfeet were forced to end the practice of polygamy, stop the Sun Dances, and cease using medicine bags during illness or burying their dead in trees or lodges. Instead, reservation officials and missionaries insisted that they attend Christian services, consult physicians when sick, and bury their dead in traditional Catholic cemeteries after appropriate Catholic burial services. Federal officials also went after the peyote cult with a passion, trying to destroy it everywhere. On reservations throughout the country, government agents punished Native American children for speaking native dialects and prohibited tribal dances, drumming, body painting, and chants. They also tried to end the custom of extended visits to relatives and friends. Since success as an individual farmer required daily labors on the land, the tribal practice of spending weeks on the road visiting loved ones seemed inefficient to most reformers. Only by confining visits to a few holidays each year could a Native American farmer expect to succeed on his land. Since the federal government was at this same time trying to stamp out polygamy among Utah Mormons, reservation agents dissolved plural marriages among Native Americans, with little thought given to the plight of women deprived of their husbands. Some agents even insisted that former warriors cut their hair short.

Reformers wanted nothing less than a complete transformation of Native American culture.

By 1880 many reformers were questioning whether the reservation approach really was the best way of bringing about the transformation. In 1858 John Beeson, an increasingly vocal critic of government policy toward Native Americans, published *A Plea for the Indian,* which condemned the reservation system because of repeated encroachments on the land by European American settlers. The Sand Creek Massacre of more than one hundred Southern Cheyennes and Arapahos by Colorado militia in 1864 had exposed the tragedy of military confrontation, and subsequent congressional hearings had revealed the horrible conditions on most reservations. In 1868 Lydia M. Child had written *An Appeal for the Indians,* and Peter Cooper had founded the United States Indian Commission to bring an end to the frontier wars. The American Anti-Slavery Society changed its name to the Reform League in 1870 and took on the Native American question as a new crusade.

For most reformers, the reservation policy had become a national scandal, not only because of the extensive poverty but because Native Americans were remaining doggedly loyal to tribal ways. Most of them preferred their own religious ceremonies to sectarian Christianity, and the once-proud hunters viewed farming as demeaning. Their children, even those educated at distant boarding schools, showed a marked propensity for staying on or returning to the reservations. Expecting eradication of Native American society in a single generation, not through violence but through conversion, reformers were dumbfounded at its tenacity. As alcohol, peyote, and the Sun, Ghost, and Dream dances became more popular, reformers slowly came to the conclusion that the reservation was actually insulating tribal culture from the dominant society. Something had to be done.

The Ponca controversy, following so quickly on the heels of the flight of Chief Joseph and the Nez Perces in 1877 and Dull Knife and the Northern Cheyennes in 1878, transformed those feelings into convictions. In 1868 the federal government had given the Sioux ninety-six thousand acres of Ponca tribal land in the Dakota Territory; and when the Sioux began occupying the area in 1877, the Bureau of Indian Affairs decided to remove the Poncas and settle them in Indian Territory (Oklahoma). Most Poncas hated the idea, especially after a delegation had visited Indian Territory. They refused to move there, but the government insisted, and by July 1877 most Poncas had reached their new reservation. Eighteen months later, the oppressive heat, poverty, hunger, malaria, and inadequate housing had become intolerable. Standing Bear, a Ponca chief, left Indian Territory early in 1879 with thirty tribesmen and headed back for the Dakotas.

Standing Bear's flight soon became a national controversy—an indictment, as far as many reformers were concerned—over United States policy toward Native Americans. Despite repeated requests by the Bureau of Indian Affairs, Standing Bear refused to return to Indian Territory. A number of influential people and organizations came to his defense, including Mary Morgan of the Indian Hope Association, Senator Henry L. Dawes of Massachusetts, Senator Algernon Paddock of Nebraska, abolitionist Wendell Phillips, Lydia Child, the American Missionary Association, and the Reform League. Alfred B. Meacham, a federal negotiator almost killed during the Modoc War in California (1872–74), began publishing a pro–Native American journal named *Council Fire Magazine* in 1878. In 1881, after lobbying in behalf of Standing Bear, Helen Hunt Jackson wrote *A Century of Dishonor,* bitterly denouncing federal policies. Herbert Welsh and Henry S. Pancoast founded the Indian Rights Association in 1882; Mary L. Bonney founded the Women's National Indian Association in 1883; and Alfred and Albert Smiley began holding annual meetings of the Friends of the Indian at Lake Mohonk, New York, in 1883. Under enormous pressure, the government returned the confiscated land to the Poncas in 1881, but the controversy convinced many reformers that drastic change was necessary. By isolating Native Americans on reservations the government was perpetuating tribal values, poverty, and economic dependence. Only in the absence of tribal values and government assistance, the reformers believed, could Native Americans be reasonably expected to shed their own culture. Thus, another assault on tribalism was launched.

Native Americans were ill prepared for the reform campaign. Although their rich cultural diversity had provided each tribe with a highly integrated set of values and a powerful sense of ethnic loyalty, that same diversity weakened them in their resistance to European culture. Throughout the eighteenth and nineteenth centuries, the historical rivalries between various tribes had prevented any military unity against non–Native Americans, placing each tribe in the impossible position of resisting European and American expansion all by itself. After the end of the military wars in the 1880s, these same tribal rivalries, as well as intratribal disputes, left Native Americans similarly impotent to resist the reform assault on tribalism. Full-blood Native Americans who still spoke the native dialect and existed emotionally outside the framework of European values generally hated the whole idea of assimilation. But mixed-bloods, the children of Native American and non–Native American parents, tended to be more acculturated to the dominant society, often speaking English and functioning in the commercial economy. They were usually not so opposed to the basic idea of assimilation. So when sincere reformers genuinely solicited Native American opinions about assimilation programs, they often received contradictory replies. No firm "Indian position" ever materialized. The lack of Native American unity reinforced the widespread assumption that only paternalistic non–Native American reformers could solve Native American problems.

While most liberal reformers were beginning to see the reservations as cultural failures, economic interests viewed them as economic failures as well—unnatural obstacles to economic progress. In the 1880s, for example, the railroads were accelerating their demands for rights-of-way through Indian Territory, negotiating at first through the various tribal councils. The St. Louis and San Francisco Railway system wanted to build a road through the Choctaw Nation, and the Missouri, Kansas, and Texas Railroad wanted to connect its Memphis branch with Texas. The Southern Kansas Railroad hoped to build through the new Ponca Reservation, and the Kansas and Arkansas Valley Railroad planned a line through Cherokee land. The Atchison, Topeka, and Santa Fe, and the Chicago, Texas, and Mexican Central were also lobbying for building rights in Indian Territory. Although many mixed-bloods wanted to give the railroads right-of-way through tribal land to raise property values, most full-bloods opposed the corporations; so company lawyers began demanding congressional violations of tribal sovereignty. Many lawyers wanted to deal directly with Congress on the issue of right-of-way rather than go through the various tribal councils.

Cattle ranchers made similar demands. In 1867, for example, the Kiowas, Comanches, and Kiowa-Apaches signed a treaty giving them nearly three million acres of joint reservation land bordering the Red River in eastern Oklahoma. The treaty closed the reservation to all non–Native Americans; but Texas ranchers, driving their herds north to Kansas, looked enviously on the land as a place to graze their cattle. They were doing so with impunity by the 1870s; and although Native American police had the authority to fine them, the reservation was so immense that enforcement was all but impossible. Also, beef suppliers distributing meat to the Native Americans under government contracts had the right to graze cattle on reservation land, but they took advantage of the law by grazing far more cattle there than they actually delivered to the Native Americans.

In 1881, when a severe drought in north Texas eroded pasture capacity, ranchers began moving even more cattle onto the reservation. By 1882 more than fifty thousand head of cattle were on the reservation illegally, and cattlemen began demanding grazing leases for them. Once again, the Native Americans were divided on the issue. Many mixed-bloods favored the leases as a means of increasing their monetary income, while many full-bloods opposed it as an intrusion of tribal land. Because their camps were in the northern part of the reservation, far from the pastures coveted by Texas ranchers, the Kiowas opposed all forms of leasing and bitterly resented the willingness of many Comanches to lease out their joint lands. In addition to their political divisions, many Native Americans were forced by economic circumstance to acquiesce. Government agents expected them to supplement their beef rations by hunting and farming, but the Plains tribes did not take well to farming and by 1880 the buffalo herds were nearly extinct in Oklahoma. The tribes needed money or beef (or both) to support themselves; and in 1882, when beef prices rose dramatically, government fiscal problems dictated ration cuts to the Kiowas, Kiowa-Apaches, Comanches, Cheyennes, and Arapahos in Indian Territory. Strained economically, tribes became more inclined to sign grazing leases with cattlemen. Desperate for the grazing land and tired of bickering over the merits of leasing, cattlemen demanded that the federal government approve long leases on Native American grazing land in Indian Territory.

With the reservation policy clearly bankrupt, both culturally and economically, reformers and economic interest groups abandoned it and launched instead a triple assault on Native American sovereignty: the creation of a federal school system for Native Americans, the extension of federal law to all tribes, and the allotment of all tribal lands. By breaking up the reservations and distributing the land in allotments to individual Native Americans, the reformers hoped to destroy tribal economic power and reorient Native Americans to European American commercial values. With tribal economic power gone, tribal political power would also wane; the reformers planned to grant allotted Native Americans citizenship in the United States and subject them to local and state laws. Reservation land left over was to be sold to non–Native American settlers, the proceeds from the sales to finance federal schools for Native American children where even the residues of tribal culture could be eradicated. After this economic, legal, and cultural assault on tribalism, reformers believed that federal supervision of Native Americans would disappear. Economically self-sufficient, legally subjugated, and finally acculturated, Native Americans would soon become fully assimilated, truly "Americans" in the European American sense of the word.

But like the Native Americans, reformers disagreed about the nature of government policy. Most of the reformers agreed that assimilation was the ultimate solution to the "Indian problem," and that education, allotment, and citizenship were the most effective ways of bringing it about. Some reformers were quite certain that total assimilation was possible immediately, or at least within a single generation. Railroads, cattle syndicates, oil companies, homesteaders, and politicians agreed, demanding immediate placement of Native American children in schools, immediate awards of citizenship, and, of course, immediate allotment of tribal land. Other reformers, however, were not so sanguine about the prospects for immediate assimilation. They insisted on a more gradual approach, one that emphasized citizenship and allotment only when individual Native Americans were culturally prepared for both. Between 1880 and 1934, policy toward Native Americans vacillated between the wishes of the "immediatists" and the "gradualists."

Ever since the eighteenth century, reformers had looked to education as the solution to the "Indian problem," but not until 1865 did the federal government become actively engaged in Native American education, finally concluding that a universal government school system was the only way of assimilating Native American children. Reformers hotly debated the nature of that school system. Richard Pratt, an army officer and founder of the Carlisle Indian Industrial School in 1879, believed in immediate assimilation by removing Native American children from the reservations and teaching them at boarding schools in the East. Distant boarding schools, he thought, would break ties to tribal culture; and by learning English and receiving a classical as well as industrial education, Native American children would be prepared for immediate assimilation. Other reformers, such as John Oberly, who served as superintendent of Indian Education in the Department of the Interior, doubted Pratt's faith in non-reservation boarding schools. In his view, they were unrealistically expensive and their teaching staffs were naive in their intention to transform Native American children in a single generation. These reformers wanted the federal government to establish instead a complete system of reservation day and boarding schools to train all Native American children, maintaining the nonreservation boarding schools for the most able graduates of the reservation schools. But in the 1880s the advocates of immediate assimilation held the upper hand, especially because of their support from western economic interests. The Bureau of Indian Affairs established dozens of non-reservation boarding schools, including Sante Fe (1890), Carson (1890), Phoenix (1890), Pierre (1891), and Flandreau (1893). Eventually, John Oberly's ideas became increasingly influential; but throughout the 1880s and 1890s Richard Pratt's vision of non-reservation boarding schools transforming thousands of Native American children remained the dominant model for Native American education.

Although the reformers argued intensely about the type of schools the federal government should establish, they generally agreed, in the 1880s at least, on the proper content of Native American education. Convinced that Native American children needed academic skills as well as training in the work habits of modern civilization, the reformers insisted on a traditional curriculum of science, mathematics, and working skills. Certain that tribal identity was intricately linked to tribal languages, the reformers prohibited use of native languages at the reservation schools and taught the students English with crusading zeal. In order to wean them from tribal laws and customs, they also taught students the principles of American history and American government.

The reformers also wanted to end tribal authority and extend federal, state, and local laws to all Native Americans. As long as the federal government treated the tribes as separate, insular communities independent of "civilized" law and subject to their own legal constraints, assimilation would never occur. Tribal lands would never be open for development, and the "Indian problem" would never be solved. Ezra Hayt, Commissioner of Indian Affairs, remarked in 1879 that a

civilized community could not exist . . . without law, and a semi-civilized and barbarous people are in a hopeless state of anarchy without its protection and sanctions. It is true that the various tribes have regulations and customs of their own, which, however, are founded on superstition and ignorance of the usages of civilized communities, and generally tend to perpetuate feuds and keep alive animosities.*

The first step in the legal subjugation of Native Americans came in 1871 when an amendment to the annual Indian Appropriations Bill nullified tribal sovereignty. Ever since the colonial period the English and then the United States governments had treated the tribes as sovereign, independent nations free to regulate their own internal affairs. Although the United States government did not recognize fee simple title to tribal lands, officials still negotiated treaties with the various tribes and treated them as part of the international community. All that ended in 1871 with a simple congressional declaration:

Hereafter no Indian nation or tribe within the territory of the United States shall be acknowledged or recognized as an independent nation, tribe, or power with whom the United States may contract by treaty.†

Instead of negotiating with the tribes, the federal government simply began to legislate for them, sometimes requesting and sometimes ignoring the advice of tribal chieftains. The era of treaty making was over.

Throughout the post–Civil War era, reformers continued to discuss the merits of legal change, and they presented a number of bills to Congress during those years. In 1882 Congress granted the Atlantic

---

*Quoted in Francis Paul Prucha, *American Indian Policy in Crisis: Christian Reformers and the Indian, 1865–1900* (Norman: University of Oklahoma Press, 1976), 331.

†Quoted in ibid., 69.

and Pacific–Frisco Railway system a right-of-way even though no previous treaty had permitted it, establishing the precedent that private corporations could receive legal privileges on Native American land without securing tribal consent. Three years later, after considerable debate and compromise, Congress extended criminal jurisdiction from tribal to federal courts. All cases of murder, manslaughter, rape, attempted murder, burglary, larceny, and arson were made subject to federal courts, completely nullifying tribal jurisdiction. Internal relations between Native Americans were thereby invaded, and the Supreme Court upheld the constitutionality of the law in 1886. The erosion of tribal authority continued through the 1880s. In December 1888, for example, after years of lobbying and contentious negotiations with cattle syndicates, the Cherokees legally leased the Outlet, a huge tract of tribal land in northern Oklahoma, to the Cherokee Strip Live Stock Association. Pressured by competing cattle interests who had lost in the bidding, the federal government voided the lease, forced the Association to remove its cattle in 1890, and finally purchased the Outlet in 1891 for $1.40 per acre.

The end of tribal sovereignty and the extension of federal criminal jurisdiction to the tribes accelerated the drive for Native American citizenship, not only to promote assimilation but to protect Native Americans from greedy settlers bent on seizing their property. Congress had awarded citizenship to the Wyandots in 1855, the Potawatomis in 1861, and the Kickapoos in 1862; but many other tribes remained in an intolerable legal position. Without legal standing as individuals or as nations they had no recourse in the courts. They had no way, other than periodic violence and mass protests, to protect themselves from encroachments on their land.

Regarding the extension of citizenship, there was much disagreement as to timing; and once again the immediatists and gradualists locked in debate. Reformers such as the Reverend William J. Harsha of the Omaha Citizenship Committee, or members of the Boston Indian Citizenship Committee and the Indian Rights Association, advocated immediate citizenship as the most effective way of promoting assimilation. Others, including former Secretary of the Interior Carl Schurz and the famous anthropologist John Wesley Powell, felt that Native Americans should remain as wards of the federal government for several generations until they had proven their ability to take advantage of American citizenship. Congress at least temporarily opted in favor of the gradualists in 1881 when it decided to delay legislation.

Three years later the debate over Native American citizenship heated up again and placed the advocates of gradual citizenship on more difficult ground. In 1884 the Supreme Court upheld the elected officials of Omaha, Nebraska, who had denied John Elk, a "civilized

Indian," the right to vote in a local election. Arguing that Elk had neither been "born" under United States jurisdiction nor naturalized by
an act of Congress, the Court agreed with Omaha officials that he did
not have the right to vote. To the advocates of immediate citizenship,
the decision was an outrage. An English-speaking farmer and family
man, Elk was acculturated to European American society and certainly deserving of citizenship, even according to the expectations of
people like Schurz and Powell. Something had to be done, and the
advocates of gradual citizenship were pressured to begin merging the
question of Native American citizenship with their drive for allotment
of Native American lands.

Dissolving tribal lands and allotting small farms to Native American families—the third part of the reform campaign—was not a new
idea. The first real allotment program came in 1839 when Congress
divided the lands of the Brotherton tribe in Wisconsin, and similar
programs occurred later on the reservations of the Chippewas,
Shawnees, Wyandots, Omahas, Ottawas, and Potawatomis. In each
case the negotiated treaties provided that, once allotment was complete, the Native Americans would become citizens of the United
States and be subject to the laws of the land. Lyman Abbott, a well-
known reformer and editor of the *Christian Union,* declared at the Lake
Mohonk conference in 1885:

If this reservation system was only doing a positive injury to us, then we
might endure it. But it holds back civilization and isolates the Indian, and
denies him any right which justice demands for him. . . . It is hopelessly wrong
. . . it cannot be amended or modified; . . . it can only be uprooted, root and
branch and leaf, and a new system put in its place.*

Non–Native American liberals in the Indian Rights Association and
the Lake Mohonk Conference of Friends of the Indian viewed allotment of land in severalty as that new system.

By the nineteenth century two agrarian ideologies had emerged in
the United States: one committed to the southern image of genteel
plantations worked by African slaves and presided over by aristocratic
"cavaliers," and the other committed to a fee simple empire of small
"yeoman" farmers. The Civil War, in some ways a product of the
competition between these two philosophies, helped resolve the question. After 1865 the southern aristocracy gave way to the fee simple
empire, and in the 1880s Native American communalism came face-
to-face with the national faith in a world of independent "yeoman
farmers." Most of the eighteenth-century immigrants had arrived in

---

*Quoted in Frederick E. Hoxie, "Beyond Savagery: The Campaign to
Assimilate the American Indians, 1880–1920" (Ph.D. diss., Brandeis
University, 1977), 191.

the colonies as indentured servants, contractually bound to work for several years in payment of their passage. Except for African slaves, they were the poorest people in the New World. But the abundance of land permitted most of them eventually to acquire property of their own—farms so large that in England they would have been considered handsome estates. Embracing the theories of English philosopher John Locke, the colonists saw liberty in property, a personal world free of political capriciousness, governmental interference, and economic dependence. The Fifth Amendment to the Constitution guaranteed to everyone the right to "life, liberty, and property," and the foundations of Jeffersonian and Jacksonian democracy were millions of yeoman farmers with fee simple title to their land. Free to speak their mind and do their pleasure, they were the backbone of the republic. James K. Paulding's poem *The Backwoodsman,* published in 1818, illustrates that conviction.

> Hence it comes, that our meanest farmer's boy
> Aspires to taste the proud and manly joy
> That springs from holding in his own dear right
> The land he plows, the home he seeks at night;
> And hence it comes, he leaves his friends and home,
> Mid distant wilds and dangers drear to roam,
> To seek a competence, or find a grave,
> Rather than live a hireling or a slave.*

As long as independent property owners filled the nation, liberty would defeat oppression. European American reformers wanted Native Americans to embrace this vision as well.

Thousands of Native Americans had tilled the land before the European conquest; but they had been communal farmers, producing just enough to meet their immediate needs, and commercial production of surpluses was almost totally alien to them. For most of the hunting and gathering tribes, farming of any kind was degrading—a humiliating way of life. The chances of ever converting them to farming were remote indeed. Finally, enormous problems existed with agricultural techniques in the West where most of the reservations were located. On the dry, windy plains of the Midwest, the semideserts of the Great Basin, and the deserts of the Southwest, agricultural success depended upon heavy capital investment and access to sophisticated technology, neither of which the Native Americans possessed. Most of their efforts at farming were destined to failure at worst and meager subsistence at best. Still, European Americans were determined that Native Americans join their fee simple empire, and in 1875 Congress

---

*Quoted in Henry Nash Smith, *Virgin Land: The American West as Symbol and Myth* (New York: Alfred A. Knopf, 1950), 155.

passed the Indian Homestead Act, permitting individual Native Americans to take ownership of up to 160 acres of land.

The reformers received a major boost in 1880 when Congress passed an allotment bill governing the Ute tribes of Colorado. Under the leadership of Chief Ouray, the Utes had been guaranteed a reservation in western Colorado in 1868, but the expansion of the mining frontier and the admission of Colorado as a state in 1876 had increased demands for their removal. When the Utes attacked in 1879, killing over twenty people, Coloradans demanded a war of extermination on the entire tribe. Fearing a genocidal assault on the Ute reservation, Secretary of the Interior Carl Schurz proposed

the settlement of the Utes in severalty allotments, so as to promote the civilization of the Indians, and to open the main part of the Ute reservation to development by white citizens, thus removing a source of constant irritation between the latter and the Utes.*

After some debate, Congress passed the Ute severalty bill in 1880. Under its provisions, the White River Utes moved to a reservation in the Uintah Basin of eastern Utah, and the Uncompahgre and Southern Utes moved to lands on the Grand and La Plata rivers in Colorado. Each Ute head of family received 160 acres, and the rest of the land went back to the federal government.

Between 1880 and 1887 a number of allotment bills, patterned after the Ute settlement, were submitted to Congress. In 1882, for example, Congress allotted 76,000 acres of land held by the Nebraska Omahas, and by 1887 Congress had allotted 584,423 acres of Native American land. Reformers were pleased, but so were land-hungry speculators, who soon joined them in supporting allotment. If reservations were divided into individual holdings, it would be easier to purchase land from the Native Americans. The reservations, totaling 155 million acres in 1881, were controlled by fewer than three hundred thousand Native Americans. Even the most generous arithmetic showed that, if every Native American received 160 acres, the total would only amount to about 50 million acres. What was to become of the other 105 million acres? Speculators saw a windfall in the making, and the allotment approach seemed an efficient way of transferring the titles on Native American land to European American owners.

During the early 1880s Congress considered a number of general allotment bills designed to break up all of the reservations, but reformers again disagreed on the timing. For the most part, reformers such as Lyman Abbott, anthropologist Alice Fletcher, and Richard Henry Pratt, who had also favored immediate citizenship, favored

---

*Quoted in Prucha, *American Indian Policy in Crisis*, 237.

immediate allotment in severalty of all reservation lands. Land developers and homesteaders, of course, sided with the immediatists. But other reformers found immediate allotment too precipitous, too naive about assimilation, and too dangerous to Native American welfare. They doubted that Native Americans could adjust so quickly to European American ways and feared that immediate allotment would only lead to more Native American poverty. General George Crook remarked in 1887, "We must not try to drive the Indian too fast in effecting these changes. We must not force him to take civilization immediately in its complete form."* Senators Richard Coke of Texas and Henry L. Dawes of Massachusetts favored more gradual allotment programs, and both men submitted bills to Congress early in the 1880s. Still others opposed allotment altogether, but they were voices in the wilderness. Alfred B. Meacham and the *Council Fire Magazine* regularly denounced compulsory allotment, as did the noted ethnologist Lewis H. Morgan. Although government agents regularly reported that some Native Americans also favored allotment, most of the tribes were totally opposed. The Senecas, Creeks, Omahas, Choctaws, Shawnees, Cherokees, Chickasaws, Umatillas, Poncas, Potawatomis, and others made formal protests to Congress and to the Bureau of Indian Affairs. But the frustration of non–Native Americans with the reservation system was too great and the momentum for allotment too strong. Under the sponsorship of Senator Henry L. Dawes a compromise bill, known as the General Allotment Act—later known as the Dawes Severalty Act, or Dawes Act—passed Congress on February 8, 1887. Elated with the law, the Indian Rights Association proclaimed:

So long as the cosmopolitan population of this country shall remember and celebrate Runnymede and Magna Carta, Independence and Emancipation, will the 8th of February, 1887, also come in for proportionate claim for honorable mention and thrilling memories.†

The Dawes Severalty Act did not require the immediate allotment of Native American land; instead, it first permitted the President to select the tribes most suited for allotment before dividing up their lands. Once allotment was implemented, each Native American adult head of family received 160 acres; single adults over eighteen years old and orphans under eighteen got 80 acres; and other single youths under eighteen received 40 acres. The Native Americans could choose their land; but if they failed to do so in four years, the Department of the Interior could do it for them. If the land was suitable only for grazing, the President could allot twice that amount of land in each

---

*Boston Post, February 28, 1887.

†Quoted in Prucha, *American Indian Policy in Crisis,* 255.

category. To prevent the Native Americans from selling their individual holdings, title to the property was placed in trust for twenty-five years. Additionally, Native Americans accepting allotment and leaving their tribes were awarded American citizenship and came under the laws of the states in which they lived. Finally, the Dawes Act provided that surplus lands not allotted could be sold by the federal government to settlers. Because of their intense opposition to the allotment plan, the Creeks, Cherokees, Chickasaws, Choctaws, Seminoles, Osages, Miamis, Peorias, and Sacs and Foxes, all in Indian Territory; the Senecas in New York; and the Sioux in Nebraska were exempted.

With the passage of the Dawes Act, reformers finally had the tools, they believed, to bring about the assimilation of the Native Americans. Still, they debated the pace of allotment, and some insisted on immediate allotment while others remained loyal to gradual allotment. By the end of 1888 only 3,349 Native Americans had received an allotment, and it appeared that the gradualists had the upper hand.

However, troubles on the Sioux reservations late in the 1880s reinforced European American frustrations with the whole reservation policy and helped accelerate the allotment program. The 1880s were bleak years for the Sioux. Stress and discontent prevailed between mixed-bloods embracing assimilation and full-bloods rejecting it, and cuts in government rations made the Sioux reservations powder kegs primed for explosion. The tragedy at Wounded Knee in December 1890 was a result.

News of the tragedy sent a shudder throughout the country, convincing reformers even more certainly of the need for drastic change in national policy. The Dawes Act of 1887 seemed ever more likely to be the right solution.

Passage of the Dawes Act, however, had not resolved the disputes between the immediatists and gradualists. The purpose of the Dawes Act had been to transform Native Americans into practical, property-owning farmers, but the gradualists had realized that most Native Americans would resist the change, preferring to lease or sell their newly allotted land to European American farmers or ranchers for cash. If that happened, Native Americans would become utterly landless and destitute. To guard against that probability, guarantees were written into the Dawes Act prohibiting the leasing of allotted land and postponing any sale of the land for at least twenty-five years. Not tempted or even able to part with their allotment, conventional reasoning maintained, Native Americans would have no choice but to put it into practical use. This was the principle of "inalienability," and it had represented a victory for the gradualists.

Almost immediately after President Grover Cleveland signed the Dawes Act in 1887, however, other reformers and western economic interests began questioning the restrictions against leasing and selling land. Reformers interested in immediate assimilation argued that many Native American women, children, and disabled men were not capable of strenuous work and that, because of the leasing and sale restrictions, they were unable to benefit from their property. In 1890, for example, more than 60 percent of Winnebago land belonged to women, children, and infirm men. Other Native Americans physically able to work did not possess the farm implements they needed to cultivate the land. On the Kiowa, Comanche, and Wichita reservations, the government supplied only one plow for every three farmers. Reacting to these problems and to the slaughter at Wounded Knee, some reformers demanded changes in the leasing and sale restrictions so that women, children, and the disabled could generate a cash income off their land, and so that Native Americans capable of farming could get enough cash to buy equipment. Speculators and settlers, who were not content to allow even the allotted land to remain unexploited and who chafed at the exemption of Native Americans from local property taxes, heartily supported the campaign to ease the leasing and sale restrictions. Once again, the immediatist reformers and land developers, for different reasons, joined to alter Native American land tenure.

In 1891 Congress gave in to the pressure and passed a law permitting aged and disabled Native Americans to lease their allotted land for three years to farmers and ranchers and for ten years to miners. John Noble, Secretary of the Interior, had to approve each lease, and at first he was very conservative, approving only two applications in 1892. In 1894 Congress eased leasing restrictions and permitted any Native American "unable" to work to lease his or her land for five years to farmers and ranchers and for ten years to miners and "businessmen." The pace of leasing quickened even more when Hoke Smith, the new Secretary of the Interior, delegated leasing approval to reservation agents. They approved 295 leases in 1894, 1,287 leases in 1897, and 2,590 in 1900. Of the 140,000 acres allotted on the Omaha and Winnebago reservations in Nebraska, more than 112,000 acres were leased to European Americans.

Restrictions on selling land outright followed a similar pattern. In 1893 Congress reduced the allotment trust period for the Puyallup Indians, located near Tacoma, Washington, from twenty-five to ten years. Tacoma's fast-growing economy, coupled with the fact that the allotted lands straddled the western terminus of the Northern Pacific Railroad, led to the trust period reduction in the name of economic progress. One year later, Congress authorized the Shawnees and Potawatomis in Indian Territory to sell all or part of their allotted land in excess of eighty acres. Gradualists predicted an enormous loss of Native American land, but the erosion of inalienability was too well underway to be stopped, and more new legislation was passed to accelerate the process, such as the 1902 Dead Indian Land Act, which permitted Native Americans to sell allotted lands they had inherited.

With allotment underway and leasing and sale restrictions eased, reformers, settlers, and speculators turned their attention to the last bastion of tribalism—Indian Territory. Although Congress had exempted Indian Territory from the Dawes Act, most reformers thought that those tribes were especially ready for assimilation. Having experienced high intermarriage rates to non–Native Americans and successful adjustment to the commercial economy, the Five Civilized Tribes seemed on the verge of assimilation—and by 1890 private oil companies hungered for the land much as the railroads and cattle syndicates had in the 1870s and 1880s. Negotiations for oil leases would be much more "rational" and consistent, the petroleum companies argued, if the federal government, rather than various tribal councils, approved the contracts. Additionally, tens of thousands of settlers were looking on Indian Territory as a farming bonanza, and their demands for the opening of tribal lands to non–Native American homesteaders grew more and more intense throughout the 1880s. All three groups—reformers, corporations, and settlers—joined forces in the 1890s to liquidate tribal sovereignty in Indian Territory.

In 1889, after years of agitation by homesteaders and railroads, President Benjamin Harrison opened the vacant lands of the "Oklahoma District" in central Oklahoma for settlement, and fifty thousand "sooners" poured into the area. The next year Congress formed a territorial government there and attached the Oklahoma panhandle to the older "Oklahoma District." In 1893, two years after purchasing the Cherokee Outlet, Congress opened the land to more than one hundred thousand homesteaders who quickly swamped the area.

Inevitably, as settlers moved to Oklahoma, demands for the extension of federal jurisdiction over the remainder of Indian Territory intensified. Original jurisdiction in criminal cases rested with federal district courts in Fort Smith, Arkansas, and Paris, Texas; but in 1890 Congress appointed nine commissioners for Indian Territory, giving them authority as justices of the peace to enforce the state laws of Arkansas there. By 1895, with European American settlement in Oklahoma continuing unabated, Congress established two federal district courts in Indian Territory, nullifying the authority of the district courts in Arkansas and Texas. Two years later, Congress decided that all civil and criminal cases in Indian Territory had to be handled by United States courts.

Ultimately, settlers' hopes for Indian Territory rested on allotment. Shortly after the opening of Oklahoma, the Sacs and Foxes, Citizen Potawatomis, Absentee Shawnees, Kickapoos, and Pawnees all had to cede some of their tribal lands to the federal government. Between

1891 and 1893 federal agents established more than three thousand allotments on Cheyenne and Arapaho land in Indian Territory. At the same time the federal government was attempting forcefully to allot the reservations of the Kiowa and Comanche. Although an older Kiowa treaty had promised that no future land cessions could occur without tribal ratification, the federal government ignored the agreement. Lone Wolf, a Kiowa chief, brought suit against the federal government, arguing that allotment implied eventual cession of tribal lands and that tribal members had rejected the idea. In 1903, after years of litigation, the United States Supreme Court decided against Lone Wolf, arguing that Congress possessed sovereignty over tribal affairs and the power to legislate for them. Native American consent to allotment would no longer be considered, even if prior treaty arrangements demanded tribal ratification.

Although the Five Civilized Tribes had appeared safe from allotment when they were declared exempt from the Dawes Act, as early as 1893 Congress established a commission to negotiate allotment agreements with those tribes, and President Grover Cleveland appointed Dawes himself, now retired from the Senate, to head the commission. Once again, Native American political divisiveness gave reformers and economic interests the upper hand because both advocates and opponents of allotment could find some Native Americans who supported their positions. Intermarriage among the Five Civilized Tribes had been common. In 1906, for example, there were 1,538 full-bloods, 4,146 mixed-bloods, and 635 intermarried whites in the Chickasaw Nation. Although most full-bloods bitterly opposed allotment as an assault on communal lands, mixed-bloods and white relatives offered conflicting opinions. Some mixed-bloods, able to farm or graze livestock on huge tracts of tribal land and keep the profits themselves, opposed allotment because it would deprive them of the use of much land and force them to work only their 160-acre (or less) parcels. Other mixed-bloods and whites, excluded from the use of any land at all, saw allotment as a way to gain some personal control over tribal lands, especially if leasing and early sale of allotments by full-bloods was permitted. With the Native Americans arguing among themselves about the merits of allotment, and with some mixed-bloods clearly exploiting tribal lands for personal gain, the reformers were even more convinced that rapid allotment was essential to assimilation and assimilation essential to solving the "Indian problem." Dawes perfectly summarized the passion and conviction of the Christian reformers.

Remember that your work is not for the regeneration of a locality, but for a race. And until in every Indian home, wherever situated, the wife shall sit by her hearthstone clothed in the habiliments of true womanhood, and the husband shall stand sentinel at the threshold panoplied in the armor of a self-supporting citizen of the United States,—then and not till then, will your work be done.*

Supported by the Lake Mohonk Conferences and the policy statements of the Indian Rights Association, and pressured by settlers and the petroleum companies, Congress pushed ahead with allotment in 1896, ordering the Dawes Commission to make a list of the members of each tribe. With more than three hundred thousand people claiming tribal membership, the enrollment list was necessary to protect Native American property. Full-bloods opposed enrollment and any allotment surveys, harassed land surveyors, and, in the case of full-blood Cherokees, threatened violence to any Native American giving his name to the Dawes Commission. Still, leaders of the Five Civilized Tribes, divided in their opinions and under severe political pressure, began giving up the fight. The Choctaws and Chickasaws signed the Atoka Agreement with the Dawes Commission in 1897, thereby accepting allotments of 320 acres each. The Seminoles agreed to 120-acre allotments in 1898, the Creeks accepted 160 acres each in 1901, and the Cherokees signed for 110-acre allotments in 1902. Allotment in severalty, the great reform panacea, had conquered Indian Territory.

The Curtis Act of 1898 then terminated tribal sovereignty in Indian Territory. Confirming the allotment surveys and agreements of the Dawes Commission, the Curtis Act voided tribal control of mineral leasing in favor of federal government control, abolished tribal laws and courts as of 1906, and imposed United States civil and criminal jurisdiction over all people living in Indian Territory. Congress completed the legal assault on tribal sovereignty in Indian Territory in 1901 by awarding citizenship to every Native American living there. Between 1898 and 1907 in Indian Territory, the Dawes Commission enrolled 101,506 Native Americans, surveyed more than 19.5 million acres of land, and allotted nearly 16 million acres to individual Native Americans. When Oklahoma Territory and Indian Territory were merged and admitted to statehood in 1907, more than 1.3 million European Americans were living there. The railroads had their rights-of-way; the cattle syndicates had their pastures; the petroleum companies had their leases; and the settlers had their land. D. W. C. Duncan, a Cherokee, testified before Congress in 1906 that

I am in a fix, . . . you will not forget now that when I use the word "I" I mean the whole Cherokee people. I am in that fix. What am I to do? I have a piece of property that doesn't support me, and is not worth a cent to me, under the

---

Lake Mohonk Conference of Friends of the Indian, 1897, 43.

same inexorable, cruel provisions of the Curtis law that swept away our treaties, our system of nationality, our very existence, and wrested out of our possession our vast territory.*

The Dawes Act, despite the temporary victories of the gradualists, proved to be a disaster for Native Americans. Before 1887 the federal government had approved 7,463 individual allotments totaling 584,423 acres; but between 1887 and 1900, Department of the Interior officials approved 53,168 allotments totaling 5,409,530 acres. That opened huge amounts of "surplus" Native American land to settlers. In 1881 Native Americans owned 155,632,312 acres, but their holdings dropped to 104,319,349 acres in 1890 and 77,865,373 acres in 1900.

Along with allotment, the reformers continued to pursue their legal and educational policies. Citizenship increased rapidly after the 1887 Dawes Act, which granted citizenship to those accepting allotments, and the 1888 decision by Congress to extend citizenship to all Native Americans who married American citizens. By 1890 citizenship had been extended to 5,307 allotted Native Americans, and by 1900 to 53,168. In 1901 Congress awarded citizenship to another 101,506 Native Americans in Indian Territory, and by 1905 more than half of all Native Americans had become citizens of the United States.

In order to render these newly allotted citizens capable of full participation in American society, the federal government continued its efforts to establish a universal school system for them. Between 1895 and 1905, the number of nonreservation boarding schools patterned after Carlisle increased from 19 to 25, and enrollment increased from 4,673 to 9,736. In the same period, the number of reservation boarding schools increased from 75 to 93, and the number of students from 8,068 to 11,402. Finally, the number of day schools on the reservations increased from 125 to 139 and enrollment from 3,843 to 4,399. As allotment occurred on each reservation, the federal government took over local schools. Between 1898 and 1906, for example, when the Chickasaw Nation was allotted, the Bureau of Indian Affairs assumed control of all tribal schools, dictating new curricula, hiring new teachers, and reforming daily schedules. At the government schools, Native American children were treated with strict discipline, forced to speak English and ignore tribal languages, forced to accept Christianity and deny tribal religions, required to patriotically celebrate American holidays (including the anniversary of the Dawes Act), and required to learn work habits to prepare themselves for life in the dominant society.

---

*Wayne Moquin and Charles Van Doren, eds., *Great Documents in American Indian History* (New York: Praeger, 1973), 288.

Great faith in the assimilation of Native Americans continued intact into the early 1900s, when the reform troika of education, citizenship, and allotment reached its zenith. Native Americans were in the process of losing huge amounts of land, but most European Americans believed that such losses were necessary for the transformation of Native American culture. Open violence and tragic confrontations were now part of the past; and reformers looked to the day, perhaps in the near future, when Native Americans would quietly disappear into the larger society. But most Native Americans determined not to accommodate.

Suggested Readings

Aberle, David F. *The Peyote Religion among the Navajo.* Chicago: University of Chicago Press, 1982.

Adams, David Wallace. "Schooling the Hopi: Federal Indian Policy Writ Small, 1887–1917." *Pacific Historical Review* 48 (August 1979).

Anderson, Edward F. *Peyote: The Divine Cactus.* Tucson: University of Arizona Press, 1980.

Andrist, Ralph K. *The Long Death: The Last Days of the Plains Indians.* New York: Macmillan, 1964.

Berkhofer, Robert F., Jr. *Salvation and the Savage: An Analysis of Protestant Missions and American Indian Response, 1787–1862.* Lexington: University of Kentucky Press, 1965.

Berthrong, Donald J. *The Cheyenne and Arapaho Ordeal: Reservation and Agency Life in the Indian Territory, 1875–1907.* Norman: University of Oklahoma Press, 1976.

Boston Post. February 28, 1887.

Carlson, Leonard A. *Indians, Bureaucrats, and Land: The Dawes Act and the Decline of Indian Farming.* Westport, Conn.: Greenwood Press, 1981.

Clifton, James A. *The Prairie People: Continuity and Change in Potawatomi Indian Culture, 1665–1965.* Lawrence: Regents Press of Kansas, 1977.

Cotroneo, Ross R., and Jack Dozier. "A Time of Disintegration: The Coeur d'Alene and the Dawes Act." *Western Historical Quarterly* 5 (October 1974).

Edmunds, R. David. *The Potawatomis: Keepers of the Fire.* Norman: University of Oklahoma Press, 1978.

Freeman, John F. "The Indian Convert: Theme and Variation." *Ethnohistory* 12 (Spring 1965).

Fritz, Henry E. *The Movement for Indian Assimilation, 1860–1890.* Philadelphia: University of Pennsylvania Press, 1963.

Gibson, Arrell Morgan. *The American Indian: Prehistory to the Present.* Lexington, Mass.: D. C. Heath, 1980.

Gilcreast, Everett Arthur. "Richard Henry Pratt and American Indian Policy, 1877–1906: A Study of the Assimilation Movement." Ph.D. diss., Yale University, 1967.

Gilles, Albert S. "The Southwestern Indian and His Drugs." *Southwest Review* 55 (Spring 1970).

Greenway, John. "The Ghost Dance: Some Reflections, with Evidence, on a Cult of Despair among the Indians of North America." *American West* 6 (July 1969).

Hagan, William T. *Indian Police and Judges: Experiments in Acculturation and Control.* New Haven, Conn.: Yale University Press, 1966.

————. "Indian Policy after the Civil War: The Reservation Experience." In *American Indian Policy: Indiana Historical Society Lectures, 1970–1971.* Indianapolis: Indiana Historical Society, 1971.

————. "Kiowas, Comanches, and Cattlemen, 1867–1906: A Case Study of the Failure of U.S. Reservation Policy." *Pacific Historical Review* 40 (August 1971).

————. *United States-Comanche Relations: The Reservation Years.* New Haven, Conn.: Yale University Press, 1976.

Hassrick, Royal B. "Alcohol and Indians." *American Indian* 4 (1947).

Hauptman, Laurence M. "Senecas and Subdividers: Resistance to Allotment of Indian Lands in New York, 1875–1906." *Prologue* 9 (Summer 1977).

Hendrick, Irving G. "Federal Policy Affecting the Education of Indians in California, 1849–1934." *History of Education Quarterly* 16 (Summer 1976).

Hoig, Stanley. *The Sand Creek Massacre.* Norman: University of Oklahoma Press, 1961.

Holford, David M. "The Subversion of the Indian Land Allotment System, 1887–1934." *Indian Historian* 8 (Spring 1975).

Hoxie, Frederick E. "Beyond Savagery: The Campaign to Assimilate the American Indians, 1880–1920." Ph.D. diss., Brandeis University, 1977.

Jorgensen, Joseph G. *The Sun Dance Religion: Power for the Powerless.* Chicago: University of Chicago Press, 1972.

La Barre, Weston. *The Peyote Cult.* Hamden, Conn.: Archon Books, 1975.

————. *The Ghost Dance: The Origins of Religion.* Garden City, N.Y.: Doubleday, 1970.

Laubin, Reginald, and Gladys Laubin. *Indian Dances of North America: Their Importance to Indian Life.* Norman: University of Oklahoma Press, 1977.

Lee, R. Alton. "Indian Citizenship and the Fourteenth Amendment." *South Dakota History* 4 (Spring 1974).

Levy, Jerrold E., and Stephen J. Kunitz. *Indian Drinking: Navajo Practices and Anglo-American Theories.* New York: John Wiley, 1974.

Lurie, Nancy O. "The World's Oldest On-Going Protest Demonstration: Native American Drinking Patterns." *Pacific Historical Review* 40 (August 1971).

Mardock, Robert W. *The Reformers and the American Indian.* Columbia: University of Missouri Press, 1971.

McNickle, D'Arcy. *Native American Tribalism: Indian Survivals and Renewals.* New York: Oxford University Press, 1973.

————. "Peyote and the Indian." *Scientific Monthly* 57 (September 1943).

McRae, William E. "Peyote Rituals of the Kiowas." *Southwest Review* 60 (Summer 1975).

Melody, Michael E. "The Lakota Sun Dance: A Composite View and Analysis." *South Dakota History* 6 (Fall 1976).

Miner, H. Craig. *The Corporation and the Indian: Tribal Sovereignty and Industrial Civilization in Indian Territory, 1865–1907.* Columbia: University of Missouri Press, 1976.

Mooney, James. *The Ghost-Dance Religion and the Sioux Outbreak of 1890.* Chicago: University of Chicago Press, 1965.

Moquin, Wayne, and Charles Van Doren, eds. *Great Documents in American Indian History.* New York: Praeger, 1973.

Murdock, Donald B. "The Case for Native American Tribal Citizenship." *Indian Historian* 8 (Fall 1975).

Otis, D. S. *The Dawes Act and the Allotment of Indian Lands.* Norman: University of Oklahoma Press, 1973.

Priest, Loring Benson. *Uncle Sam's Stepchildren: The Reformation of United States Indian Policy, 1865–1887.* New Brunswick, N.J.: Rutgers University Press, 1942.

Prucha, Francis Paul. *American Indian Policy in Crisis: Christian Reformers and the Indian, 1865–1900.* Norman: University of Oklahoma Press, 1976.

———. *The Churches and the Indian Schools, 1888–1912.* Lincoln: University of Nebraska Press, 1979.

Savage, William W., Jr. *The Cherokee Strip Live Stock Association: Federal Regulation and the Cattlemen's Last Frontier.* Columbia: University of Missouri Press, 1973.

Smith, Burton M. "The Politics of Allotment: The Flathead Indian Reservation as a Test Case." *Pacific Northwest Quarterly* 70 (July 1979).

Smith, Henry Nash. *Virgin Land: The American West as Symbol and Myth.* New York: Alfred A. Knopf, 1950.

Smith, Michael T. "The History of Indian Citizenship." *Great Plains Journal* 10 (Fall 1970).

Stein, Gary C. "The Indian Citizenship Act of 1924." *New Mexico Historical Review* 47 (July 1972).

Stewart, Omer C. "The Native American Church and the Law with Description of Peyote Religious Services." *Brand Book* (Denver Westerners) 17 (1961).

Tibbles, Thomas Henry. *The Ponca Chiefs: An Account of the Trial of Standing Bear.* Lincoln: University of Nebraska Press, 1972.

Waddell, Jack O., and Michael W. Everett, eds. *Drinking Behavior among Southwestern Indians: An Anthropological Perspective.* Tucson: University of Arizona Press, 1980.

Washburn, Wilcomb E. *The Assault on Indian Tribalism: The General Allotment Law (Dawes Act) of 1887.* Philadelphia: J. B. Lippincott, 1975.

Whittaker, James O. "Alcohol and the Standing Rock Sioux Tribe: The Pattern of Drinking." *Quarterly Journal of Studies on Alcohol* 23 (September 1962).

Young, Mary Elizabeth. *Redskins, Ruffleshirts, and Rednecks: Indian Allotments in Alabama and Mississippi, 1830–1860.* Norman: University of Oklahoma Press, 1961.

Chapter Four

Native American Reaction
and the Seeds of Reform

As the twentieth century dawned, the United States was swept up into a vast reform movement known as Progressivism. Generally representing the economic and social interests of the middle and professional classes, the Progressives were especially concerned about the concentration of power in the United States and the survival of democratic individualism. Politically, they hoped to guarantee the future of democracy through the secret ballot, direct election of senators, primary nominating elections in each party, the initiative, the referendum, the recall, and women's suffrage. In economic terms they wanted to preserve competition against the rise of big business monopolies; only through government regulation of the major corporations, as in the Federal Reserve Act of 1913 or creation of the Federal Trade Commission, could small businesses survive and consumers enjoy reasonable prices. Politically and economically, they wanted to preserve an America of small interest groups competing on equal terms for success.

But these Progressives were hardly so forward-looking regarding similar aspirations among ethnic and religious minorities. Most Progressives were very concerned with preserving the dominance of white Anglo-Saxon Protestant values, especially in view of the flood of African Americans from the American South and southern and eastern European immigrants coming into the major cities during the early 1900s. Jim Crow laws became rampant throughout the South and racist ideologies became more and more popular everywhere in the United States. Additionally, the acquisition of a territorial empire in the Caribbean and the Pacific after 1898 brought millions of "brown people" under United States sovereignty, seriously challenging the traditionally assumed policy of incorporating new territories equally into the republic. Prominent scholars like Herbert Baxter Adams and Robert Knox argued that different groups of people had fixed characteristics beyond change—that Anglo-Saxon, Nordic, and Germanic people were fitted for free-enterprise capitalism, technological development, and political liberty, while "native" people were forever limited by their genetic heritage to lives of subsistence poverty and political subservience. More popular writers like Madison Grant in books like his *The Passing of the Great Race* (1916), sounded similar themes.

Under the impact of these new ideas during the Progressive period, the older faith in the possibilities of rapid assimilation of Native Americans weakened somewhat, raising doubts in the minds of some reformers. Francis Ellington Leupp, Commissioner of Indian Affairs under President Theodore Roosevelt between 1905 and 1909, wondered about the new racial theories and their meaning for assimilation policies. In 1905 he remarked:

If nature has set a different physical stamp upon different races of men it is fair to assume that the variation of types extends below the surface and is manifested in mental and moral traits as well. . . . What good end shall we serve by trying to blot out these distinctions . . . ? Nothing is gained by trying to undo nature's work and do it over, but grand results are possible, if we simply turn her forces into the best channels.*

Assimilationists did not surrender, of course, but they became somewhat more realistic about the time it would take to absorb Native Americans completely into the larger society. Their long-standing faith in the efficacy of allotment, education, and citizenship remained intact, but they were willing to make some adjustments in the timing and nature of assimilation to accommodate the prevailing racial and social attitudes. Gradualism, once a euphemism for delay and exploitation, became increasingly more palatable to them.

The allotment and leasing programs continued into the twentieth century, even though changes in both programs reflected some concern about whether Native Americans were ready for assimilation. Spurred on by speculators who wanted still more Native American land, by assimilated mixed-bloods who wanted cash payments, and by a number of liberal reformers who hoped to improve Native American income, Congress had passed the Dead Indian Land Act in 1902. The law waived the trust status of inherited allotments, permitting individual Native Americans to sell their land. Interest in further altering the trust status of Native American land continued. Four years after the Dead Indian Act, Congressman Charles Burke of South Dakota pushed the Burke Act through Congress, eliminating the twenty-five-year trust period altogether when the Secretary of the Interior declared individual Native Americans competent to manage their own affairs. Other provisions of the act allowed the extension of the trust period beyond twenty-five years in certain cases and withdrew the granting of citizenship to Native American allottees until they received their fee simple titles. After receiving such titles, Native Americans could sell their allotments. Western economic interests saw

---

Annual Report of the Commissioner of Indian Affairs (Washington, D.C.: U.S. Government Printing Office, 1905), 7–9.

the Burke Act as a means of getting more Native American land; liberals supported it too, afraid that, with the Dawes Act's twenty-five-year trust period expiring in 1912, many Native Americans might want to sell their allotments. By requiring individual Native Americans to receive permission from the Secretary of the Interior before they could sell, the Burke Act, they presumed, would slow the alienation of Native American land after 1912. To stop the wholesale leasing of this land, Congress had also passed new restrictions in 1900, permitting only five-year leases on farming property.

Although under the impact of the Dawes Act of 1887 and the Curtis Act of 1898 more than 53,000 Native Americans had received allotments totaling 5,409,530 acres, Native American land holdings had declined from 155,632,312 acres (in 1881) to 77,865,373 acres in 1900. After 1900, under the continuing influence of the Dawes Act and the Curtis Act, as well as the Dead Indian Land Act of 1902 and the Burke Act of 1906, the loss of Native American land went on largely unabated. During the presidential administrations of Theodore Roosevelt and William Howard Taft, the Secretary of the Interior issued competency patents under the Burke Act cautiously. By 1917 only 9,984 Native Americans had received patents permitting them to sell their allotments; but when President Woodrow Wilson appointed Franklin K. Lane, an arch-assimilationist, as Secretary of the Interior in 1917, the number of patents issued increased dramatically, totaling more than twenty thousand between 1917 and 1921. Real estate salesmen, government agents, land speculators, and European American farmers eagerly bought up allotments from the Native American owners.

The extension of citizenship, by exposing Native Americans to state and local statutes, only accelerated the sale or exploitation of allotments. On the White Earth Reservation in northern Minnesota, a 1906 congressional law permitting all mixed-bloods to sell their allotments created a bonanza for several major timber corporations. On Flathead land in Montana, local officials often encouraged members of the tribe to sell inherited allotments, and since the allotments were often so small the Native Americans usually acquiesced. In Indian Territory the loss of allotments was even more extensive because of the enormous value of farming, grazing, and timber land and the rich deposits of lead, zinc, coal, and petroleum. Under pressure from local non–Native American interest groups, in 1908 Congress ended all restrictions on the allotments of intermarried Native Americans and many mixed-bloods, releasing almost thirteen million more acres for sale. Settlers and speculators were jubilant. The measure also turned over control of the remaining restricted allotments to the county courts, where corrupt judges soon declared all Native Americans incompetent to manage their property. Judges then appointed guardians to oversee each Native American allotment. With nearly one hundred thousand allotments still restricted, and their value totaling more than one billion dollars, corrupt trafficking in guardianships became common. In some cases attorneys were awarded fees of 50 percent of the annual royalties off the allotment for "managing" them. The bonanza was so lucrative that forgery, blackmail, kidnapping, embezzlement, and even murder became common occurrences to prevent Native Americans from enjoying the financial profits from their land, to keep rival attorneys and guardians from increasing the amount of land they controlled, and to stop reformers from protesting the criminality of it all. It was not uncommon for some attorneys to have guardianship over fifty or even one hundred Native American children and, consequently, control over the proceeds from their allotments. It was no wonder that many reformers referred to that original congressional statute as the "Crime of 1908."

Under the various allotment programs, the most valuable land was first to go. Settlers went after the rich grasslands of Kansas, Nebraska, and the Dakotas; the dense, black-soil forests of Minnesota and Wisconsin; and the wealthy oil and gas lands of Oklahoma. In 1887, for example, the Sisseton Sioux of South Dakota owned 918,000 acres of rich virgin land on their reservation. But since there were only two thousand of them, allotment left more than 600,000 acres for European American settlers. Between 1887 and 1930 the Sisseton lost nearly 200,000 of the remaining 300,000 allotted acres through sales under the Dead Indian Land Act and the Burke Act. The Chippewas of Minnesota lost their rich timber lands; once each member had claimed his land, the government leased the rest to timber corporations. The Colvilles of northeastern Washington lost their lands to cattlemen, who fraudulently claimed mineral rights there. In Montana and Wyoming the Crows lost more than two million acres, and the Nez Perces had to cede communal grazing ranges in Idaho. All sixty-seven of the tribes in Indian Territory underwent allotment. Eventually the Kickapoos there sold most of their allotted lands to settlers for less than thirty cents an acre. The Coeur d'Alenes of Idaho owned more than 400,000 acres in rich land; but by 1930, after allotment and the sale of individual parcels, they owned only 62,400 acres, with more than 45,000 of those acres leased to non–Native Americans. After all the rhetoric about transforming Native Americans into farmers, the Coeur d'Alenes were actually farming only 17,280 acres of land. On the Flathead Reservation—which included Flatheads, Pend Oreilles, Kutenais, and Spokanes—government agents enrolled 2,133 people on allotment lists, 901 of whom were full-bloods, 1,149 mixed-bloods, and 83 adopted Native Americans or intermarried European Americans. When the actual allotments were distributed in 1909, the Flatheads received a maximum of 380,000 acres; another 2,524 acres were reserved for tribal use, 6,774 more acres for the government agency, 4,977 acres for power installations, and 18,521 acres for a national bison range. On April 1, 1910, the federal government opened 1.1 million acres of "surplus" land on the Flathead Reservation to settlers. A similar story prevailed throughout the country.

Some tribes managed to evade the assault, including the Cherokees in North Carolina; Seminoles in Florida; Senecas in New York; Alabamas and Coushattas in Texas; Sacs and Foxes in Iowa; Pueblos and Mescalero Apaches in New Mexico; Yumas in Arizona; and Zuñis, Hopis, and Navajos in Arizona and New Mexico. But they were the exceptions. In 1500 Native Americans of what is now the United States controlled billions of acres of land; that heritage had shrunk to about 140 million acres in 1887 and less than 48 million acres in 1931, one-third of which was leased to non–Native Americans.

The reformers also continued their emphasis on education, always in hope of decreasing federal control over Native Americans and integrating them into the larger society. But even as enrollment in nonreservation boarding schools rose in the early 1900s, new doubts about the prospects of immediate assimilation brought changes. Critics of Richard Henry Pratt had always claimed that nonreservation boarding schools were too expensive, but some critics also questioned the alleged success of schools such as Carlisle. The students remained doggedly loyal to tribal ways. They preferred their own religious ceremonies to Christianity and often disdained farming. After graduating from nonreservation boarding schools, they showed a marked propensity for returning to the reservations, even though they supposedly had acquired the intellectual and cultural equipment to survive in European American society. Many non–Native Americans were dumbfounded at the tenacity of Native American culture.

With immediate assimilation seemingly an impossible goal, nonreservation boarding schools seemed more and more impractical. Just as Booker T. Washington was emphasizing vocational education for African Americans, reformers began to argue that Native American children should be given specific vocational training in day schools near their homes. Rather than try to transform the children in nonreservation boarding schools, the federal school system dedicated its resources after 1905 to providing minimal job skills so that Native American students would be able to support themselves someday in the mainstream national economy. The federal government also attached employment bureaus to many of the school systems to help students find suitable jobs. With the shift in emphasis away from nonreservation boarding schools and classical education, enrollment in those schools peaked at 9,736 in 1905 and then began to decline.

Because public schools throughout the country were also in the midst of changing curricula concepts—"tracking" students according to intellectual abilities and providing vocational training for academically weak children—many reformers interested in gradual assimilation saw an opportunity to integrate Native Americans into local schools and gradually terminate federal supervision of Native American education. In 1908 only twenty-four Native American children attended public schools, but after 1910 the Bureau of Indian Affairs accelerated its program to place them in surrounding public schools. By 1928 there were 79,000 Native American children of school age. Nearly 11,000 were not in school, and another 6,000 attended church mission schools. More than 5,000 children were at federal day schools, and 21,000 more attended boarding schools. The remaining 36,000 children attended public schools near the reservations, and the vast majority of them were tracked into slow learning groups receiving vocational education.

After 1900 the reformers had managed to change direction, slowing the drive toward immediate assimilation through nonreservation boarding schools emphasizing classical education to federal day schools and public schools interested in gradually integrating Native Americans into the dominant economy through vocational education. However, Christian industrial education, despite all the rhetoric and some of the post-1900 changes in approach, still dominated the expectations of reformers and remained an important weapon in the assault on tribalism.

Extension of citizenship also continued, even increasing after 1900. By 1917 more than two-thirds of all Native Americans were citizens of the United States. Because thousands of Native Americans had loyally volunteered to serve in the military during World War I, Congress passed a law in 1919 also permitting Native American veterans to apply for citizenship. Still, in 1920 nearly 125,000 Native Americans remained without the "benefits and responsibilities" of citizenship. As was so often the case in the past, the citizenship question was caught up in a conflicting network of feelings on the part of non–Native American "benefactors." Some favored citizenship on moral grounds, arguing that common sense and decency dictated citizenship. Other reformers, like the members of the Indian Rights Association, continued their forty-year campaign for citizenship as the final step toward integrating Native Americans into the general society. Still others, such as Congressman Edgar Howard of Nebraska or Gale Stalker of New York, were equally interested in ending the special trust status on Native American land and advocated blanket, immediate citizenship to break BIA control of the reservations. Supported by such diverse sentiments, Stalker and Howard introduced those citizenship bills to the House of Representatives in 1923, and political maneuvering began immediately.

They encountered a good deal of hostility from other European Americans—and a number of Native Americans. Many reformers had by 1923 become doubtful of the prognosis for rapid assimilation; they feared that immediate citizenship of those still not "emancipated" might subject them to widespread, concerted exploitation by state and local interest groups. Elizabeth S. Sergeant, writing for *The New Republic* in 1924, argued that any citizenship law should be accompanied by a strict federal guardianship over Native American property. Herbert J. Spinden, an anthropologist and reformer, worried that blanket citizenship, by severing the legal relationship between Native Americans and the federal government, would give Native Americans some "vague rights" and guarantee "greater profits for someone else."* Favoring gradual assimilation and some form of citizenship, they also wanted to preserve the wardship status of Native American land tenure in order to prevent economic abuse and the wholesale transfer of Native American property to non–Native Americans. At the same time, full-bloods in many tribes were extraordinarily suspicious of the proposal. Potawatomi full-bloods bitterly rejected the whole idea of citizenship as just another step toward the ultimate elimination of tribal values. The Iroquois were even more suspicious and protective of tribal prerogatives. Ever since the colonial period they had nurtured a strong sense of sovereignty and independence, and that sense had endured through all of the assimilation programs since. Rather than docilely accepting the federal government's declaration of war on Germany in 1917, the Iroquois formally declared war themselves and then claimed status as one of the allied nations. During the citizenship debates of the early 1920s they protected any attempts to grant them citizenship and declared that they would not accept citizenship if Congress granted it in the future.

Out of these conflicting points of view came a compromise. In January 1924 Congressman Homer P. Snyder of New York introduced House Resolution 6355 authorizing the Secretary of the Interior to grant citizenship to all Native Americans requesting it if they were "individually prepared" for the responsibilities. Since such a bill would leave federal supervision intact, opponents of the Bureau of Indian Affairs insisted on changes. The Senate Committee on Indian Affairs then proposed a blanket, immediate-citizenship law which predictably raised the ire of many full-blood Native Americans and non–Native Americans who were skeptical about rapid assimilation. Finally, out of the conference committee emerged the Snyder Act, which stated

---

*Herbert J. Spinden, "What about the Indian?," *World's Work* 47 (February 1924):384.

that all noncitizen Indians born within the territorial limits of the United States be, and they are hereby, declared to be citizens of the United States: Provided, that the granting of such citizenship shall not in any manner impair or otherwise affect the right of any Indian to tribal or other property.*

Citizenship, of course, did not always guarantee the right to vote. Because states possessed the power to determine voting eligibility, Congress had little power to protect the right to vote, and states such as New Mexico and Arizona kept erecting voting barriers and did not allow most of their Native Americans to vote until after World War II.

Yet by the mid-1920s reformers had largely fulfilled their three goals of allotting tribal lands, incorporating Native Americans into the body politic, and providing them with educational systems geared to integration with European American society.

The assault on tribalism had a clearly negative effect on Native American life. Conversion of tribal land into individual allotments did not lead to family self-sufficiency. For the Cheyennes and Arapahos, only sixteen years had passed between their confinement on the reservation in 1875 and allotment of their lands in 1891. Except for the most assimilated mixed-bloods, they had not made the transition from independent nomadism to settled commercial farming, nor had many of the men come to accept agricultural labor as anything more than complete humiliation. In 1906–7, for example, the combined Cheyenne and Arapaho income was $217,312. Only $5,312 of that money, however, came from the sale of farm commodities; about two-thirds came from the sale of inherited allotments and one-third from the leasing of allotments. Both tribes were selling their birthright for current consumption. Per capita tribal income declined from $139 in fiscal year 1904–5 to only $78 in fiscal 1906–7. Farm machinery was unavailable, technical assistance from the federal government was inadequate, and crops failed year after year. In the process, they lost the economic rationale of their existence: the independent freedom of the buffalo hunts. Poverty, disease, and lethargy plagued the Cheyenne and Arapaho people as their land base eroded.

Native Americans also paid a heavy price culturally during the assault on tribalism. In the nonreservation boarding schools, reservation day schools, and local public schools, teachers and missionaries had for years attacked Native American values. Among the Southern Cheyennes, teachers and federal agents prohibited the Sun Dance, the Renewal of the Sacred Arrows, peyotism, large camp meetings, and the use of alcohol, and vigorously condemned multiple marriages, use of the native language, and living arrangements involving anything

---

*Quoted in Gary C. Stein, "The Indian Citizenship Act of 1924," *New Mexico Historical Review* 47 (July 1972):257.

other than the nuclear family. Cheyenne dedication to the old ways was strong, but these constant cultural pressures created an atmosphere of tension, frustration, fear, and chronic lack of purpose. In the name of assimilation, European Americans demanded conformity, but even then Native Americans knew that European American society would never accept them. When Native American children returned from schools like Carlisle or Haskell with good educations and economic skills, they still could not secure jobs in the European American economy and instead were destined to a few jobs at the local agency, seasonal farm labor, or limited work as scouts or Native American police. Social equality never materialized.

Finally, the assimilation crusade often weakened the old traditions of tribal consensus and intensified bitter factionalisms. By 1910 the Southern Cheyennes' old tribal and war chiefs, such as Little Robe, Stone Calf, and Bull Bear, were dead, and federal agents had replaced them on the tribal council with men such as Old Crow, Young Whirlwind, and Three Fingers. The agents insisted that the new leaders attend a Christian church; send their children to a local school; and avoid alcohol, peyote, and the Sun Dance. And they were to marry only one woman, cut their hair, wear European-style clothing, and work their own allotments. Often too willing to acquiesce to the agent's demands, the new chiefs lost credibility and prestige among the full-bloods of the tribe. Everyone realized that the real source of power for the tribe was no longer the chiefs but the government agents who approved selection of their tribal leaders. Factions developed between full-bloods, who generally resisted cultural change, and mixed-bloods, who were generally willing to accept the new ways. Among the Southern Cheyennes, for example, the mixed-blood leader George Balenti demanded complete individual control over leasing of allotments, while most of the full-bloods, hoping to keep European Americans out of the community, demanded tribal approval of leasing arrangements. Conservative Prairie Band Potawatomis, led by Wakwaboshkok, refused to accept individual allotments, send their children to school, or permit the fencing of mixed-blood allotments. Most mixed-bloods accepted and fenced their allotments, cooperated closely with federal agents, and sent their children to local schools. Conflict between the two groups has defined much of Potawatomi history in the twentieth century. In tribe after tribe throughout the United States, the assimilationist crusade introduced a kind of bitter factionalism which undermined traditional forms of conflict resolution.

Throughout this assault on tribalism, Native Americans reacted in a number of ways to the political, cultural, and economic pressures they were facing as European American civilization advanced. In the nineteenth century, these reactions included violent resistance (of such as the Chiricahua Apaches), spectacular flights (of such as Chief Joseph and the Nez Perces or Standing Bear and the Poncas), and passive resistance through alcoholism and spiritualism (such as peyotism, the Ghost Dance, the Sun Dance, and the Dream Dance). In the twentieth century the responses were far different. Native Americans resorted to violence only rarely and in very limited numbers, this owing primarily to the drastic decrease of tribal power brought about by the ever more powerful and dominant European American society. Rather, resistance took the forms of religious revival, stubborn loyalty to traditional customs, and the beginnings of political organization and interest-group lobbying.

There was some violent resistance to assimilation, however. Chitto Harjo, a full-blood Creek, formed a society of "Snakes," revived Creek tribal government, and claimed that all United States treaties guaranteeing the tribal land base "forever" were still in effect, regardless of allotment legislation. In 1901 the reorganized tribal council prohibited all Creeks from accepting allotments and, at Harjo's direction, groups of Snakes physically assaulted all Creeks who did. The "Snake Uprising," after delaying the allotment process for a few months, was finally crushed by federal troops—but not before it inspired more insurgency among the Choctaws and Cherokees. For years, even after federal authorities had ended overt violent resistance, full-bloods of the Five Civilized Tribes refused to live on their allotments, camping instead on school, tribal, church, or government property. Many of Chitto Harjo's Snakes even refused to accept government royalty checks on petroleum drilled from their allotted lands.

The Ghost Dance religion had died by 1900—primarily due to the 1890 tragedy at Wounded Knee—and the Dream Dance was withering among the Potawatomis and other Algonquian-speaking peoples. But for many Native Americans, the Sun Dance religion and peyotism continued to bring comfort in the changing circumstances of twentieth-century America. After its revival in the 1890s, the Sun Dance became an important religious movement for many Great Plains and Great Basin tribes, but especially for the Shoshones, Utes, Paiutes, and Gosiutes because it helped them resolve the tension between their older collective world and the individualistic ethos of the dominant society. The Sun Dance ceremony promised individual satisfaction and personal power to all the participants, but the communitarian ideology of the dance—emphasis on loyalty, fidelity, service, and sacrifice—fulfilled the collective expectations so central to Native American culture. In some ways, the Sun Dance even fostered a pan-Indian spirit when several tribes began joining together for inter-reservation ceremonies. By 1910 the Fort Hall, Wind River, and Western Shoshones were meeting with the Southern Paiutes, Gosiutes,

Northern Utes, Southern Utes, and Ute Mountain Utes, and occasionally since 1910 they have been joined by Pueblos, Arapahos, Navajos, and Apaches. The common theme at the joint ceremonies was that, before Europeans arrived in America, all Native Americans were one people; and the Sun Dance was a means for reuniting all the tribes.

But even more important than the Sun Dance was the growth of the peyote cult among Native Americans. Originating in Mexico, the peyote cult spread to the Mescalero Apaches and Comanches and, apparently, from them to the Kiowas and Caddos. Quanah Parker, a Comanche chief, was the unofficial high priest of peyotism in the 1870s; and, after the decline of the Ghost Dance in the 1890s, the religion converted thousands of Cheyennes, Shawnees, Arapahos, Pawnees, Delawares, Osages, and Winnebagos. Between 1900 and 1920 the religion continued to meet the needs of many Native Americans and gained new supporters among the Omahas, Utes, Crows, Menominees, Iowas, Sioux, and Shoshones; and in the 1920s and 1930s peyotism continued to spread—among the Gosiutes, Paiutes, Navajos, Blackfeet, Creeks, Cherokees, Seminoles, and Chippewas. By 1955 nearly eighty Native American tribes practiced some form of peyotism.

In the nineteenth century the peyote rite was a simple meditative exercise. By chewing the peyote "bean," adherents enjoyed a mild hallucinatory experience, one that brought different feelings to different people. The great vitality of peyote culture was its ability to meet a wide variety of needs. For some peyotists the religion offered certainty—a testimony of God's revelatory powers and spiritual concern and of the meaning of life. Consistent with the communal values of most tribes, Native Americans using peyote often experienced a sense of unity with the universe and close identification with other peyotists. Finally, for some Native Americans, peyote provided an escape from the pains of reservation life, a momentary sense of peace and harmony in a world of poverty and dependence. Among some tribes, peyotism seemed to ameliorate the more disturbing consequences of reservation life, particularly crime, alcoholism, and divorce. By the early twentieth century an ethical code known as the "Peyote Road" had developed in the religion, emphasizing brotherly love, honesty, marital fidelity, hard work and economic self-reliance, trustworthiness, family responsibility, and strict avoidance of alcohol. By following the Peyote Road, Native Americans could live successfully and peacefully in an alien world.

The spread of peyotism early in the twentieth century raised a storm of protest from non–Native Americans and nonpracticing Native Americans alike. To most non–Native Americans who were intent on eliminating the "bizarre" elements of Native American culture altogether, peyote use was an especially dangerous aberration, one that would surely retard assimilation by "making the Indian contented with his present attainments . . . cutting off from him the possibility of healthful aspirations."* They were also convinced that use of peyote on the reservations would only intensify such social problems as crime, sexual deviancy, and laziness. Many Native Americans also opposed peyote—including numerous Christian converts, who felt that the peyote cult was sacrilegious, a blasphemous deviation from the gospel of Jesus Christ. In 1940, for example, the Navajo Tribal Council, led by Jacob Morgan and Howard Gorman, both Christians, outlawed the possession and use of peyote on the reservation. Other Native Americans, most of them full-blood traditionalists, opposed peyotism because it seemed to contradict and weaken older tribal religions. The Taos Pueblos, White Mountain Apaches, and several Sioux tribes in South Dakota passed ordinances prohibiting the use of peyote as a means of protecting tribal culture.

Thus supported by most non–Native Americans and many Native Americans, territorial, state, and federal legislatures and agencies vigorously attempted to eradicate the practice. The territorial legislature of Oklahoma outlawed peyote use in 1898, and by 1923 fourteen states had passed similar laws. United States Public Health Service hospitals refused to treat Native Americans suffering from symptoms of peyote addiction, federal agents working the Mexican border confiscated all peyote being imported, and between 1917 and 1940 Congress prohibited the shipment of peyote through the mails. Beginning in 1906 the Bureau of Indian Affairs tried, though unsuccessfully, to secure congressional statutes outlawing peyote use nationwide.

Rather uncharacteristically, small groups of Native Americans nationwide joined hands to save peyotism. This banding together, and some development of an organizational base early on, made possible a successful resistance to the combined assault. Peyote missionaries traveled widely to bring the faith to other tribes, and by 1906 a very loose organization of peyote users existed in several states. The Winnebagos in Nebraska organized the Mescal Bean Eaters in 1906. By 1909 they were using the Christian Bible in their peyote ceremonies and calling themselves the Union Church. At approximately the same time the Omahas formed the American Indian Church Brother Association and the Kiowas organized the Kiowa United American Church. In 1914 Jonathan Koshiway, a member of the Oto tribe, formed the Church of the First Born in Oklahoma. All used peyote in their services or rituals. In 1918 peyotists agreed to combine on a national scale, largely as a means of protecting their First Amendment right to freedom of religion. Under the leadership of Mack Haag (Cheyenne),

---

Annual Report of the Commissioner of Indian Affairs (Washington, D.C.: U.S. Government Printing Office, 1912), 35.

Charles Dailey (Oto), George Pipestem (Oto), Frank Eagle (Ponca), Wilbur Peawa (Comanche), Apache Ben (Apache), James Waldo (Kiowa), and others, the Native American Church was formed. A loose umbrella organization of peyote groups throughout the country, the Native American Church promoted the use of peyote as a religious experience and claimed the constitutional right to do so.

Perhaps encouraged by the survival of peyotism as the result of intertribal cooperation and coordination, more and more Native Americans organized politically to lobby for their rights. Eufaula Harjo and Red Bird Smith founded the Four Mothers Society, a pan-Indian group of Cherokees, Creeks, Choctaws, and Chickasaws, to protest the allotment of Indian Territory. With small amounts of money they went to Washington and demanded that Congress permit the preservation of tribal customs, guarantee the communal ownership of tribal property, and/or remove all restrictions on allotments so that Native Americans could sell their land and create trust funds. Additionally, they demanded the right to purchase land for relocation in Mexico. When the Dawes Commission began enrolling too many non–Native Americans as tribal members in preparation for allotment, the Chickasaws protested, sent a delegation to Congress, and eventually retained a law firm to investigate the backgrounds of people claiming tribal membership. In response, Congress created the Choctaw-Chickasaw Citizenship Court in 1902, a body which eventually allowed only 156 of the 3,679 contested applications to be added to tribal rolls. With money and lawyers, the Osages managed to retain tribal ownership of all mineral rights even while Congress was allotting tribal land.

The Society of American Indians, the first major pan-Indian organization, appeared in 1911, even though plans to form such a group had been discussed as early as 1899 by Dr. Charles Alexander Eastman, the Sioux physician, author, and lecturer; his brother John Eastman, a Sioux Presbyterian minister; and Sherman Coolidge, an Arapaho Episcopal minister. At that time they decided to postpone establishing such an organization because they feared it would not garner sufficient support from Native Americans, non–Native Americans, and the Bureau of Indian Affairs to form a strong enough coalition of those groups they thought necessary for success. Twelve years later those fears had vanished, and a renewed impetus came from a European American, Dr. Fayette A. McKenzie, a professor of economics and sociology at Ohio State University. An avid student of relations between Native Americans and European Americans, McKenzie invited six prominent Native Americans to attend an organizational meeting in Columbus, Ohio, in April 1911: Dr. Charles A. Eastman; Dr. Carlos Montezuma, a Yavapai physician; Thomas L. Sloan, a lawyer from the Omaha tribe; Charles E. Daganett, a Peoria and supervisor of employment for the Bureau of Indian Affairs; Laura M. Cornelius, an Oneida from Wisconsin; and Henry Standing Bear, a Sioux from the Pine Ridge Reservation. At first calling themselves the American Indian Association, they drafted a preamble outlining their major goals and describing the general purpose of their organization.

The American Indian Association declares that the time has come when the American Indian race should contribute, in a more united way, its influence and exertion with the rest of the citizens of the United States in all lines of progress and reform, for the welfare of the Indian race in particular, and humanity in general.*

Before the meeting adjourned, the president of Ohio State University, the mayor of Columbus, and several other city officials invited the participants to hold their first annual conference in Columbus in October 1911. The offer was accepted and, symbolically, the conference convened on October 12, 1911—Columbus Day.

As their first order of business, the American Indian Association became the Society of American Indians, a name to indicate that the organization was run by Native Americans. (Membership without voting rights was to be open to non–Native Americans.) Both Native American and non–Native American participants listened to the opening address by Commissioner of Indian Affairs Robert G. Valentine, who stated that he hoped that the Society of American Indians would become a body that would express a united Native American point of view on matters affecting their welfare.

Laura Cornelius proposed to the conference the converting of reservations into "self-governing industrial villages" that would tap natural and human resources there. She believed that, since most Native Americans were at different levels of technological development, reservation industries should be selected accordingly. Arthur C. Parker, a Seneca, argued that if European Americans and Native Americans learned more about each other culturally, they would become more tolerant and understanding, and mutual acceptance would be more likely. He proposed the establishment of "social betterment stations" on reservations. These "stations," similar to the settlement houses being established among the urban poor, would help Native Americans enjoy higher educational and "social standards." (Gertrude Bonnin, a Sioux, established one such station for the Utes at Fort Duchesne, Utah. Ute women there learned English, domestic

---

*Quoted in Hazel W. Hertzberg, *The Search for an American Indian Identity: Modern Pan-Indian Movements* (Syracuse, N.Y.: Syracuse University Press, 1971), 36.

skills, first aid, and health education. Additionally, they enjoyed inexpensive lunches and recreational activities.)

Other speakers at the Columbus conference addressed the legal and political problems facing Native Americans, especially the confusing status of tribal sovereignty and American citizenship. At the close of the conference they selected Washington, D.C., as their headquarters, primarily so that they could monitor congressional legislation and the activities of the Bureau of Indian Affairs.

The Society of American Indians had an auspicious beginning. Supported by many non–Native American friends and groups like the Indian Rights Association, SAI leaders were proud of tribal values and wanted European Americans to recognize Native Americans for their accomplishments and their potential as functioning members of the larger society. They emphasized that Native Americans should be more involved in their own self-betterment, and, at first, mildly criticized the Bureau of Indian Affairs for failing to assist in that direction. Since nearly all of the SAI leaders had attended college, they also stressed education as the primary avenue of social progress.

The members of the Society of American Indians held subsequent conferences in Columbus in 1912; Denver, Colorado, in 1913; Madison, Wisconsin, in 1914; Lawrence, Kansas, in 1915; Cedar Rapids, Iowa, in 1916; Pierre, South Dakota, in 1918; Minneapolis, Minnesota, in 1919; St. Louis, Missouri, in 1920; Detroit, Michigan, in 1921; and Chicago, Illinois, in 1923. At each conference they reiterated most of the challenges raised at the first meeting in 1911. In 1913 the SAI began publishing *The Quarterly Journal of the Society of American Indians* (renamed *The American Indian Magazine* in 1916), under the editorial direction of Arthur C. Parker. The journal stressed the development of a pan-Indian spirit, American patriotism, and a reform zeal among European Americans.

Eventually, the Society of American Indians proved no more successful than previous Native American groups in dealing with the dominant society because factionalism, only slightly present at the first meeting in 1911, intensified as the years passed, crippling and ultimately destroying the organization. Led by Dr. Charles Eastman, some members of the Society of American Indians worried that the organization was not truly representative of the larger Native American community; that is, it reflected only the interests of highly educated, more assimilated Native Americans from the Sioux, Apache, Arapaho, Oneida, and Omaha tribes. Eastman wanted the SAI to serve as an organization committed to promoting Native American welfare, but he knew that any group claiming to represent *all* Native Americans had to enjoy a very broad base of support. So he advocated transforming the Society into an "Indian Congress" with elected delegates from each tribe. Thus speaking with a united voice, the SAI could become the most powerful Native American organization in American history. But Eastman's proposal troubled other people in the SAI who preferred to maintain the group as primarily an educational organization committed to annual meetings, publications, and public relations.

Far more debilitating to the SAI was the dispute over relations with the Bureau of Indian Affairs. Carlos Montezuma led the attack on the BIA, which eventually became an assault on the Society itself. An assimilationist and advocate of citizenship and public education, Montezuma opposed any attempt to preserve Native American culture and wardship status in the United States. When the SAI began calling for legislative enactment of an annual American Indian Day, Montezuma bitterly attacked the proposal as a cruel farce that would only prolong Native American suffering in the United States. Montezuma similarly criticized reservation schools where tribal crafts and culture were taught, calling instead for integrated education in public schools so that Native American children could rapidly become assimilated. He blamed the Bureau of Indian Affairs for being the central agency in preserving the isolation of Native American society and called for immediate abolition of the BIA. Montezuma then directed his condemnation at the SAI for becoming a tool of the BIA campaign to dominate and manipulate Native Americans. He demanded that the SAI join him in calling for the destruction of the Bureau of Indian Affairs. Arthur C. Parker, who became president of the SAI in 1916 while retaining editorship of the journal, refused to acquiesce to Montezuma's demands. In response, in 1916 Montezuma started his own monthly publication, *Wassaja,* in which he continued his diatribes against both the Bureau of Indian Affairs and the SAI.

The peyote question proved more damaging still to the SAI, especially to its hope of becoming a legitimate pan-Indian organization. Hostility toward the use of peyote was strong among many Native Americans as well as non–Native Americans, and state campaigns against it were well underway by 1915. When representatives of twenty-five tribes gathered at Lawrence, Kansas, in 1915 for the fifth annual conference of the SAI, many peyotists joined them, demanding that the Society of American Indians formally protest all attempts to outlaw peyote as unconstitutional violations of freedom of religion. After a number of bitter exchanges between peyotists and anti-peyotists, the SAI formally called for federal legislation to prohibit the use of peyote.

At hearings held on a bill sponsored by Congressman Carl M. Hayden of Arizona to suppress liquor traffic and peyote among Native Americans, both Native Americans and non–Native Americans, many of whom were members of the SAI, testified in Washington, D.C., in 1918 on the effects of peyote. Among the leading figures taking sides in the controversy were the supporters of the bill: Charles A. Eastman, General Richard Henry Pratt, and Gertrude Bonnin. Those opposing the bill were Thomas Sloan, Francis LaFlesche (an Omaha), and James Mooney of the Bureau of American Ethnology. Eventually, Congress refused to pass the bill, preferring to leave the matter up to state and local legislation, and the peyote controversy continued. The intense factionalism developing within the SAI over peyote all but destroyed the organization.

No annual conference was held in 1917—ostensibly because of World War I, but actually because Arthur Parker feared losing control of the SAI. He wanted to make the journal a forum for pan-Indianism, but in 1918 the convention ousted him, named Charles Eastman the new president, and handed editorship of the magazine over to another Sioux, Gertrude Bonnin. During that year the SAI still opposed peyote, became more vocal in calling for the abolition of the BIA, and campaigned for Native American citizenship. But in 1919, at the eighth annual conference held in Minneapolis, the SAI replaced Eastman with Thomas Sloan, a peyotist. Sloan tried to convert the SAI into a national lobbying group, but continued factionalism over peyote and the BIA sapped the SAI of the rest of its strength.

Torn by dissension, the Society of American Indians declined after the end of World War I. Its last annual conference was held in 1923. In calling for educational reform, codification of Native American laws, citizenship for Native Americans, and simplified procedures enabling Native Americans to sue the federal government, the SAI was ahead of its time; but like other Native American groups, it was unable to transcend tribal and intratribal rivalries.

Led by remnants of SAI membership, especially Gertrude Bonnin, several Native Americans organized the National Council of American Indians in 1926. They continued the campaign against peyote, calling for the abolition of the Native American Church, and tried unsuccessfully to organize Native Americans into a powerful voting bloc in Oklahoma and South Dakota. But like the SAI, the National Council of American Indians became a victim of factionalism and disintegrated in the mid-1930s.

Although the Society of American Indians and the National Council of American Indians failed in their attempts to represent all Native Americans in the United States, they were—like the Four Mothers Society among the Five Civilized Tribes, or the Native American Church—new forms of Native American organizations ready to struggle for civil rights and self-determination. Importantly, such organizations were joined in the 1920s by a new generation of non–Native American reformers whose doubts about the virtues of assimilation had been transformed into strong convictions about the virtues of tribal sovereignty. This coalition of reformers and politically aroused Native Americans developed just in time, for in the early 1920s western economic interests launched another assault on Native American land.

After winning the presidential election of 1920, President Warren G. Harding named Albert Fall, a former U.S. senator from New Mexico, to be Secretary of the Interior, and Fall in turn selected Charles H. Burke, former South Dakota congressman and author of the Burke Act of 1906, as Commissioner of Indian Affairs. Both Fall and Burke were convinced (or so they rationalized) that Native Americans were technologically primitive people unable to use their land effectively; consequently, non–Native American business interests should have access to all mineral and petroleum deposits on the reservations, as well as to good farming land and water supplies. When Fall resigned in disgrace in 1923 because of the Teapot Dome scandal, Hubert Work became the new Secretary of the Interior. Although incorruptible politically, Work, who had been postmaster general under President Harding, continued to support assimilation policies.

In 1921, and again in 1922, Senator Holm O. Bursum of New Mexico introduced a bill to divest the Pueblos, who numbered about eight thousand, of large sections of their land along the Rio Grande in New Mexico in favor of twelve thousand squatters who had settled there. By placing the burden of proof on the Pueblos, the bill virtually confirmed land title to the squatters. Whether the Pueblos had the right to sell their land was the crux of the matter. With confirmed land grants issued by the Spanish crown, the Pueblos became Mexican citizens after the Mexican Revolution. The Treaty of Guadalupe Hidalgo, ending the Mexican War, contained a provision granting American citizenship to Mexican nationals living in the newly acquired territory and confirming Pueblo ownership of seven hundred thousand acres of land. Most settlers then assumed that the Pueblos were free to sell their land without federal interference, and, in the Joseph Case of 1876, the United States Supreme Court sustained that view, declaring that the Pueblos were not wards of the government as were other Native American tribes. But in 1913, in the Sandoval Case, the Supreme Court reversed itself and declared that the Pueblo Indians were wards of the federal government and could not dispose of their assets freely; thus, all land transactions since 1848 were illegal. By 1920 there were more than twelve thousand settlers living on Pueblo land; some had purchased the land legally, some had moved there thinking it was part of the public domain, and others had simply encroached on Pueblo property illegally. Secretary Fall and Senator Bursum moved to legalize these settlers' claims to the land.

Secretary Fall supported two other measures which brought cries of foul play. In 1922 he declared that the General Leasing Act of 1920, which provided for the leasing of mineral deposits on the public domain by private business interests, applied to executive order reservations—reservations established by executive order after 1871 when the treaty-making process between the federal government and Native American tribes was terminated. Fall viewed executive order reservations, which comprised over 22 million acres of land, as public lands which were only "temporarily withdrawn" by presidential decree and open to exploitation under the General Leasing Act. However, he declared, the tribes involved were entitled to a portion of the royalties. Soon after Fall's decision, the General Land Office received more than four hundred applications to explore for mineral resources on tribal lands.

Finally, Commissioner Burke issued Circular 1665 in 1921 ordering BIA superintendents (agents) to suppress tribal dances and ceremonies that were deemed morally and socially unacceptable to the standards of European American society. Ever since the 1870s assimilationists had wanted, along with citizenship and allotment, to divest Native Americans of their tribal cultures. Temperance groups wanted to eliminate alcohol and peyote; teachers wanted to wipe out tribal languages and tribal dress; Christian missionaries and affiliated groups like the YMCA and YWCA hoped to end all "primitive dances and ceremonies." Fall, Work, and Burke believed that tribal dances were "lascivious and immoral," characterized by all forms of sexual depravity and violence. Government testimonies, for example, alleged that at one sacred Zuñi dance every female who participated became pregnant and that religious leaders among the Pueblos conducted a "two-year course in sodomy." Circular 1665 was simply another attack on Native American cultures, although its language exceeded the norm in viciousness.

Protests against the Bursum Bill, Fall's interpretation of executive order reservations, and Circular 1665 developed immediately. Ever since the turn of the century a number of reformers had been nursing doubts about the merits and even the practicality of rapid assimilation, and the history of government allotment and education programs after 1900 had only magnified their suspicions. By 1920 John Collier, an eastern social worker now concerned about the plight of Native Americans, had emerged as one of the leaders of those who advocated the retention of tribal sovereignty. Opposition to the Bursum Bill came from a variety of sources, however. More traditional assimilationists in the Indian Rights Association condemned it as outright robbery; the General Federation of Women's Clubs openly questioned Bursum's motives; members of the Society of American Indians protested it; and in 1923 John Collier organized the American Indian Defense Association to stop the measure. The AIDA reflected Collier's views on Native American reform: the end of land allotments in severalty, improvement of educational and health services, legislation allowing Native Americans to participate in decisions affecting their welfare, establishment of tribal governments, and recognition for tribal customs. Collier called on the New Mexico intellectual community for support, particularly writers and artists who had moved to Taos and Santa Fe after World War I. People such as Mabel Dodge, Mary Austin, D. H. Lawrence, Edgar Lee Masters, Zane Grey, and Carl Sandburg signed petitions, provided funds, made public appearances, and wrote articles in such prestigious newspapers and periodicals as the *New York Times, Christian Science Monitor, Outlook, New Republic, Nation, Forum, Sunset Magazine,* and *Survey* on behalf of the Pueblos. Finally, the Pueblos organized as well. On November 5, 1922, 121 delegates met at Santo Domingo, where, after forming an All Pueblo Indian Council, they decided to protest the Bursum Bill by appealing to the American people and sending a delegation to Washington to appear before the Senate.

The Bursum Bill could not survive such a chorus of protest. In its place, Congress passed the Pueblo Lands Act in 1924 to resolve the dispute. The act established the Pueblo Lands Board, located in Santa Fe, to determine ownership and to compensate claimants, both Native American and non–Native American. When the board found in favor of a settler, Congress made cash compensation to the Pueblos. The initial Pueblo award was about $600,000—a paltry sum when compared to the real value of the land. Collier protested the inadequate compensation and later, as Commissioner of Indian Affairs, supported a bill which made additional payments to both Native American and non–Native American claimants. The Pueblo Relief Act, passed on May 31, 1933, appropriated $761,958 to the Pueblos and $232,086 to the settlers.

Fall's proposal on executive order reservations fared no better. Again, the Indian Rights Association and Collier were in the vanguard of protest. Hostility to the measure was so intense that after Fall's resignation in 1923 Commissioner Charles Burke urged the new Secretary of the Interior, Hubert Work, to reverse the interpretation. Attempting to settle the issue, Attorney General Harlan F. Stone ruled in May 1924 that executive order reservations belonged to the tribes and were not part of the public domain. Congress followed that legal opinion in 1926 with a law placing executive order reservations on the same statutory basis as treaty reservations. The bonanza expected by mineral and petroleum concerns did not materialize.

Congress continued to enact legislation favorable to Native American interests. In 1925 it passed the Osage Guardianship Act to end the scandalous plunder of Osage petroleum land by Oklahoma district courts. No longer could district court judges freely appoint guardians to manage the property and royalties of Osage minors; federal agents now had to approve all guardian nominations. Albert

Fall's administrative directive concerning Native American dances survived longer because of divisions among Native Americans themselves. Long a leading advocate of assimilation as the answer to the "Indian problem," the Indian Rights Association, along with a number of Christian missionary societies, supported the ban on dances and ceremonies they considered immoral. Fall, Burke, and Work all sustained the bans throughout the 1920s. John Collier and the American Indian Defense Association, on the other hand, rejected the notion that the dances were obscene. A staunch believer in preserving and recognizing tribal culture as the only way of maintaining social stability within Native American communities, Collier claimed that reports emphasizing promiscuity and depravity were grossly inaccurate. He also emphasized that, since many of the dances were an integral part of native religions, the prohibition was unconstitutional and violated religious freedom. Collier felt the same about peyote and the Native American Church, but not until he became Commissioner of Indian Affairs in 1933 did the bans on tribal customs disappear.

The pressure to change the direction of Native American policy had other results in the 1920s. Criticism by writers, lobbyists, and reformers in general helped to generate a new respect for tribalism in the United States. Eager to expose corruption, journalists turned their attention to the plight of Native Americans. Criticisms via newspapers, magazines, radio, and lecture circuits described how the Dawes Act had plundered tribal land and destroyed Native American culture. Apparently, the media counterattack had an effect. The issuing of fee simple patents by the Department of the Interior was greatly reduced, which had the effect of ending the rapid alienation of Native American allotments under the Burke Act. Additionally, in 1923 Interior Secretary Work appointed the National Advisory Committee, also called the Committee of One Hundred, to review federal policy toward Native Americans.

A mixed group of traditional assimilationists and people committed to tribal sovereignty, the Committee of One Hundred included such prominent non–Native Americans as Bernard Baruch, General John J. Pershing, William Jennings Bryan, Mark Sullivan, William Allen White, John Collier, Clark Wissler, Frederick W. Hodge, and Warren K. Moorehead, and such well-known Native Americans as Charles A. Eastman, Arthur C. Parker, Sherman Coolidge, and Thomas L. Sloan. Gathering in Washington in December 1923, the committee elected Arthur Parker as presiding officer and Fayette McKenzie as chairman of the resolutions committee. Their findings were published in 1924 as *The Indian Problem.* They recommended curricula and physical facilities improvements in Native American schools, admittance of more Native Americans to public schools, federal government scholarships for Native American students to attend high schools and colleges, and better health services on the reservations. The committee also called for establishment of a federal commission to settle tribal financial claims against the government, a thorough investigation of the effects of peyote, and a more cautious approach toward the banning of Native American dances and rituals. Finally, the committee upheld the right of the Pueblos to their land, opposed Fall's insistence on corporate access to executive order reservations, and called for the Department of the Interior to be much more careful about issuing fee simple patents to allotted Native Americans.

In response to a special request by the Board of Indian Commissioners, Work then asked the Institute for Government Research, a private research group later known as the Brookings Institution, to conduct a more comprehensive study of Native American affairs. The Institute for Government Research accepted the assignment in 1926 and oil magnate John D. Rockefeller, Jr., financed it. Dr. Lewis Meriam, a social scientist employed by the Institute, directed the study and assembled a staff of nine specialists, each known for his or her expertise in education, health, sociology, economics, law, and Native American affairs. After preparing for a month in Washington, the group left on a seven-month field trip to reservations throughout the United States, visiting over ninety agencies and jurisdictions in all. Returning to Washington, Meriam and his staff spent several more months compiling their findings and drafting recommendations to improve Native American conditions. Published in 1928 as *The Problem of Indian Administration,* more commonly called the Meriam Report, the 872-page study provided details on the shocking and deplorable conditions endured by hundreds of thousands of Native Americans.

They reported alarming information concerning Native American health. Mortality rates were higher than those of any other ethnic group in the United States. Infant mortality rates were 190.7 per 1,000 among Native Americans, compared to only 70.8 per 1,000 among European Americans as a group. Measles, pneumonia, and tuberculosis were cited as major causes of Native American deaths, and thousands of Native Americans suffered from trachoma, an eye disease often resulting in blindness. The Meriam staff discovered that Native Americans suffered from diets that lacked fruits, vegetables, and milk. Most hospitals and medical facilities on reservations were understaffed, ill equipped, and insufficiently funded.

Schools, in addition to operating on an average eleven-cent daily allotment for each student for food, were poorly staffed, weak in curriculum offerings, unsanitary, and overcrowded. Per capita income for Native Americans was less than $200 per year, compared to the national average of $1,350. Often unable to comprehend the value of money and of land, they were barely able to eke out a living from land sales, leases, and annuities.

The Meriam Report singled out allotment as the main cause of Native American poverty. Blaming the BIA for neglecting Native American needs and Congress for failing to appropriate sufficient funds, the Meriam staff called for an increase in congressional funding for Native American health and educational needs, recruitment of more qualified BIA personnel through higher salaries, establishment of follow-up programs and placement services for educated students, establishment of programs to train tribal leaders for political and business affairs, establishment of a loan fund to promote tribal business ventures, and utmost restraint in supervision and regulation of allotted land. Severely criticizing the assimilation-by-allotment philosophy, the Meriam report still held out the hope of incorporating Native Americans into the dominant society, but not at the expense of ruining tribal values. Indeed, the Meriam staff recommended that

the fundamental requirement is that the task of the Indian Service [BIA] be recognized as primarily educational in the broadest sense of the word, and that it be made an efficient educational agency, devoting its main energies to the social and educational advancement of the Indians, so that they may be absorbed into the prevailing civilization or be fitted to live in the presence of that civilization at least in accordance with a minimum standard of health and decency.*

Two other major investigations of Native American life also appeared in the 1920s. The Preston-Engle Irrigation Report was a joint survey by the Bureau of Indian Affairs and the Bureau of Reclamation on Native American irrigation projects. Published in 1928, the report recommended transferring the major tribal irrigation projects to the Bureau of Reclamation and abandoning irrigation services that were too expensive or of no value to Native American agriculture. The other study was a Senate investigation requested by Senator William H. King of Utah. Most of the findings of the Senate investigation substantiated the conclusions of the Meriam Report.

The pace of the reform movement accelerated with the election of Herbert Hoover as president in 1928. A new direction in federal policy toward Native Americans became more clear. President Hoover selected Ray Lyman Wilbur, president of Stanford University, as his Secretary of the Interior. He also chose Charles J. Rhoads as Commissioner of Indian Affairs and J. Henry Scattergood as Assistant Commissioner of Indian Affairs. Both men, no doubt influenced by their Quaker faith, were reformers interested in improving the living standards of Native Americans.

---

*Lewis Meriam et al., *The Problem of Indian Administration* (Baltimore: Johns Hopkins Press, 1928), 21.

The new team tried to implement many of the recommendations made by the various studies on Native American living conditions, particularly those put forth by the Meriam Report. Secretary Wilbur hoped that within twenty-five years the Bureau of Indian Affairs would no longer be necessary and that Native Americans would be integrated into the mainstream of the larger society. He proposed that the government rapidly accelerate its programs to achieve those goals. Rhoads and Scattergood moved more cautiously, not nearly so convinced of the prospects of rapid assimilation. They realized the need to gauge results before implementing new programs too hastily.

In their attempts to convince Congress to pass legislation, Wilbur and Rhoads had limited success. Congress failed to pass such measures as the Leavitt Bill of 1929, which proposed creating a special court to adjudicate tribal claims against the federal government for past wrongs, or the Swing-Johnson Bill of 1930, which proposed the transfer of some of the responsibilities for health, education, and welfare services to states where Native Americans resided. After World War II, however, this "termination" philosophy would gain strength. Congressional appropriations to the BIA did increase from $15 million in 1928 to $28 million in 1931, but those gains were largely offset by the hiring of two thousand more employees for the BIA and salary increases of 25 percent.

In accordance with recommendations made by the Meriam Report, the BIA was reorganized into five divisions—health, education, agricultural extension, forestry, and irrigation—to better serve Native American needs. The Bureau also worked for health reform. They proposed improvement of Native American hospitals, initiated disease prevention and hygiene instruction programs, and coordinated improved cooperation between state and local health agencies and the Public Health Service. One result was that Native Americans became less reluctant to use government hospitals, especially when non–Native American doctors recognized tribal beliefs and consulted with native medicine men on the proper procedures to follow. The number of Native American babies born in BIA hospitals increased from 595 in 1928 to 2,277 in 1933.

The Hoover administration also named Dr. W. Carson Ryan, Jr., a professor of education at Swarthmore College, as Director of Indian Education. Ryan initiated several important changes. The BIA began providing health examinations for Native American students on a regular basis, expanded classroom facilities to eliminate overcrowding, and ordered more nutritious lunches in reservation schools. The old policy of a disciplined and regimented military system of instruction was relaxed, and Ryan hired hundreds of better-qualified teachers at higher salaries. He pushed to decrease the number of boarding schools, to build more government day schools, and to enroll more Native American students in public schools. By 1932 government day school enrollment had increased by over 2,000 students. Curriculum changes allowed more emphasis on tribal culture and more practical vocational instruction. The BIA also established placement services to help graduates find suitable jobs.

The Hoover administration also managed a few minor steps toward economic reform. Although Secretary Wilbur failed to have Native American irrigation and reclamation projects transferred to the Bureau of Reclamation, he did form a Division of Agricultural Extension and Industries in 1930. Agricultural specialists and others visited reservations in an effort to help Native Americans become more self-supporting. Wilbur also endorsed the development of tribal arts and crafts. But he achieved little in ending the allotment program. Indeed, both Wilbur and, to a lesser extent, Rhoads supported the continuation of granting allotments. Although they wanted changes to protect Native American title to the allotted lands, they still viewed allotment as a means of integrating Native Americans into European American society.

Had the Great Depression not hit the United States in 1929, discrediting the Hoover administration and making the economy-minded Congress even more niggardly, perhaps Wilbur and Rhoads could have accomplished more. Certainly they were attempting to carry out many of the recommendations of the Meriam Report and the other investigations, and many of their proposals were passed in later sessions of Congress. The decade of the 1920s was a time of reform, even though their view on retaining the allotment policy constituted a major break between them and John Collier, a fervent enemy of the whole severalty concept. In 1933 John Collier became the new Commissioner of Indian Affairs, and he enthusiastically continued to implement suggestions made in the Meriam Report as well as bringing the allotment policy to an end. Although Native Americans would not always support Collier's policies—and not all of Collier's policies were well-conceived or successful—the years of Native American resistance and reform were about to bear fruit.

Suggested Readings

Aberle, David F. *The Peyote Religion among the Navajo.* Chicago: University of Chicago Press, 1982.

Adams, David Wallace. "Schooling the Hopi: Federal Indian Policy Writ Small, 1887–1917." *Pacific Historical Review* 48 (August 1979).

Anderson, Edward F. *Peyote: The Divine Cactus.* Tucson: University of Arizona Press, 1980.

Annual Report of the Commissioner of Indian Affairs. Washington, D.C.: U.S. Government Printing Office, 1905 and 1912.

Berens, John F. "Old Campaigners, New Realities: Indian Policy Reform in the Progressive Era, 1900–1912." *Mid-America* 59 (January 1977).

Carlson, Leonard A. *Indians, Bureaucrats, and Land: The Dawes Act and the Decline of Indian Farming.* Westport, Conn.: Greenwood Press, 1981.

Collier, John. *From Every Zenith: A Memoir and Some Essays on Life and Thought.* Denver: Sage Books, 1963.

———. *The Indians of the Americas.* New York: W. W. Norton, 1947.

Corbett, William P. "The Red Pipestone Quarry: The Yanktons Defend a Sacred Tradition, 1858–1929." *South Dakota History* 8 (Spring 1978).

Cotroneo, Ross T., and Jack Dozier. "A Time of Disintegration: The Coeur d'Alene and the Dawes Act." *Western Historical Quarterly* 5 (October 1974).

Dale, Edward Everett. *The Indians of the Southwest: A Century of Development under the United States.* Norman: University of Oklahoma Press, 1949.

Downes, Randolph C. "A Crusade for Indian Reform, 1922–1934." *Mississippi Valley Historical Review* 32 (December 1945).

Edmunds, R. David. *The Potawatomis: Keepers of the Fire.* Norman: University of Oklahoma Press, 1978.

Fey, Harold E., and D'Arcy McNickle. *Indians and Other Americans: Two Ways of Life Meet.* New York: Harper and Row, 1970.

Gibson, Arrell Morgan. *The American Indian: Prehistory to the Present.* Lexington, Mass.: D. C. Heath, 1980.

Hertzberg, Hazel W. "Nationality, Anthropology, and Pan-Indianism in the Life of Arthur C. Parker (Seneca)." *Proceedings of the American Philosophical Society* 123 (February 1979).

———. *The Search for an American Indian Identity: Modern Pan-Indian Movements.* Syracuse, N.Y.: Syracuse University Press, 1971.

Holford, David M. "The Subversion of the Indian Land Allotment System, 1887–1934." *Indian Historian* 8 (Spring 1975).

Hundley, Norris, Jr. "The 'Winters' Decision and Indian Water Rights: A Mystery Reexamined." *Western Historical Quarterly* 13 (January 1982).

Iverson, Peters. *Carlos Montezuma and the Changing World of American Indians*. Albuquerque: University of New Mexico Press, 1982.

Kelly, Lawrence C. *The Assault on Assimilation: John Collier and the Origins of Indian Policy Reform*. Albuquerque: University of New Mexico Press, 1983.

————. *The Navajo Indians and Federal Indian Policy, 1900–1935*. Tucson: University of Arizona Press, 1968.

La Barre, Weston. *The Peyote Cult*. Hamden, Conn.: Archon Books, 1975.

Littlefield, Daniel F., Jr., and Lonnie E. Underhill. "The 'Crazy Snake Uprising' of 1909: A Red, Black, or White Affair?" *Arizona and the West* 20 (Winter 1978).

McDonnell, Janet. "Competency Commissions and Indian Land Policy, 1913–1920." *South Dakota History* 11 (Winter 1980).

McNickle, D'Arcy. *Native American Tribalism: Indian Survivals and Renewals*. New York: Oxford University Press, 1973.

Meriam, Lewis, et al. *The Problem of Indian Administration*. Baltimore: Johns Hopkins Press, 1928.

Moses, Lester George. "James Mooney, U.S. Ethnologist: A Biography." Ph.D. diss., University of New Mexico, 1977.

Philp, Kenneth R. "Albert B. Fall and the Protest from the Pueblos, 1921–1923." *Arizona and the West* 12 (Autumn 1970).

————. *John Collier's Crusade for Indian Reform, 1920–1954*. Tucson: University of Arizona Press, 1977.

————. "John Collier and the Indians of the Americas: The Dream and the Reality." *Prologue* 11 (Spring 1979).

Prucha, Francis Paul. "The Board of Indian Commissioners and the Delegates of the Five Tribes." *Chronicles of Oklahoma* 56 (Fall 1978).

Robbins, William G. "Herbert Hoover's Indian Reformers under Attack: The Failures of Administrative Reform." *Mid-America* 63 (October 1981).

Smith, Burton M. "The Politics of Allotment: The Flathead Indian Reservation as a Test Case." *Pacific Northwest Quarterly* 70 (July 1979).

Spinden, Herbert J. "What about the Indian?" *World's Work* 47 (February 1924).

Stein, Gary C. "The Indian Citizenship Act of 1924." *New Mexico Historical Review* 47 (July 1972).

Szasz, Margaret Connell. *Education and the American Indian: The Road to Self-Determination since 1928*. Albuquerque: University of New Mexico Press, 1977.

————. "Indian Reform in a Decade of Prosperity." *Montana: The Magazine of Western History* 20 (January 1970).

Tyler, S. Lyman. *A History of Indian Policy*. Washington, D.C.: U.S. Government Printing Office, 1973.

Washburn, Wilcomb E. *Red Man's Land/White Man's Law: A Study of the Past and Present Status of the American Indian.* New York: Charles Scribner's Sons, 1971.

————. *The Assault on Indian Tribalism: The General Allotment Law (Dawes Act) of 1887.* Philadelphia: J. B. Lippincott, 1975.

Wilson, Raymond. *Ohiyesa: Charles Eastman, Santee Sioux.* Urbana: University of Illinois Press, 1983.

Wise, Jennings C. *The Red Man in the New World Drama: A Politico-Legal Study with a Pageantry of American Indian History.* New York: Macmillan, 1971.

Chapter Five

The "Indian New Deal"

John Collier became Commissioner of Indian Affairs on April 21, 1933, and he held the position for twelve years—longer than any other person. He became the most controversial and influential commissioner in United States history. His ideas invited debate and controversy, polarizing both the Native American communities and the European American community, with some of each group hailing him as a great reformer and others despising him as just another assimilationist, albeit a subtle one. Few people, however, questioned the profound influence he had on non–Native American opinion and on hundreds of thousands of Native Americans. Even now, nearly four decades after he left office, historians are still debating his career.

Born in Atlanta, Georgia, in 1884, Collier attended both Columbia University and the Collège de France in Paris, but he did not complete his studies at either place. In 1907 he found a job as civic secretary for the People's Institute in New York City, a job that shaped his ideas about ethnicity and social policy. The People's Institute worked to improve life for urban immigrants by promoting cooperative community action and preserving cultural traditions and communal lifestyles. Collier joined other social reformers at the Institute in the belief that cultural tradition tended to solidify and strengthen ethnic groups and that the vitality of such tradition in the process collectively enhanced political and social stability in American society as a whole. Ideally, cultural pluralism was a unifying force which represented ethnic differences and promoted a feeling of universal brotherhood. That belief strongly influenced his later service as Commissioner of Indian Affairs.

In September 1919 Collier moved to Los Angeles, where he accepted the directorship of public adult education in California. In his new post he stressed the importance of preserving community life in urban America and often cited the Bolshevik Revolution in Russia as a prime example of cooperative community action. State legislators in California frowned on Collier's "un-American" attitudes, and in 1920 he became a victim of the Red Scare and was forced to resign. Collier traveled to New Mexico to visit Mabel Dodge, an old friend from New York known for her support of the arts and the weekly salons she held in her Fifth Avenue apartment. Taos, New Mexico, where she had moved, had become a gathering place for hundreds of artists and writers. There Collier discovered his "Red Atlantis," the homeland of Pueblos still living together in a communal setting despite more than three centuries of attacks on their culture by generation after generation of Spanish, Mexican, and American settlers. For Collier, their cultural endurance demonstrated the vitality of communal relationships and ethnic pride.

Collier returned to California in 1921 and took a teaching post at San Francisco State College. But after a year of teaching psychology and sociology, he abandoned the academic life and joined the Indian Welfare Committee of the General Federation of Women's Clubs as a research agent. He quickly gained national recognition because of his efforts to block the passage of the Bursum Bill threatening the Spanish land grants to the Pueblos. In 1923 Collier became executive secretary of the newly formed American Indian Defense Association, an organization opposing the Bursum Bill, calling for termination of the Dawes Act, and encouraging preservation of Native American culture. In addition to organizing political lobbying efforts, in 1925 Collier began editing the magazine *American Indian Life,* a reform journal reflecting his basic values.

Throughout the 1920s Collier was in the vanguard of the reform movement, frequently publishing articles critical of the Bureau of Indian Affairs. He was also instrumental in convincing Secretary of the Interior Hubert Work to call upon the Brookings Institution to investigate reservation conditions, a proposal resulting in the Meriam Report in 1928. The Senate then decided to conduct its own investigation, and Collier served as a Senate investigator, an assignment which gave him an opportunity to visit a number of reservations and to observe the generally deplorable conditions. Among other things, he became convinced of the disastrous effects of the allotment and rapid assimilation policies.

When Franklin D. Roosevelt entered the White House in 1933, he selected Harold L. Ickes, a political liberal and former head of the American Indian Defense Association, as Secretary of the Interior. Ickes let it be known to the Senate and to Roosevelt that he wanted Collier to be his Commissioner of Indian Affairs. There was some opposition to Collier, especially from Senate Majority Leader Joseph T. Robinson of Arkansas, who wanted his brother-in-law, Edgar B. Meritt, a BIA employee for many years, as the new commissioner. With diplomatic skill, President Roosevelt informed Robinson that Collier was the choice, Robinson acquiesced, and Collier received Senate confirmation on April 21, 1933.

Collier enjoyed excellent rapport with Roosevelt and Ickes. Both men were willing to experiment with new and unconventional ideas, and because of their trust in Collier and the pressing duties imposed by the Great Depression they gave him virtually a free hand in making government policy. Collier immediately launched a new and, according to many people, revolutionary approach to Native American reform. Ever conscious of the importance of ethnic values and community solidarity, Collier attacked the concept of rapid assimilation of Native Americans into mainstream society. Instead of "getting the Indian out of the Indian," Collier sought to preserve tribal heritage and culture. Although many assimilationists cried that Collier was trying to "return Indians to the blanket," he was actually advocating more of an acculturated approach to solving the "Indian problem" based on his faith in cultural pluralism. The traditional goal was still the same: absorption of Native Americans into the dominant society, but at a slower and more equitable pace. Although some Native American critics would later call him an assimilationist, Collier was not committed to an inflexible timetable and believed that Native American culture, in the decades and even centuries before assimilation was complete, was absolutely necessary to Native American survival.

When he assumed office in April 1933, Collier had already developed a set of ideas about Native American affairs. He viewed the Bureau of Indian Affairs as an advisory rather than a supervisory agency and hoped to change the prevailing view among many full-bloods that the BIA was a manipulative, self-serving government bureaucracy. Collier was also adamant that the allotment program had been an economic and social disaster for Native Americans. Rather than breaking up tribes and distributing their land, Collier wanted to reconstitute the tribes politically, incorporate them economically, and restore their traditional land base. In one of Collier's earliest programs for self-determination, he wanted Native Americans to play a more active role in decisions affecting reservation life and to receive better training in the proper management of their land and natural resources. Regarding education, Collier believed that Native American children should attend community day schools or public schools on or near reservations instead of the distant boarding schools which separated them from their parents for long periods of time. Finally, Collier insisted that the federal government should no longer attempt to suppress Native American customs in the name of assimilation. The years of cultural imperialism had to come to an end. As a first step toward realizing his hopes, Collier convinced President Roosevelt to abolish by executive order the Board of Indian Commissioners, an agency created in 1869 to oversee the Bureau of Indian Affairs. Both Collier and Ickes considered the board an obstacle to reform, since its members and supporters remained intensely committed to the Dawes Act and to the eradication of tribal traditions. Roosevelt acted on Collier's request within days of his confirmation as commissioner.

With the influence of the presidency solidly behind him, Collier wasted no time in putting into motion a number of relief measures. On May 31, 1933, at Collier's request, Congress passed the Pueblo Relief Act granting additional payments to Native Americans and settlers who had been inadequately compensated by the Pueblo Lands Board in the 1920s. Collier also moved quickly to extend New Deal legislation to destitute Native Americans suffering from the effects of the Great Depression. Seasonal work for Native Americans in southern California and parts of Arizona, for example, had nearly disappeared. Many were also facing new difficulties in selling their products. The Navajos were receiving very low prices for their handicrafts, wool, lambs, and piñon nuts. Blistering summer heat and drought, as well as severe winter temperatures in 1932–33, increased the misery on the reservations. Although Native Americans were participating in the Civilian Conservation Corps established by Congress (in March 1933) to provide employment for young men in conservation work, Collier was instrumental in establishing the Indian Emergency Conservation Work program. Congress initially appropriated $5.9 million to the program, which funded the establishment of seventy-two camps on thirty-three reservations. Not only did the program permit Native Americans to work close to their families, but the conservation projects directly helped the reservation ecology. In New Mexico, Arizona, Oklahoma, Montana, South Dakota, and Washington, where reservation conservation programs were desperately needed, Native Americans constructed roads, storage dams, fences, and wells and put into effect proper fire control methods to protect their forests. Each worker received thirty dollars per month and many learned to operate machines and heavy equipment. Between 1933 and 1942 the more than eighty-five thousand Native Americans employed in the Indian Emergency Conservation Work program built a total of 1,742 dams and reservoirs, 12,230 miles of fences, 91 lookout towers, and 9,737 miles of truck trails. They conducted pest control projects on 1,315,870 acres of land and removed poisonous weeds from 263,129 acres of reservation farm and grazing land. Collier also established a magazine, *Indians at Work*, which promoted the "Indian CCC" and later served as a vehicle to garner support for Collier's other legislation.

Collier also managed to channel funds from other government agencies to benefit Native Americans. Secretary of Agriculture Henry A. Wallace used his influence to help Native Americans purchase purebred cattle from non–Native Americans through an eight-hundred-thousand-dollar allocation from the Agricultural Adjustment Administration. Between 1933 and 1939 Native American cattle herds increased from 167,373 to 267,551 head. Collier convinced Harry Hopkins, director of the Federal Emergency Relief Administration, to supply relief money to the reservations not included in the original legislation of May 1933. From the Department of War, poverty-stricken Native Americans received army surplus clothing, including 35,000 pairs of pants, 33,000 shirts, 40,000 coats, and 24,000 pairs of shoes. Under the Civil Works Administration, thousands of Native Americans were employed during the winter of 1934—such employment in addition to that made possible through the IECW program. The CWA also employed fifteen Native American artists and twenty-five craftsmen to paint pictures and make jewelry, rugs, and pottery. The Bureau of Indian Affairs then displayed the finished products in its offices.

The Public Works Administration, the Works Progress Administration, the National Youth Administration, and the Resettlement Administration provided more relief in the form of jobs and improved reservation conditions. The PWA, for example, employed Native Americans in building or improving reservation hospitals, schools, and sewage systems. The WPA hired over ten thousand Native Americans a year to index and file records for the Bureau of Indian Affairs, while the NYA provided six dollars monthly to each Native American student enrolled in day school for clothing, supplies, and lunches. The Resettlement Administration assisted Native Americans in North and South Dakota by constructing needed water wells. The agency also purchased nearly one million acres of grazing land for the Pueblos and Navajos. Finally, the Resettlement Administration encouraged Native Americans to help themselves and allocated money to instruct them in developing root cellars, canning centers, and low-cost housing.

To further assist Native Americans, Collier convinced Secretary Ickes to cancel their debts to the federal government. Ickes had authority to do so through an act of Congress passed on July 1, 1932. In 1933 the Roosevelt administration canceled debts worth more than $3 million; by 1936, debts exceeding $12 million for the construction of roads, bridges, irrigation projects, and the purchase of tribal herds had been eliminated. Because of the debt cancellation and the appropriation of more than $100 million in relief programs, Native Americans were able to survive the worst years of the Great Depression. Indeed, many Native Americans enjoyed a higher standard of living during the 1930s than they had in the 1920s, in large measure due to Collier's efforts to make available to them a healthy share of such depression relief.

In the field of education Collier followed the recommendations of the Meriam Report. Will Carson Ryan, Jr., remained as director of Native American education until 1936, when Willard W. Beatty, an educator from Illinois, succeeded him. Collier, Ryan, and Beatty continued to close boarding schools in favor of day schools. Using $3.6 million in PWA Funds, Collier ordered the construction of one hundred day schools. Consistent with Collier's philosophy, the day schools served as community activity centers where both children and adults could learn domestic skills and health care and participate in preserving tribal culture. Beatty also worked to improve the quality of teachers hired, and he expanded curricula by inaugurating summer school classes in anthropology, home economics, arts and crafts, rural sociology, health, and tribal languages. He also supported bilingual education as one of the best ways to increase literacy among Native Americans.

In addition to relief measures and educational reform, Collier tried to improve health conditions. Securing $1.7 million from the Public Works Administration in 1933, he ordered the construction of eleven reservation hospitals and the substantial improvement of ten others. He also saw to the employment of more part-time doctors, nurses, and dentists. More comprehensive treatment programs for trachoma and tuberculosis were soon made available. Between 1939 and 1943 the incidence of trachoma dropped from 20.2 percent to 7.2 percent. And throughout the 1930s and early 1940s, Collier recognized the inadequacy of government health programs on the reservations and demanded increased appropriations for the Indian Medical Service.

Many New Dealers felt that Collier had achieved some remarkable results in 1933 and early 1934. But he was not without his critics. Many Native Americans and non–Native Americans complained that either too much money was spent on programs that were not needed or that too little money went to critically necessary programs. Others complained of government-sponsored blunders, such as the time when inexperienced work parties of Klamaths in Oregon mistakenly destroyed timber on their reservation. Problems still plagued Native American education. Appropriations were inadequate to provide needed teachers, classrooms, and lunch programs. Navajo students at day schools in 1937 received only thirteen cents per day for lunches, a figure well below the minimum recommended in the Meriam Report. Day schools among the Navajos were largely unsuccessful because the lack of reservation roads and the Navajos' nomadic ways meant low attendance. Additionally, many Navajos preferred boarding schools simply because their children had received better meals there. Flora Warren Seymour, a staunch opponent of Collier and formerly a member of the Board of Indian Commissioners, tried to ruin him politically when it became clear that the Navajos preferred boarding schools. Christian missionaries greatly resented Collier's decision to extend religious freedom to Native Americans by restricting religious instruction in day and boarding schools. He also angered them by ending compulsory religious services and providing voluntary instruction in native religions. Some Christian Native Americans also protested Collier's orders. At the Pine Ridge Reservation in South Dakota, 962 people signed a petition addressed to Eleanor Roosevelt expressing the fear that their children would no longer receive Christian instruction in BIA schools. Collier had to remind all these critics that he was not anti-Christian but was merely concerned that native religions receive equal time. Religious freedom, he argued, was not limited to instruction in the tenets of Christianity. To soothe any misgivings President Roosevelt had about the criticisms, Secretary Ickes wrote to him that he had been

a real White Father to the Indians and they appreciated it deeply. . . . Your administration will go down in history as the most humane and far seeing with respect to the Indians that this country ever had.*

Despite the gains of 1933, Collier still felt that the overall approach had been piecemeal and that a more carefully planned and comprehensive approach to Native American affairs still had to be developed. The relief measures passed in 1933 had been absolutely necessary, as had the changes in education policy in reservation schools. Preservation of Native American culture, new support for Native American education, and the end of the allotment program were all keys to Collier's philosophy; and in 1934 and 1935 the federal government took major steps toward implementing his ideas in these regards.

In 1934 Secretary Ickes named a committee to study means of protecting and marketing Native American arts and crafts, and the next year Congress authorized the Department of the Interior to create an Indian Arts and Crafts Board, operating on an initial budget of $45,000. The five-member board was to improve the quality and widen the distribution of tribal arts and crafts and, through the use of government trademarks on products, to guarantee to purchasers that the items were Native American–made. The board created craft guilds on reservations to operate as "training centers" for Native American artists and craftsmen and as direct marketing outlets, bypassing middlemen who siphoned off profits. It sponsored art classes in BIA schools, helping to inspire young artists and to preserve native traditions. The board also conducted weaving, silverwork, leatherwork, and beadwork projects. Collier took great pride in the board's work. He was delighted with the superb products exhibited by the Navajo Arts and Crafts Guild at the 1939 World's Fair in San Francisco.

The New Deal launched a new approach to Native American education on April 16, 1934, when Congress passed the Johnson-O'Malley Act, which authorized the Secretary of the Interior to negotiate contracts with any state or territory for monetary relief in the areas of

*Quoted in Kenneth R. Philp, *John Collier's Crusade for Indian Reform, 1920–1954* (Tucson: University of Arizona Press, 1977), 126.

Native American education, medical aid, agricultural assistance, and social welfare. Although Collier had high hopes that the Johnson-O'Malley Act would improve conditions and provide better services to Native Americans, especially in the field of education, there were several problems inherent in the law. The act was passed on the assumption that state administrators and federal officials could work together. Collier believed that better programs could be developed by combining federal and state resources. But the Bureau of Indian Affairs was deeply concerned that the states would be more interested in the money they received from the act than in providing special programs and classes for Native American students. State administrators, on the other hand, guarded their authority jealously and resented any federal interference with their schools.

The idea of Native Americans attending public schools was hardly new. Since the end of the nineteenth century, Native American students had attended public schools through federal contracts with individual school districts, and by 1928 more of them were in public schools than in BIA schools. Before the Johnson-O'Malley Act, however, the funding method was cumbersome and inefficient, with the BIA Education Division responsible for contracting with hundreds of individual school districts instead of working directly with officials of the state departments of education. Will Carson Ryan, Jr., director of the BIA Education Division, complained that the method was "administratively absurd" and violated "every right principle of Federal-State relationship in education."* With the passage of the Johnson-O'Malley Act, the BIA was able to contract on a federal-state basis.

The Education Division of the BIA stressed the importance of handling each state's situation individually because of the complex differences in local tribal groups. Both Arizona and Oklahoma, for example, had large Native American communities, but only a small number of Native American children in Arizona went to public schools, while more than three-fourths of them in Oklahoma attended public schools. Federal funding for these educational programs had to be different because of the number of Native American students involved and because the sources from which the states drew their revenue varied greatly.

Between 1934 and 1941, California, Washington, Minnesota, and Arizona negotiated contracts with the Bureau of Indian Affairs. Except in Minnesota, the harmonious working relationship Collier had so desperately wanted never materialized. California was the first state to receive federal funding under the new act. Mary Steward, the BIA

---

*Quoted in Margaret Connell Szasz, *Education and the American Indian: The Road to Self-Determination since 1928* (Albuquerque: University of New Mexico Press, 1977), 90.

Superintendent of Indian Education for California and a well-known educator, immediately encountered difficulties with state education officials who did not want the federal government to "dictate" educational policy to them. She finally resigned in disgust in 1941, and the next year her position was eliminated. State officials then played a much more active role in allocating Johnson-O'Malley funds. Similar problems erupted in Washington between Homer L. Morrison, the BIA superintendent, and the state Superintendent of Public Instruction. Although there were few problems in Arizona, primarily because most Native American children were in BIA schools, it was only in Minnesota that the state department of education worked hard to cooperate with the BIA.

The competitive problem in education, of course, did not always involve state education leaders. The effectiveness of the Johnson-O'Malley Act was also limited by BIA fears as well as by local attitudes. A number of BIA officials regarded federal schools as better fit to accommodate the needs of Native American children. They felt that most public school administrators were too inexperienced to develop adequate programs for Native Americans. Public school instruction was seriously flawed in several areas. A primary problem was the anti–Native American prejudice so common to teachers and administrators. Some teachers were openly prejudiced, while others were subtly cruel. Public schools also lacked courses in tribal culture, and a capability for bilingual instruction was commonly inadequate or nonexistent. It was no wonder that Native American students did not do well in public schools. Too often their physical needs—food, clothing, shoes, and transportation—were not met, while their emotional needs—ethnic pride and a sense of belonging—were ignored completely. Yet public schools continued to draw Johnson-O'Malley money while failing to provide adequate programs for Native American children. Instead, in most instances they channeled the money into their general operating expenses and made little effort to meet specifically the needs of Native American students. Collier's hopes for drastic educational reform were dashed on the rocks of federal-state rivalry and racism.

The third and most profound piece of New Deal legislation directly affecting Native Americans was the Indian Reorganization Act of 1934. A denunciation of the allotment policy, this act was an open admission that the Dawes Act, after forty-seven years of operation, was a devastating blunder. Collier had always been an outspoken critic of land allotment, and in August 1933 he had ordered federal agents on reservations nationwide to stop selling trust land and to cease submitting certificates of competency, fee patents, or removal restrictions on Native American land to the BIA except in cases of grave distress. Early in 1934 Collier joined with William Zimmerman, Assistant

Commissioner of Indian Affairs, and Nathan Margold, Felix Cohen, and Charles Fahy, members of the Interior Department legal staff, to draw up the piece of legislation which later became the Indian Reorganization Act. The forty-eight-page bill was sent to Senator Burton K. Wheeler of Montana and Representative Edgar Howard of Nebraska, chairmen of the Senate and House Committees on Indian Affairs, and they introduced it to Congress in mid-February.

The Wheeler-Howard Bill was divided into four titles involving self-government, education, land, and a special court for Native American affairs. Title I allowed Native Americans residing on reservations to establish local self-governments and tribal corporations to develop reservation resources. The Secretary of the Interior would issue a charter of home rule and right of incorporation to a tribe after one-fourth of its adults petitioned for such a charter and after three-fifths of them ratified the charter in a tribal election. Collier hoped that these newly formed local governments would operate like municipalities, each having a voice in congressional bills affecting them and ultimately assuming most of the functions of the Bureau of Indian Affairs. Title II permitted the federal government to train Native Americans in forest management, public health, law enforcement, and record keeping and provided scholarship money for gifted students. Money was also allocated for courses in tribal culture in BIA boarding schools. Title III ended the Dawes Act and provided for the consolidation of allotted and heirship lands into productive units for chartered community use. Individuals affected by the consolidations would receive either compensation or interest of equal worth in tribal lands. Those holding fee patent titles could participate on a voluntary basis. The Secretary of the Interior was also authorized to buy property for Native Americans through a congressional appropriation of $2 million annually. Title IV established a special federal court, the Court of Indian Affairs, for the chartered communities. The court would have jurisdiction over reservation crimes and cases where at least one of the parties was a Native American.

In order to garner support for the bill, Collier had ten meetings with Native Americans in South Dakota, Oregon, Arizona, New Mexico, California, Oklahoma, and Wisconsin in March and April 1934. He spent most of his time at the meetings dealing one at a time with the numerous particular and often unique apprehensions and problems presented by representatives of the many tribes involved. Several Sioux delegates, for example, wanted all land exchanges under Title III to be voluntary instead of compulsory, and Collier agreed to amend the bill. Papago delegates doubted whether self-government would work among their independent farming and ranching communities; they opposed the bill. The Pimas and San Carlos Apaches feared loss of their mineral rights or tribal herds. And the Navajos tended to link the Wheeler-Howard Bill to Collier's unpopular program of stock reduction of Navajo sheep and goats, instituted to prevent overgrazing and long-term environmental damage to the reservation. Many mixed-bloods simply wanted to retain their individual allotments; they had no desire to return to communal living under tribal direction. Nevertheless, Collier later informed Congress that polls taken at the ten meetings revealed that fifty-four tribes representing 141,881 individuals approved the bill, while only twelve tribes totaling 15,106 opposed the measure.

The bill was stiffly opposed by several groups, mostly for traditional reasons. The Indian Rights Association believed that the bill perpetuated the segregation of Native Americans, isolating them forever from the mainstream of social life in the United States. Many congressmen seriously questioned the idea of communal ownership of property and feared that the creation of "independent" tribal-chartered communities would severely threaten the process of assimilation, which they felt was the only realistic way of dealing with the "Indian problem." Collier responded to them by citing the Mormon success with cooperative land allotment, agricultural, and economic programs during the early decades in the Great Basin, arguing that Native Americans too could benefit from similar programs. Some people accused Collier of attempting to restore pagan ideas and of being an advocate of communism. Joseph Bruner, a full-blood Creek and later president of the American Indian Federation, denounced Collier and considered him a communist and an atheist. Many western congressmen, reflecting the demands of economic interest groups, feared the permanent loss of reservation resources to outside development. In Arizona, for example, where certain Papago lands had been temporarily withdrawn for mineral exploitation by non–Native American mining interests, Senator Henry F. Ashurst believed that the Wheeler-Howard Bill would permanently deny non–Native American entry to these lands. He vociferously opposed the bill. Eventually, Collier agreed to thirty amendments to the Wheeler-Howard Bill, most of them based on congressional criticisms of the original draft of the bill and the proposals made at the ten regional conferences. Included in those proposed changes were the individual's consent to the transfer of allotted land to community ownership, the protection of individual mineral rights to allotted lands, and the retention of the right to partition farm lands among heirs as long as the procedure remained economically sound. Many in Congress, however, remained opposed, most of them along traditional lines: liberal reformers feared the end of assimilation; those with an eye to increased land holdings feared the permanent inaccessibility of those Native American–controlled resources that remained.

Frustrated and angry at the opposition to his proposals, Collier finally turned to President Roosevelt for assistance. The President had previously expressed his support for the bill, and both Secretary Ickes and Secretary of Agriculture Henry Wallace began soliciting Roosevelt's open support for the measure. Roosevelt insisted that Democratic congressmen join in support of the Wheeler-Howard Bill, and in June 1934 Congress passed the bill but only after reducing its benefits and protections. The appropriation for helping organize tribal governments was reduced from $500,000 annually to $250,000; benefits were denied to all Native American groups not formally recognized by the BIA as a tribe or band; provisions to consolidate allotted lands were weakened; tribes were prevented from simply taking over heirship lands; and the provision for a special Court of Indian Affairs was eliminated. Despite Collier's hopes, Congress had very little interest in restoring Native Americans to a position of political, economic, and cultural independence.

In its final version, the Indian Reorganization Act repealed the allotment laws, restored certain surplus reservation lands to tribal ownership, and permitted voluntary exchanges of allotments for interests in tribal corporations. Congress agreed to appropriate $2 million annually to the Secretary of the Interior for the acquisition of additional lands for tribes. Congress also authorized the expenditure of $250,000 a year for the organization of tribal governments and tribal corporations, which could then borrow money from a $10 million revolving credit fund—later increased to $12 million—to finance economic development of reservation resources. The law also created a $250,000 annual scholarship fund for Native American students and gave Native Americans preferential treatment in securing civil service positions in the Bureau of Indian Affairs.

The Indian Reorganization Act required tribes to accept or reject the act through referenda. Similarly, the provision establishing tribal self-governments was decided through referenda. When a majority of the adult members of a tribe voted to approve the Indian Reorganization Act, they could then write a constitution which had to be approved by another majority vote of the tribe and by the Secretary of the Interior. At first, in order to expedite implementation of the Indian Reorganization Act and avoid delays that would inevitably arise because of tribal factionalism, the Interior Department arbitrarily counted all eligible adult voters who failed to vote as favoring the measure. As could be expected, the results were extremely biased in favor of acceptance. At least seventeen tribes who voted to reject the act were considered as being in favor of it because a high number of qualified adult voters did not cast ballots. California Mission Native Americans at the Santa Ysabel Reservation, for example, overwhelmingly voted to reject the Indian Reorganization Act by a vote of forty-three to nine; but since sixty-two eligible members did not vote, the Secretary of the Interior declared the tribe in favor of the new law. Thousands of Native Americans denounced the election method, claiming that it favored mixed-bloods, who were more likely to vote, over full-bloods, many of whom were isolated in distant parts of the reservations and were less likely to vote. The last thing Collier wanted was to appear dictatorial, so in 1935 he convinced Congress to pass legislation defining "majority" as half plus one of those Native Americans actually participating in the election.

Tribes accepting the Indian Reorganization Act could then, by majority vote, elect a tribal council which possessed all powers already vested in the tribe by "existing law." The tribal council had a right to hire legal counsel, to prevent the sale or lease of tribal lands without its consent, to enter into negotiations with federal or state agencies for public services, and to review federal appropriations affecting the tribe before such measures were submitted to either Congress or to the Bureau of Indian Affairs. In the 1960s and 1970s Native American activists built on this idea of tribal self-determination. When one-third of the adult tribal members petitioned the Secretary of the Interior for a tribal charter of incorporation, and a simple majority of tribal voters ratified the charter, tribes could then form corporations to develop reservation resources and business enterprises.

To assist Collier in his efforts to organize tribal self-government and restore tribal life, the federal government sought help from recognized anthropologists. Dr. Duncan Strong, an employee of the Bureau of American Ethnology, and several university anthropology professors agreed to serve as consultants. The Bureau of Indian Affairs established the Applied Anthropology Unit in 1935 under the direction of Dr. H. Scudder Mekeel, a former Harvard anthropology professor. Mekeel's staff conducted reservation fieldwork in an effort to prepare tribes to adopt the Indian Reorganization Act and to write constitutions. But over the years, internal conflicts over policy decisions between BIA administrators and anthropologists, including Collier and Mekeel, weakened the effectiveness of the division, and in 1937 Congress cut appropriations and disbanded the unit. Collier continued, however, to consult anthropologists and other social scientists. Their expertise was especially useful in instructing employees and teachers in the BIA Education Division on Native American culture.

To further assist tribes in drawing up constitutions, Nathan Margold, Felix Cohen, and other members of the Interior Department's legal staff prepared a model constitution to follow. The model helped some tribes, but its abundance of "legalese" made it difficult to comprehend, and it was too general to take into account the particular needs and expectations of individual tribes.

In 1936 the Bureau of Indian Affairs established an Indian Organization Division to aid tribes in administrative details after they had prepared their constitutions. Division field representatives—most of them Native American employees of the BIA—provided political, economic, and social assistance to tribal councils. For example, they examined how well the tribal councils operated, helped settle some problems the tribal councils faced, and assisted them in their efforts to develop economic and social programs.

As Collier and others in the Bureau of Indian Affairs tried to implement the Indian Reorganization Act, critics attacked it on the grounds that the law segregated Native Americans from European American society, prevented "efficient" development of reservation resources, ignored tribal prerogatives and customs, or supported anti-Christian and communistic principles. Such criticism was effective to the extent that congressional appropriations to the Indian Reorganization Act programs were cut beginning in 1935.

Still, Collier had other successes. For example, he convinced Congress to pass legislation in 1936 providing self-government and financial assistance to Native Americans in Alaska and Oklahoma. Native Americans in Alaska, due to an oversight in the law, had not been permitted to establish constitutions or tribal corporations or to draw from the revolving credit fund under the Indian Reorganization Act. To remedy the situation, Congress passed the Alaska Reorganization Act in 1936, extending these privileges to Alaskan natives and authorizing the creation of reservations on land occupied by Native Americans. With Native American approval, the Secretary of the Interior established six reservations in Alaska in 1944. Since Alaskan Native Americans were more village than tribal oriented, villages were allowed to establish corporations and constitutions. Forty-nine villages with a total native population of 10,899 drew up constitutions and charters of incorporation. An Alaska Native Industries Cooperative Association was created to borrow money from the revolving credit fund for the promotion of Native American business ventures.

Oklahoma congressmen objected so bitterly to the Indian Reorganization Act—on the grounds that it would retard assimilation—that the tribes there were excluded from many of the act's provisions. But Collier was not satisfied, and in the fall of 1934 he went with Senator Elmer Thomas, who had been opposed to the act initially, and visited many tribes, soliciting their opinions, especially about the right to establish tribal governments and tribal corporations. He met with very mixed feelings. Some of the delegates from the Five Civilized Tribes, for example, favored the establishment of self-government and charters of incorporation, while others, wishing to be left alone on their individual allotments, rejected all or most programs of a communal nature. Delegates representing the Kiowas and Potawatomis also voiced disapproval and supported the older allotment policies. Shawnee, Sac and Fox, and Iowa delegates tended to approve of the creation of tribal corporations, and the Pawnees and Comanches were bitterly divided.

Convinced that Native Americans in Oklahoma could benefit from the extension of certain provisions of the Indian Reorganization Act to them, Senator Thomas and Representative Will Rogers introduced a bill drafted by Collier. The Thomas-Rogers Bill proposed to place Native Americans in Oklahoma under federal guardianship; but in order to satisfy non–Native American assimilationists, mixed-bloods, and assimilated Native Americans, the bill allowed Native Americans of less than one-half Native American ancestry to be "relieved of all restrictions" on their property. The Secretary of the Interior would make the final decision in lifting such restrictions, based on recommendations from a special competency commission. Other provisions involved better protection of heirship lands, tribal self-government, tribal incorporation charters, communal ownership of land, acquisition of additional property (which would be tax exempt), reservation expansion, and increased educational and health care.

The bill encountered stiff opposition from Native Americans and non–Native Americans at congressional hearings. Joseph Bruner, the Creek president of the American Indian Federation, again argued that such a bill would retard assimilation. Legislators and businessmen in Oklahoma echoed similar sentiments and complained about the loss of state taxes on withdrawn tribal lands and mineral deposits. Others feared that the competency commission would function like previous commissions and indiscriminately give fee patent titles to "incompetent" Native Americans who would then lose their lands to European Americans or mixed-bloods. As had been the case in many previous pieces of Native American reform legislation, the Thomas-Rogers Bill was controversial for both Native Americans and non–Native Americans.

Collier revised the Thomas-Rogers Bill to meet many of the criticisms, and Congress passed it as the Oklahoma Indian Welfare Act in June 1936. The law permitted the state of Oklahoma to levy a "gross production tax" on oil and gas leases on reservation land and deleted all provisions regarding the degree of Native American blood required to remove restrictions on Native American land. The act made no mention of improving educational and health services but did provide for communal ownership of property and the creation of tribal constitutions and corporations. The Oklahoma Indian Welfare Act also permitted ten or more Native Americans to establish local cooperatives and secure money from a special $2 million credit fund.

For a variety of reasons, only a minority of Native Americans ever really came under the umbrella of the Indian Reorganization Act and the Oklahoma Indian Welfare Act. Because the Indian Reorganization Act denied eligibility to all groups not officially recognized as tribes or bands by the Bureau of Indian Affairs, more than 50,000 Native Americans were excluded at the outset. The 103,000 Native Americans in Oklahoma were similarly excluded from the IRA. With the vote counted, approximately 181 tribes numbering 129,750 people accepted the Indian Reorganization Act, while 77 tribes with a total population of 86,365 rejected it. Less than 40 percent of all Native Americans were eligible for IRA benefits from the beginning.

Moreover, not all tribes approving the Indian Reorganization Act or the Oklahoma Indian Welfare Act adopted constitutions or incorporated. Ninety-three tribes or bands ultimately adopted constitutions under the IRA, and only seventy-three had charters of incorporation. Despite Collier's hard work on the Oklahoma Indian Welfare Act, most Oklahoma Native Americans did not avail themselves of the law, preferring instead to keep their own land allotments. Indeed, between 1936 and 1945 only eighteen Oklahoma tribes or bands numbering 13,241 people wrote tribal constitutions, and only thirteen of them, numbering 5,741 people, set up charters of incorporation. Among the Five Civilized Tribes, for example, only the Cherokee Keetoowah band and the three Creek towns adopted constitutions and corporate charters. By 1945 tribes representing only a small percent of Native Americans had opted for the provisions of the Indian Reorganization Act and the Oklahoma Welfare Act. Most individuals continue to live on allotted lands in Oklahoma. Only one reservation remains, and that for mineral rights only. (Only 12 percent of its residents were Native Americans in 1980.)

Despite his understanding of and respect for Native American culture, Collier had underestimated its diversity, as well as the intensity of Native American factionalism. His ideas had come from his experience with the isolated, high-context cultures of the Navajos and Pueblos—the "Red Atlantis" of the Southwest. But relatively few Native Americans lived in such highly integrated, monolithic cultures. The idea that Native Americans functioned as unified tribes was an inherent flaw of the Indian Reorganization Act, since many Native Americans were more band (even family) oriented than tribal oriented. Thus, the formal tribal governments on the level envisioned by the architects of the Indian Reorganization Act never really existed among many tribes, even before the time of European or European American contact. The Indian Reorganization Act imposed rigid political and economic systems which were often alien to Native American peoples. Voting by majority rule posed problems for a people who had a long tradition of reaching decisions by consensus or persuasion. To them, majority rule was arbitrary, rigid, and inconsiderate of the feelings of the minority; and the result, even when the tribe approved the Indian Reorganization Act, was considerable dis-affection among many members of the tribe. Rivalries and faction-alism on the reservations militated against the Indian Reorganization Act as well. Native American factionalism, not always clear-cut or well defined, was as common in the 1930s as it had been throughout American history. Simply stated, it usually pitted full-bloods against mixed-bloods and traditionalists against progressives.

The Crows of Montana, for example, rejected the Indian Reorga-nization Act even though their native superintendent, Robert Yellowtail, urged support. Full- and mixed-bloods united to defeat the measure, believing that acceptance would inevitably result in the loss of their lands. Full-blood Northern Cheyennes in Montana supported the Indian Reorganization Act because they viewed it as a means of gaining control of the tribal business committee which mixed-bloods, a numerical minority, had controlled for years. At the Rosebud Reservation in South Dakota, the full-blood Sioux, who generally still retained their land allotments, opposed the act, charging that it would favor the mixed-bloods who had disposed of their allotments. In the referendum voting, both the Northern Cheyennes and the Rosebud Sioux accepted the Indian Reorganization Act; but the full-blood Northern Cheyennes gained control of tribal enterprises while the mixed-blood Sioux gained more control over tribal decisions and property.

In the Southwest, the Papagos voted to accept the Indian Reorgani-zation Act; but they had no tradition of tribal unity. Their language had no word equivalents for "representative" and "budget" and only one word to describe a superintendent or commissioner, a president, or a king. The Hopis were also village-oriented people and had little knowledge of centralized tribal government. Their constitution estab-lished a tribal government respecting the authority of individual vil-lages in certain matters, but intervillage rivalries undermined its effec-tiveness. Although most of the New Mexico Pueblos accepted the act, it was only a token gesture. Very few of the Pueblo communities wrote constitutions because most Pueblo leaders held tenaciously to their traditional forms of authority and feared that those powers would be threatened if they wrote constitutions establishing self-governments based on majority rule.

Another major disappointment to Collier was the rejection of the Indian Reorganization Act by the Navajos, the largest tribe in the United States. They turned down the act by a close vote of 8,197 to 7,679 in June 1935, largely because they related it to the unpopular government programs to reduce their stock herds. The BIA had rec-ommended the reduction of Navajo livestock because reservation land was being damaged by overgrazing. But the number of animals a Navajo owned was a status symbol among tribesmen, and, although the stock reductions could be seen to be a long-range benefit, Navajos still resented the decreases. Collier visited the Navajos in 1933 and convinced their tribal council, which had been created by the Interior Department in 1922 to represent the tribe in oil leasing of reservation land, to accept the stock reductions. Securing a grant of $200,000 from the Federal Emergency Relief Administration, the Bureau of Indian Affairs purchased 100,000 head of sheep; but the reductions were done on an across-the-board scale rather than a graduated one, which favored the large herd owners at the expense of the smaller owners.

In March 1934 Collier again visited the Navajos and explained the proposed Indian Reorganization Act to them. He also requested a second stock reduction. Although the Navajo Council finally agreed to a reduction of 150,000 goats and 50,000 sheep, the BIA again implemented the program too rapidly, and the Navajos used the livestock reduction programs in their campaign against the Indian Reorganization Act. Jacob C. Morgan, a Navajo graduate of Hampton Institute and a staunch assimilationist, led the faction opposing the Indian Reorganization Act. Chee Dodge, a recognized tribal leader of long standing and an avid traditionalist, was Morgan's archrival and threw his support behind Collier and the Indian Reorganization Act.

Morgan argued that acceptance of the Indian Reorganization Act would segregate the Navajos from the dominant society and "return them to the blanket." He condemned the closing of boarding schools (he had had a successful experience as a boarding school student) and the increased enrollment of Navajo children in day schools. In his campaign of opposition Morgan effectively converted hostility to the livestock reductions into resentment for both the Bureau of Indian Affairs and the Indian Reorganization Act.

Most traders and missionaries among the Navajos similarly disapproved of the new law. The traders worried about their own economic survival, fearing that the Navajos, under the Indian Reorganization Act programs, would banish them and establish cooperatives. The Protestant missionaries also harbored fears of expulsion and viewed the new tribal independence and tribal governments as a threat to Christian assimilation.

Dodge, on the other hand, believed that acceptance of the Indian Reorganization Act would create genuine self-government for the Navajos. But Dodge was not nearly as effective a campaigner as Morgan, who especially influenced the eastern and northern Navajos. Their votes proved decisive in defeating the Indian Reorganization Act in June 1935. Collier was deeply disappointed over the rejection; he tried repeatedly to persuade the Navajos to hold another election on the act—to no avail. Throughout the 1930s and early 1940s the Navajos, outside the provisions of the act, argued with Collier and the BIA over such issues as land management, livestock regulation, and the power of the Navajo Tribal Council.

Other tribes, however, took advantage of the Indian Reorganization Act by forming tribal corporations and borrowing money from the revolving credit fund. The Manchester Band of the Pomos in California, for example, established a dairy and farming business, and the Chippewas at the Lac du Flambeau Reservation in Wisconsin built a number of tourist cabins to generate income. Native Americans on the Swinomish Reservation in Washington started an oyster fishing project, and in Montana the Northern Cheyennes and Rocky Boy Band of Chippewa Crees received loans to increase and feed their cattle herds. In the Southwest, the Chiricahua and Mescalero Apaches (on the Mescalero Apache Reservation) secured loans of more than $240,000 for the improvement of reservation housing and agricultural and livestock production, while the Jicarilla Apaches used a loan from the revolving credit fund to establish a tribal store, the first of its kind operated exclusively by Native Americans. Tribal corporations also gave loans to individual Native Americans so that they could improve their own economic situations. These loans were repaid promptly; by 1945 less than 1 percent of the loans from the revolving credit fund were in default. Still, only 8 percent of adult Native American males in the United States ever participated in the revolving credit fund program.

Further problems magnified Collier's unpopularity. The creation of the Technical Cooperation–Bureau of Indian Affairs project in December 1935, a joint venture by the Department of Agriculture and the Interior Department to survey reservation resources and recommend means of economic development, caused many Native Americans to fear reductions of their lands and livestock. At Zuñi Pueblo, tribal members complained that Collier had placed them under the jurisdiction of the United Pueblo Agency and had appointed a woman—medical doctor Sophie Aberle—as general superintendent without their consent. At Taos Pueblo, where Collier had first encountered his "Red Atlantis" in the 1920s, disputes over the use of peyote brought more controversy and bitterness. The peyotists were a minority there, but problems between the two factions had existed for years. In February 1936 the antipeyotist majority stopped a peyote ceremony, and the peyotists protested vehemently. Collier went to Taos Pueblo in June and managed to arrange a compromise that allowed the peyotists to practice their religion on a restricted basis, but the agreement soon degenerated into more bitterness and contention. More serious for Collier, the antipeyotists among the Pueblos resented his interference, as did Mabel Dodge, his old friend. She had long viewed peyote as a dangerous drug and believed that Collier's unilateral decisions regarding the Zuñis were deplorable. At an All Pueblo Council meeting in April 1936, Collier defended his actions, while Dodge and the antipeyotists criticized him. Their arguments were carried nationally in the media, and in August the United States Senate held hearings in Santa Fe. Although Collier's decision on peyote stood, along with his willingness to let the Native American Church function on the reservations, his popularity suffered a serious setback.

As the 1930s drew to a close, the "Indian New Deal" had become the object of intense criticism. Even Burton K. Wheeler, one of the sponsors of the original Indian Reorganization Act, began expressing misgivings about the program. He had never really supported Collier's views on communal societies and the values of ethnic pluralism, and he had become critical of BIA controls over Native Americans. By the late 1930s he also came to believe that the tribal corporations were becoming too powerful and that the Bureau of Indian Affairs was discriminating against the tribes which had rejected the Indian Reorganization Act. Wheeler's disaffection from Collier grew more intense in 1937 when Collier wrote an editorial in *Indians at Work* supporting Roosevelt's attempt to pack the United States Supreme Court. To Collier's great dismay, Wheeler introduced a bill in the Senate in 1937 to repeal the Indian Reorganization Act. Collier fought the repeal, arguing that Native Americans were not being segregated from European Americans, that tribal corporations were only exercising powers specifically granted to them in previous laws and in the provisions of the Indian Reorganization Act, and that those Native Americans rejecting the New Deal program were not being mistreated or ignored. The repeal was defeated, but it was a continuing sign of congressional resentment over the "Indian New Deal."

The American Indian Federation also remained a major critic of the "Indian New Deal." Leaders of that organization even solicited aid from the Nazis, who had declared that Native Americans were members of the Aryan race and a suppressed minority in the United States. (The German-American Bund carried on a propaganda campaign, condemning Collier's "communistic" reforms and the presence of Jewish employees in the Department of the Interior.) Federation spokesmen were allowed to express their views at Senate Indian Affairs Committee meetings, and in 1939 they managed to submit a bill exempting certain tribes from the Indian Reorganization Act. However, the House revised the legislation to allow tribes who had already accepted the law to vote again on provisions they might have already approved but now found objectionable. Collier fought the bill and it died in committee, but the "Indian New Deal" barely survived the assault.

World War II eventually accomplished, however, what the critics of the 1930s had failed to do. Because of the tremendous growth of federal agencies and the shortage of office space during the war, in December 1941 the Bureau of Indian Affairs was transferred to Chicago, far from the seat of power. It became almost impossible for the BIA to work with other government departments in cooperative programs to assist Native Americans. John Collier no longer had the ear of President Roosevelt, who was too absorbed with military, diplomatic, and economic concerns to worry about Native American affairs. More than eight hundred employees of the Bureau of Indian Affairs left the agency during the war, either going to work for other federal agencies or joining the armed services. Congressional appropriations to the bureau dwindled, and deterioration of roads, housing, and medical care on the reservations ensued.

Even more significant were the ideological pressures created by total war. The Japanese attack on Pearl Harbor inspired nearly four years of patriotic fervor, anti-Axis propaganda, and obsessive concern for national unity; in the process Collier's emphasis on ethnicity and community independence seemed counterproductive at best and dangerous at worst. Between 1941 and 1945 the need for unity and consensus was overwhelming, and most Americans were simply unwilling to accept Native Americans as a permanently separate set of subcultures in the United States. Karl Mundt, a prominent congressman from South Dakota, called for a complete investigation of Native American affairs in 1943 and suggested abolition of the BIA and the end of federal control over Native Americans.

In 1944 Senator Thomas issued a scathing attack on Collier and the "Indian New Deal," and Senator Wheeler concurred. The Senate Subcommittee on Indian Affairs suggested a return to the old allotment policies. That same year Senator Harlan Bushfield of South Dakota sounded a similar theme in demanding repeal of the Indian Reorganization Act. Additionally, the National Council of Churches once again proposed a return to the traditional policies of individualism, private property, and assimilation in Native American communities. Disgusted with the criticism and the pressure, John Collier resigned on January 10, 1945.

Achievements of the Indian Reorganization Act were limited—far short of expectations. The Department of the Interior spent more than $5 million purchasing four hundred thousand new acres of land, and several pieces of congressional legislation added another nine hundred thousand acres. The Interior Department returned more than a million acres that had not been homesteaded as well as a million acres of public-domain grazing land. With their own funds Native Americans managed to purchase four hundred thousand new acres, so that in all they recovered nearly 4 million acres of land they had lost under the Dawes Act. That was not much, especially in view of what they had lost since 1887, but at least the Indian Reorganization Act had stopped the allotment program before it had done any more damage. Also, the tribal structures of some tribes had been repaired and the federal government had given at least lip service to the principle of self-determination for Native Americans.

Still, overwhelming problems remained for the more than five hundred thousand Native Americans living in the United States in 1945. They had lost over 90 million acres of land since 1887, and much of what they had recovered since 1934 was of little value—land that European American settlers had not wanted. Economic dependence on the federal government remained a fact of life. Poverty, disease, and unemployment continued to be far higher than among other Americans.

As had occurred so often in the past, European American attitudes and Native American factionalism had stalled reform movements, and the "Indian New Deal" had been no exception. Although it had many shortcomings, it was an unprecedented effort to protect Native American heritage and provide political and economic assistance. Collier failed, however, to appreciate the complexity of Native American tribalism. He expected all Native Americans to accept political and economic institutions created along European American rules of individual aggrandizement and majority rule. The "Indian New Deal" had been a noble, albeit flawed, attempt to reverse the trends of the past. A viable but mutually accommodating policy had yet to be formulated.

Suggested Readings

Clemmer, Richard O. "Land Use Patterns and Aboriginal Rights: Northern and Eastern Nevada, 1858–1971." *Indian Historian* 7 (Winter 1974).

Clow, Richmond Lee. "The Rosebud Sioux: The Federal Government and the Reservation Years, 1878–1940." Ph.D. diss., University of New Mexico, 1977.

Collier, John. *From Every Zenith: A Memoir and Some Essays on Life and Thought.* Denver: Sage Books, 1963.

Debo, Angie. *A History of the Indians of the United States.* Norman: University of Oklahoma Press, 1977.

Fey, Harold E., and D'Arcy McNickle. *Indians and Other Americans: Two Ways of Life Meet.* New York: Harper and Row, 1970.

Gibson, Arrell Morgan. *The American Indian: Prehistory to the Present.* Lexington, Mass.: D. C. Heath, 1980.

Hauptman, Laurence M. *The Iroquois and the New Deal.* Syracuse, N.Y.: Syracuse University Press, 1981.

Hertzberg, Hazel W.. *The Search for an American Indian Identity: Modern Pan-Indian Movements.* Syracuse, N.Y.: Syracuse University Press, 1971.

Jackson, Curtis E., and Marcia J. Galli. *A History of the Bureau of Indian Affairs and Its Activities among Indians.* San Francisco: R and R Research, 1977.

Kelly, Lawrence C. *The Assault on Assimilation: John Collier and the Origins of Indian Policy Reform.* Albuquerque: University of New Mexico Press, 1983.

———. "Choosing the New Deal Indian Commissioner: Ickes vs. Collier." *New Mexico Historical Review* 49 (October 1974).

———. "The Indian Reorganization Act: The Dream and the Reality." *Pacific Historical Review* 44 (May 1975).

———. *The Navajo Indians and Federal Indian Policy, 1900–1935.* Tucson: University of Arizona Press, 1968.

Koppes, Clayton R. "From New Deal to Termination: Liberalism and Indian Policy, 1933–1953." *Pacific Historical Review* 46 (November 1977).

McNickle, D'Arcy. *Native American Tribalism: Indian Survivals and Renewals.* New York: Oxford University Press, 1973.

Parman, Donald L. "The Indian and the Civilian Conservation Corps." *Pacific Historical Review* 40 (February 1971).

———. *The Navajos and the New Deal.* New Haven, Conn.: Yale University Press, 1976.

Philp, Kenneth R. "The New Deal and Alaskan Natives, 1936–1945." *Pacific Historical Review* 50 (August 1981).

————. *John Collier's Crusade for Indian Reform, 1920–1954.* Tucson: University of Arizona Press, 1977.

Schrader, Robert Fay. *The Indian Arts & Crafts Board: An Aspect of New Deal Indian Policy.* Albuquerque: University of New Mexico Press, 1983.

Smith, Michael T. "The Wheeler-Howard Act of 1934: The Indian New Deal." *Journal of the West* 10 (July 1971).

Szasz, Margaret Connell. *Education and the American Indian: The Road to Self-Determination since 1928.* Albuquerque: University of New Mexico Press, 1977.

Taylor, Graham D. *The New Deal and American Indian Tribalism: The Administration of the Indian Reorganization Act, 1934–1945.* Lincoln: University of Nebraska Press, 1980.

Tyler, S. Lyman. *A History of Indian Policy.* Washington, D.C.: U.S. Government Printing Office, 1973.

Washburn, Wilcomb E. *Red Man's Land/White Man's Law: A Study of the Past and Present Status of the American Indian.* New York: Charles Scribner's Sons, 1971.

————. *The Indian in America.* New York: Harper and Row, 1975.

Weeks, Charles J. "The Eastern Cherokee and the New Deal." *North Carolina Historical Review* 53 (July 1976).

Wise, Jennings C. *The Red Man in the New World Drama: A Politico-Legal Study with a Pageantry of American Indian History.* New York: Macmillan, 1971.

Wright, Peter M. "John Collier and the Oklahoma Indian Welfare Act of 1936." *Chronicles of Oklahoma* 50 (Autumn 1972).

Zimmerman, William, Jr. "The Role of the Bureau of Indian Affairs since 1933." *Annals of the American Academy of Political and Social Science* 311 (May 1957).

Chapter Six

Resurrection of the Past:
Compensation, Termination,
and Relocation

With the dawn of the seventeenth century Native Americans began to occupy a uniquely tenuous position in what is now the United States—the frustration and anger resulting from being forced into the role of permanent aliens in their own land. Rarely have non–Native Americans understood them or appreciated their difficulty in living in a society of competitive, individualistic values. Thousands have sympathized with Native Americans over the years, and many have maintained a paternalistic admiration for tribal life. Out of that sympathetic paternalism emerged many diligent attempts to work out an accommodation between European American and Native American civilizations, but the solutions have too often been either tragically naive or too short-lived, shifting back and forth between the panacea of assimilation and the tradition of tribal sovereignty. At the same time, others have coveted Native American land, producing strategy after strategy to transfer tribal assets to farmers and corporations. On several occasions, for quite different reasons, the liberal reformers and land developers have pursued similar policies, usually without a great deal of concern for Native American needs or opinions. This juxtaposition of sympathy and greed has produced a cyclical series of programs for Native Americans. Certain that European American ideas always fluctuate with the winds of economic pressure and social change, Native Americans have lost faith in the ability of other Americans to deal effectively with their social, political, and economic needs.

With the end of World War II—so soon after the Indian Reorganization Act of 1934—the pendulum began to swing back again, this time from Collier's emphasis on community values, tribal sovereignty, and evolutionary assimilation to the older faith in rapid assimilation as the key to the Native American future. Despite chronic poverty and stunted life spans, Native Americans had gained from John Collier's years in the Bureau of Indian Affairs. After more than three centuries, the loss of tribal property ceased and the land base stabilized. Moreover, with the investment of money from federal agencies like the Civilian Conservation Corps, the existing land was more productive than it had been in years. Federal officials and teachers in reservation schools discarded the more blatant demands for conformity and instead tried to encourage the expression of tribal values and customs. Finally, the Native American mortality rate was halved and population was growing rapidly. People no longer wondered whether the Native American community was going to survive in the United States. The years of the Great Depression, so tragic for many Americans, had precipitated aid that had partially revived Native American hopes for the future, aid that, according to Vine Deloria, Jr., provided "the greatest days of Indian life in the twentieth century."*

Yet even during the "greatest days" of the 1930s the seeds of change were already developing. Inspired by continuing unemployment problems, President Roosevelt's ill-advised assault on the Supreme Court, and the rise of totalitarian dictatorships abroad, a conservative resurgence developed in the United States. An early casualty was the Indian Reorganization Act. Late in the 1930s, with the world on the brink of another military apocalypse, most Americans desperately wanted to insulate themselves from the impending conflict and re-assert their traditional identity. The "Indian New Deal's" emphasis on community rather than private property, tribal rather than individual values, and ethnic autonomy rather than national unity seemed suspect, especially with authoritarianism enjoying a global revival. When Senator Burton K. Wheeler, an original sponsor of the Indian Reorganization Act, reversed himself in 1937 and began calling for total assimilation of Native Americans into the larger society, the outline of the future was clear: the destruction of tribal sovereignty, communal unity, and ethnic pluralism would soon be offered as "solutions" once again.

The defection of some of the original supporters of the Indian Reorganization Act, the financial and bureaucratic pressures created by World War II, the growing ideological fear of radicalism, and the resignation of John Collier in 1945 cut the political props from under the "Indian New Deal." Its existence had been precarious all along, dependent in many ways on the special climate of opinion during the Great Depression as well as Roosevelt's willingness to experiment in social and economic policy. In short, the reform mood so prevalent during the 1930s had dissipated and change was in the wind.

After more than fifteen years of depression and war, most Americans yearned for more tranquil times when change had been slower and values more constant. They were desperate for confidence and faith in themselves again, especially as the apparent menace of "world communism" became more ominous. The "Red Scare" mania, embodied in the Truman Doctrine, the Marshall Plan, the

---

*Jennings C. Wise, *The Red Man in the New World Drama: A Politico-Legal Study with a Pageantry of American Indian History* (New York: Macmillan, 1971), 360.

Berlin blockade, the revolution in China, the Alger Hiss case, the Korean War, the Rosenburg case, and the campaigns of Senator Joseph McCarthy created an intense need for conformity and consensus. Assimilationist policies for Native Americans fit neatly into that national paranoia. At the same time, the postwar boom in the American economy turned the attention of land developers back to the reservations, which could be used for large commercial farms, highways, strip mines, resort developments, shopping centers, and suburban housing—Native American assets "productively" utilized.

Once again reformers joined the clamor for assimilation. Propelled by the electoral power of urban African Americans, the civil rights movement gained political momentum after the war. To most liberals, racial discrimination of any kind was a violation of the natural rights philosophy. So while President Truman was desegregating the armed forces and the Supreme Court was preparing for its historic assault on Jim Crow, some liberals were taking another look at the reservations, seeing them not as havens preserving tribal values but as anachronistic relics of a racist past. To them, reservations seemed another variety of *de jure* segregation—one more monument to prejudice and separatism. Caught up as they were in celebrating individualism and integration, these liberals were uneasy with ideas of tribal sovereignty, reservation autonomy, ethnic identity, and cultural pluralism; thus, they resorted to the "melting pot" ideology as the ultimate answer to American ethnicity. Assimilation would solve the "Indian problem" after all. Other liberals, preoccupied with stabilizing the economy, controlling the major corporations, and solving the problems of an urban industrial society, had little time for the concerns of America's smallest minority. This change in liberal outlook, in the face of what had been a continuous campaign by a few western politicos to repeal the Indian Reorganization Act, dissolve the tribes, nullify their corporate authority, and remove tribal land from its trust status, put the "Indian New Deal" into eclipse.

Between 1880 and 1934 the assimilationists had demanded education, allotment, and citizenship to integrate Native Americans into the larger society; but, despite their best efforts, tribalism survived. After the brief interlude of the New Deal, assimilationists developed three new "melting pot" ideas: compensation, termination, and relocation. History was about to repeat itself. Like past policies, these three programs emerged out of conflicting interests of non–Native Americans, insensitivity to Native American values, and inter- and intratribal rivalries. Each program existed in its own right with its own proponents, but in concert they became a comprehensive assault on Native American tribalism—the twentieth-century version of the nineteenth-century assimilation strategy.

Compensation was designed to settle all outstanding tribal claims against the United States government; once past controversies over fraud and treaty violations were resolved, federal responsibility for Native American welfare could be discontinued. Conservatives applauded the idea because it promised an erosion of federal power; liberals appreciated it because compensation relieved their guilt-ridden consciousness about past shabby treatment of Native Americans; and Native Americans tended to favor compensation as at least some recoupment of what had been taken from them. With these legal obstacles out of the way, the government could promote "termination" by eliminating special tribal legal status and turning Native Americans over to state and local authorities. While compensation and termination were underway, the federal government could move some Native Americans off the reservation to urban settings. Relocation was the urban industrial equivalent of allotment. Since the age of small farmers was obviously over, Native American families had to be placed in urban housing and industrial jobs before they would melt into the surrounding society. Population pressure on reservations could also be reduced in this manner. With land claims settled, federal authority scuttled, and reservations dwindling in population, the "Indian problem" would cease to exist. Such were the aspirations.

As political pressures for changes in federal policy mounted, the Bureau of Indian Affairs came under siege. In Congress the number of bills to repeal the Indian Reorganization Act, dissolve the BIA, and break up tribal lands increased dramatically after World War II. Following John Collier's resignation, Harold Ickes, the sympathetic Secretary of the Interior, left the Truman cabinet in February 1946. Ickes's successor, Julius A. Krug, had little interest in Native American affairs. William A. Brophy, successor to Collier, resigned as commissioner in 1948 because of lingering illness. William E. Zimmerman served as acting commissioner until 1949 when President Truman appointed John R. Nichols, an assimilationist and former president of New Mexico College of Agriculture and Mechanical Arts. Nichols served only eleven months before Truman replaced him with Dillon S. Myer, an archassimilationist and former head of the War Relocation Authority. After five years of bureaucratic drift and congressional hostility, the BIA was no longer prepared to protect tribal land and sovereignty against the rapidly forming coalition of liberal reformers, economic interest groups, and conservative politicians.

Intertribal conflict and intratribal competition continued to plague Native Americans after 1945, giving assimilationists the upper hand by providing some evidence of Native American support for termination. Many mixed-bloods and Native Americans who had successfully assimilated into the mainstream society favored repeal of the

Indian Reorganization Act and distribution of tribal assets to individual families. The American Indian Federation, representing highly assimilated Native Americans in Oklahoma, had opposed John Collier throughout the 1930s and 1940s and by 1944–45 demanded termination. Wade and Ida Crawford, influential members of the Klamath tribe in Oregon, wanted an end to the BIA, elimination of all trust protections on land, and distribution of Klamath timber lands to individual members of the tribe. Peter Red Elk of the Pine Ridge Reservation felt that under the Indian Reorganization Act the tribal council ignored the needs of individual landowners. Private landowners on the Colville Reservation in Washington wanted to take their individual shares of tribal assets. Many of these property owners even claimed that the Indian Reorganization Act was "communistic," an enemy to individual initiative and private property.

But at the same time, others bitterly denounced the shift in congressional sentiments. The National Congress of American Indians, a lobbying group organized in 1944 with the mission of representing Native Americans of all tribes, bitterly condemned assimilation and termination, demanding that tribal self-determination and the survival of native culture should permeate federal policies. The Association on American Indian Affairs, largely a non–Native American group, also denounced the new termination proposals in 1947 as simply a return to the Dawes Act. The Southwestern Indian Conference, representing eighteen western tribes, met in 1949 and argued that termination should not occur until Native Americans were educationally prepared and had achieved permanent legal protection of their lands. Still, although there was considerable opposition to the whole concept of assimilation, enough vocal support from mixed-bloods and assimilated Native Americans was generated to fuel the demands of congressional terminationists.

At about this time the concept of compensation appeared. Between 1784 and 1871 the United States had negotiated 377 separate treaties with various tribes; but throughout the years, Native Americans complained, treaty provisions were repeatedly violated. Annuity payments were not forwarded, guaranteed services were not rendered, tribal income was not invested properly, promises of permanent land tenure were not kept, and incompetence and corruption reigned generally. Congress had established the United States Court of Claims in 1855 to hear suits against the federal government, but an amendment eight years later prohibited Native Americans from using the courts to recover land or money. Only through special congressional legislation, such as the Choctaw Jurisdictional Act of 1881, could tribes sue the federal government; and even then the legislation was difficult to obtain. The major legal avenue for redress of grievances was closed to Native Americans.

Still, it was not impossible to secure legal compensation. In 1938 Congress appropriated $4.4 million to compensate the Shoshones for hardships they suffered when the BIA transferred the Arapahos to their reservation. Congress also reimbursed the Klamaths more than $5.3 million for tribal land given to the state of Oregon. But the possibility of congressional action by no means implied its probability. The political and legal process was extremely complicated—often beyond the cultural endurance (and financial ability) of Native Americans. Late in the nineteenth century, for example, the Yankton Sioux suffered a number of intrusions on their Pipestone Reservation in southwestern Minnesota. Settlers began moving onto reservation land; builders began developing the pipestone quarries there; the Cedar Rapids, Iowa Falls, and Northwestern Railway constructed a road across the reservation; and in 1891 the BIA built an industrial training school there. Incensed about the intrusions, tribal leaders called for compensation in the 1890s. Not until 1910 did Congress pass a jurisdictional act permitting the Court of Claims to hear the case, and when the case was finally heard (seven years later), the court denied the claim. In 1920, and again in 1925, Congress permitted further litigation on the case, and in 1928 the Court of Claims awarded the Yankton Sioux $328,558 in damages. After nearly forty years of legal and political maneuvering, the Yankton Sioux had finally won their case; the BIA then distributed the money to tribal members in per capita payments of $151.98.

The major difficulty in settling claims was Native American political impotence. As the frontier receded into the past and the United States became an urban and industrial power, the relative importance of Native Americans declined. Few in number and isolated in western reservations, they were an invisible minority, significant only when land developers periodically focused on tribal property. Native Americans were generally unorganized—a special handicap in an age when Congress responded only to campaign contributions, efficient lobbying, demonstrations, and voter clout. Native American affairs ceased to be a major congressional priority in the twentieth century. But in the 1920s liberals like John Collier and Charles Rhoads demanded settlement of those claims against the federal government. The Meriam Report of 1928 recommended that

the benevolent desire of the United States government to educate and civilize the Indian cannot be realized with a tribe which has any considerable unsatisfied bona fide claim against the government. . . . The conviction in the Indian mind that justice is being denied, renders extremely difficult any cooperation between the government and its Indian wards.*

---

*Lewis Meriam, et al., *The Problem of Indian Administration* (Baltimore: Johns Hopkins Press, 1928), 805.

Late in the 1930s and into the 1940s conservatives such as Senator Elmer Thomas of Oklahoma and Senator Arthur V. Watkins of Utah wanted to settle all Native American claims as a first step toward the ultimate "termination" of federal authority over the tribes. Temporarily united once again in their ironic coalition and supported by the National Congress of American Indians and thousands of Native Americans desperate for some form of financial compensation, non–Native American liberals and conservatives lobbied diligently until Congress passed the Indian Claims Commission Act in 1946.

The Indian Claims Commission Act created a three-person board to review all grievances against the federal government arising before 1946; decisions could be appealed to the Court of Claims. All claims filed after 1951 would be invalid, however, and Congress would no longer consider special legislation for individual tribes. The jurisdictional laws of the past were dead, and Congress permitted the Indian Claims Commission only ten years to process all claims against the United States. To protect tribes from excess attorney fees, the law mandated a 10 percent maximum on legal charges. Each tribe petitioning the commission would have to plead its case successfully in two phases. In the "title" phase they would have to prove "exclusive occupancy" of a definable territory from "time immemorial." If the tribe satisfied the commission in the title phase and received recognition of tribal ownership of the contested land, the hearing would then enter the "value phase," in which the commission would determine the value of the land at the time it was taken from the tribe. Once the commission had reached an assessment, Congress would appropriate the necessary funds, which would be distributed by the Bureau of Indian Affairs. After a careful study of tribal needs, the BIA would either award the funds to the tribe for investment in reservation development, distribute the funds on a per capita basis to individual members of the tribe, or divide the funds for both purposes. Federal responsibility would then end.

Despite some good intentions, the Indian Claims Commission was soon another monument—like the Dawes Severalty Act—to European values and naiveté about Native American tribalism. Given their materialism and inclination to quantify most problems, people of European descent saw the Indian Claims Commission as the solution to the hundreds of Native American claims against the federal government. Specifically prohibiting the return of any land to petitioning tribes, the Indian Claims Commission Act stipulated that all "valid claims would be paid in money. No lands would be returned to a tribe." For European Americans, accustomed to buying and selling land and resolving property disputes with cash settlements, the restriction was sensible and fair; but to many Native Americans monetary compensation did not fulfill their claims. Land, not money, was the source of their culture. Don Monongye, a Hopi, illustrated those feelings in 1955 when he said before a congressional committee:

This is our own, our very own, and I speak this not for the Hopis but for all Indian people who were here first. . . . We are not going to . . . give this life and land to anyone but will continue this life that our forefathers have followed so that we will not make a mistake.*

A government check could hardly compensate for a way of life.

Two cases clearly illustrate the inadequacy of monetary compensation. In 1906 the federal government had incorporated Blue Lake and the surrounding forty-eight thousand acres into the Kit Carson National Forest in northwestern New Mexico; later, the Forest Service opened the area to non–Native American hunters, fishermen, and campers. But the Taos Indians believed that the lake was the source of life and a final resting place for the spirits of the dead. They demanded return of the lake; only then could they continue to live and think as they had for thousands of years. The Indian Claims Commission took up their case in the 1950s and in 1965 came to a decision awarding the Taos Indians $10 million and nearly three thousand acres of land near the lake. What seemed to European Americans like a most generous offer was, however, unacceptable to the Taos tribe. Paul Bernal, a Taos leader, said

My people will not sell our Blue Lake that is our church, for $10 million, and accept three thousand acres, when we know that fifty thousand acres is ours. We cannot sell what is sacred. It is not ours to sell.†

They refused the Indian Claims Commission offer and demanded return of the land and the lake, not their equivalent in money.

The Pit River Indians of northern California felt the same way. They had lost all of their land in the gold rush of 1849, and in 1951 entered their claim for the return of 3,368,000 acres. The Indian Claims Commission decided in 1956 that the land had been taken illegally, and in 1963 the federal government awarded the Pit River Indians forty-seven cents an acre. They too refused the money, insisting on the return of the land. In the late 1960s and 1970s both the Taos and Pit River Indians resorted to the politics of confrontation to regain tribal lands. For obvious cultural reasons, few European Americans could fathom such attachment to the land.

---

*Wayne Moquin and Charles Van Doren, eds., *Great Documents in American Indian History* (New York: Praeger, 1973), 335–36.

†Quoted in Stan Steiner, *The New Indians* (New York: Harper and Row, 1968), 243.

Nor did non–Native Americans appreciate the complexity of Native American tribalism and the depth of Native American alienation from Anglo-American jurisprudence. The hope that all claims—the heritage of more than a century and a half of ethnic conflict—could be resolved in only ten years was naive. During the five-year filing period the Indian Claims Commission received thousands of inquiries about fraudulent use of tribal money, illegal land cessions, exploited water rights, deprivation of hunting and fishing rights, and loss of mineral and natural resource royalties. The commission docketed 370 separate cases, but the ten-year time limit was clearly inadequate. Intense rivalries within tribes and bitter competition between tribes stalled the commission, as did a Justice Department decision to adopt an adversary role in the hearings. The vision of 1946—easy cases, mutual understanding, rapid settlements, and an end to federal supervision—was obliterated by political and legal reality.

For thousands of years Native American tribes had been divided by geography, technology, religion, and language; and, although the pan-Indian spirit gained strength in the twentieth century, tribal identities remained narrow and powerful. Native America still consisted of hundreds of ethnic groups. With the Indian Claims Commission, traditional rivalries often reasserted themselves, especially over conflicting land claims. The Indian Claims Commission Act originally required petitioning tribes to prove "exclusive occupancy" of an area from "time immemorial"; but it was a ludicrous demand, resting on the belief that tribes had been sedentary, static communities for thousands of years. Nothing was further from the truth. The Apaches and Navajos, for example, were both Athapascan-speaking tribes who had migrated from Canada to the Southwest, much to the dismay of the Pueblos and Zuñis already there. The Chippewas, Ottawas, and Potawatomis, desperate for fresh hunting grounds, left southeastern Canada late in the sixteenth century and migrated west to Lake Huron. The Potawatomis settled the Lower Peninsula of Michigan; the Ottawas occupied the area surrounding Lake Nipissing; and by the eighteenth century the Chippewas were struggling with the Santee Sioux for control of northern Minnesota. Some of the Sioux tribes may have been in the Ohio Valley in the sixteenth century, moved to the Upper Mississippi Valley by the eighteenth century, and from there scattered out across the northern plains as they domesticated the horse.

Under such circumstances, proving title to land was extremely difficult. When the Miamis petitioned the Indian Claims Commission in 1950 for more than $13 million worth of land they had lost in Indiana, the Delawares, Potawatomis, Kickapoos, and the Six Nations of the Iroquois filed counterclaims to the Miami territory. When the Upper Pend Oreilles filed a claim in 1950 for land lost in northeastern

Washington, the Kalispels were outraged, insisting that the land had once been theirs. In 1954 the Santee Sioux contested the Yankton Sioux claim to parts of southwestern Minnesota and northwestern Iowa. Settlement of these conflicting claims consumed years of archeological and anthropological research, legal maneuvering, and political compromise. The ten-year limit to Indian Claims Commission hearings was therefore grossly inadequate.

Delays caused by intertribal rivalries, however, were not nearly as important as the attitude of the Justice Department in dragging out the work of the commission. Instead of trying to distinguish between legitimate and illegitimate claims, the Justice Department became a militant defender of government interests, viewing the tribes as adversaries. To discourage the tribes by exploiting their frustrations with Anglo-American legalisms, the Justice Department repeatedly sought extensions and delays in the hearings. The Yankton Sioux, for example, filed their claim in 1951, but the government succeeded in getting more than four years of 120-day extensions to "prepare its findings." After the Santee Sioux protested Yankton Sioux claims in 1954, the Justice Department managed five more years of delays. When extensions were no longer possible, the government tried to disprove tribal claims on the ground that an "identifiable, land-holding group" had not been adequately demonstrated. The government succeeded, for example, in getting the Indian Claims Commission to rule that neither the Chippewa nor the Ottawa nations were single political entities, making them ineligible to pursue their claims at all. Then, if the Indian Claims Commission agreed that a petitioning tribe was an identifiable group, the government often tried to disqualify the claim by arguing against "exclusive occupancy" from "time immemorial." By 1951, the commission had dismissed 29 of 31 claims, and between 1946 and 1960 the commission completed work on 105 separate claim dockets, disqualifying 88 of the claims and awarding $20 million in 17 claims.

Once the Indian Claims Commission agreed to compensation for a tribe, the Justice Department vigorously tried to assess the property at its lowest possible value. The commission, for example, awarded the California tribes forty-seven cents an acre for land they had lost in the middle of the nineteenth century. The Justice Department also hired teams of accountants to search through BIA and U.S. Army records and total the value of all blankets, clothing, tools, and building materials given to the petitioning tribe over the years. The government then insisted on deducting those grants from the final settlement awarded by the commission. If the tribe felt that an award was inadequate, they could appeal, causing more delays. In 1956, for example, the commission awarded the Miamis seventy-five cents an acre for Indiana land they had lost in 1818. They appealed and in 1959 the

United States Court of Claims vacated the original settlement, remanding the case back to the Indian Claims Commission. In 1960 the commission revised its award up to $1.15 an acre, and the Miamis accepted.

Finally, once the commission had reached a financial settlement acceptable to the tribe, a series of intratribal rivalries, much like those affecting allotment earlier in the century, often caused further delays. Under the Indian Claims Commission Act, the Bureau of Indian Affairs had the responsibility of studying each tribe's economic status and advising as to whether the award should be invested in the reservation economy or distributed on a per capita basis. That decision, of course, often inspired a great deal of conflict among tribal members, especially since Congress usually insisted that the BIA support the majority position in each tribe. Mixed-bloods, assimilated Native Americans, and tribal members living off the reservation usually wanted per capita distribution of the awards so that they could have more money. Full-bloods on the reservation often wanted investment of the money in the tribal economy so that the reservations could become self-sustaining. The Prairie Potawatomis, for example, received more than one million dollars in 1961; but not until 1967, after six years of tribal debate, was the money distributed in per capita allotments of $490.50. In the process the division of opinion between reservation and nonreservation Potawatomis was so intense and the struggle so extended that tribal power shifted to the more assimilated tribal members favoring per capita payments.

Determining the legitimate recipients of per capita payments from the Indian Claims Commission became another problem intensifying tribal factionalism. When the Miamis finally accepted a settlement of $8,091,400 in 1960, the BIA and tribal council began drawing up a tribal enrollment list. They completed the first membership roll in 1965, which totaled only 317 names, but then extended the application period for another two years. By 1967 the list contained the names of 3,066 people who were confirmed as full- or mixed-blood Miamis. When the Prairie Potawatomis began to distribute their awards, the full-blood elders wanted only 204 people to receive the checks. They were upset that the final membership roll contained the names of 2,101 full- and mixed-bloods. Assimilated Potawatomis and mixed-bloods living off the reservation, the elders argued, had surrendered their right to the award when they abandoned their culture for life in the dominant society. Many full-bloods in other tribes felt the same way, resenting the decision of some Native Americans to proclaim their heritage only when it meant a cash reward.

The Indian Claims Commission failed to achieve its original goal of soothing European American guilt, strengthening the reservation economies, and preparing the way for termination. When the commission ceased to operate in 1978, over $800 million had been awarded on 285 claims out of nearly 850 originally filed. Some tribes had received very large settlements: $32 million for the Utes, $29 million for the eight claims of the California tribes, $16 million for the Chiricahua Apaches, $14,364,000 for the Oklahoma Cherokees, $10,242,000 for the Crows, $15 million for the Cheyennes-Arapahos, $8,500,000 for the Mescalero Apaches, and $15,790,000 for the northern Paiutes. Other settlements were quite small; for example, the Poncas received only $2,500.

Some tribes made prudent use of the money. After paying attorney fees, the Crow Tribal Council had $9,238,500. They distributed 50 percent of the money to individual families but insisted that the $3,019 checks be used only for improvements in housing, health, and education, or for the purchase of farming equipment. The council then invested the rest of the money in land purchases, tribal credit programs, land leasing, economic development, educational scholarships, and construction of recreational and social services facilities.

But for economically impoverished tribes divided by factionalism, the per capita payments were often used for daily living expenses— rent, utilities, and food—and did not last very long. Beyond providing tribal members with some temporary financial relief, the awards did little to raise the standard of living permanently. Much award money was consumed rather than invested. By February 1970 the commission had actually distributed only $148.9 million of the $305.2 million in awards. The Bureau of Indian Affairs had distributed $48.3 million on a per capita basis and $100.6 million to tribal entities. But the tribes had only invested $38.5 million of that money in scholarships, community development projects, local businesses, employment programs, and the construction of reservation social services facilities. The rest had either been distributed in per capita allotments or was being held up as the tribes debated how the money should be allocated. After a quarter-century of work, the Indian Claims Commission, in the words of Commissioner John T. Vance, had "failed throughout the time of its existence to exercise the initiative in hearing and determining the claims before it."* The abuses of the past had not been erased.

But long before the results of Indian Claims Commission proceedings were known, the movement for termination and relocation was well underway. For many people, the Indian Claims Commission had been a legal and moral forerunner of the new assimilation program. Senator Arthur V. Watkins, architect of the termination policy, wrote in 1957 that a

---

*John T. Vance, "The Congressional Mandate and the Indian Claims Commission," *North Dakota Law Review* 45 (Spring 1969):335.

basic purpose of Congress in setting up the Indian Claims Commission was to clear the way toward complete freedom of the Indian by assuring final settlement of all obligations—real or purported—of the Federal government to the Indian tribes.*

Late in the 1940s, with tribal claims being rapidly filed at the Indian Claims Commission, many Americans were convinced that within a few years the slate would be clear of resentment, guilt, and frustration with the past.

Throughout American history, but especially since the Supreme Court's *Worcester v. Georgia* ruling in 1832, a series of federal court decisions had insulated tribes from state jurisdiction, declaring them wards of the United States government. During those same years, assimilationists tried to eliminate that special status, extend citizenship to Native Americans, and fully integrate them legally into the body politic. In 1830, for instance, all Choctaws refusing to move to Indian Territory lost their special relationship with the federal government and went under the jurisdiction of the state of Mississippi. The whole thrust of the allotment and citizenship campaigns between 1887 and 1924 was aimed at dissolving tribal estates and tribal sovereignty—to "individualize" all Native Americans, forever severing them from federal supervision. Even during the New Deal, when Congress passed the Johnson-O'Malley Act in 1934, state governments received contracts from the Bureau of Indian Affairs to supply medical, educational, and social welfare services on the reservations. So when Senator William Langer of North Dakota called for the gradual destruction of the BIA, it was nothing more than a new version of an old theme. "Termination" was therefore the logical descendent of allotment and citizenship—the end of treaty obligations to the tribes, settlement of outstanding tribal claims against the federal government, liquidation of tribal trust funds, disenfranchisement of tribal governments, and integration of all tribal lands into the larger commercial economy.

The termination movement gained momentum late in the 1940s. In 1947 Senator Langer's Senate Civil Service Committee asked William Zimmerman and the BIA to prepare guidelines for the termination of federal services to certain tribes. Hoping to delay termination, Zimmerman opposed the guidelines, asking Congress to consider such questions as the degree of assimilation of the tribe, its economic resources and potential for self-support, its willingness to accept termination, and the willingness of the surrounding state and local governments to provide public services. The BIA then suggested that ten

---

*Arthur V. Watkins, "Termination of Federal Supervision: The Removal of Restrictions over Indian Property and Person," *Annals of the American Academy of Political and Social Science* 311 (May 1957): 50.

tribes might be ready for termination: the Osages; the Klamaths; the Menominees; the Flatheads; the Kansas and Nebraska Potawatomis; the Turtle Mountain Chippewas; the Six Nations in New York; and the Hoopas, Missions, and Sacramentos in California. In 1946 and 1947, separate termination bills were submitted to Congress for the Klamaths, Osages, and Menominees.

Also in 1947 the Hoover Commission, a special body studying government efficiency, recommended the "discontinuance of all specialized Indian activity on the part of the federal government."* In 1948 Congress passed the Assimilative Crimes Act, which supported termination by permitting the Department of Justice to prosecute Native Americans accused of certain criminal acts in federal courts but under state laws. Under Commissioner of Indian Affairs John Nichols in 1949–50, the BIA moved closer to termination by allowing individual Native Americans to receive direct payments for their land leases (rather than having the money put into tribal accounts) and by increasing the number of fee simple patents to those wanting to sell their land. By that time even the American Association on Indian Affairs was gradually shifting toward assimilation and termination, arguing that their basic strategy was to absorb Native Americans into the general population, even if they

may not be able to retain . . . their own culture. . . . Our problem is to guide and protect the process of amalgamation that it will be carried through with benefits to both groups, with justice, and with humanity.†

That same year, in 1950, Dillon S. Myer was confirmed as the new Commissioner of Indian Affairs, and termination had become national policy.

Dillon S. Myer was the quintessential administrator—confident, decisive, and committed to efficiency. A career civil servant, he was assistant director of the Soil Conservation Service in 1942 when President Roosevelt asked him to head the War Relocation Authority. The WRA operated the ten internment camps holding Japanese Americans during World War II. Myer brought to the agency all of his administrative skills as well as an undaunted faith in the "melting pot." Only complete assimilation would ever erase the ethnic conflict so central to American history. Convinced that assimilation of Japanese Americans would never occur in isolated camps, Myer was determined to prevent the postwar development of "Little Tokyos" on

---

The Hoover Commission Report on Organization of the Executive Branch of the Government (New York: McGraw-Hill, 1949), 267.

†Quoted in Larry J. Hasse, "Termination and Assimilation: Federal Indian Policy, 1943 to 1961" (Ph.D. diss., Washington State University, 1974), 114.

the West Coast by resettling the inmates widely across the country. In 1950 he applied the same idea to Native Americans.

Shortly after taking over the Bureau of Indian Affairs, Myer implemented "withdrawal programming"—the suppression of tribal culture and the scheduling of tribes for termination and relocation. Unwilling to admit that Native Americans even possessed "legitimate cultures," Myer attacked the arts and crafts boards that John Collier had so carefully established on the reservations. He also reversed the trend toward reservation day schools by transferring many full-blood children to distant boarding schools where, separated from tribal culture, they could be taught English, personal habits, health and sanitation, and vocational skills. At the same time, Myer began transferring mixed-blood children from reservation day schools to local public schools whenever possible. Urging Native Americans to mortgage individual property to private banks whenever they needed money, Myer then prohibited all access to tribal revolving credit funds. To prevent the BIA superintendents from being influenced by tribal wishes, he stripped them of their decision-making powers in favor of distant area directors. He abandoned Collier's program to retrieve land for the Pyramid Lake Paiutes; supported a statehood bill for Alaska which would have negated tribal land claims; and replaced Collier appointees in the BIA with his own former subordinates from the WRA. Only a storm of protest from the American Bar Association, the American Civil Liberties Association, the Association on American Indian Affairs, and the National Congress of American Indians prevented him from arming BIA employees on the reservations, arresting Native Americans without warrants, requiring BIA approval before tribes could retain attorneys, closing reservation hospitals or unilaterally turning them over to state or local political bodies, disposing of "surplus" reservation land, and eliminating tribal consent from BIA programming.

While Myer was moving ahead with his "withdrawal programming," Senator Arthur V. Watkins of Utah and Congressman E. Y. Berry of South Dakota were preparing bills for termination. In 1952, House Resolution 698 asked Myer to report on the status of the BIA and to prepare a termination program. The resolution also called for a list of BIA services which could be ended or transferred to the states. Myer reported that plans were progressing to hasten the transfer of Native American students from BIA to public schools. The passage of Public Law 291 in April 1952 permitted the transfer of BIA hospitals to state control. In 1953 House Concurrent Resolution 108 proposed ending federal relations with tribes in California and New York and with the Seminoles in Florida, the Alabama-Coushattas in Texas, the Menominees in Wisconsin, the Flatheads in Montana, the Klamaths in Oregon, the Potawatomis in Kansas and Nebraska, and the Turtle

Mountain Chippewas in North Dakota—the list suggested by the BIA in 1947 (less the Osages), expanded to include the Seminoles and the Alabama-Coushattas.

When Dwight D. Eisenhower defeated Adlai E. Stevenson in 1952, for the first time in twenty years political power shifted from the Democrats to the Republicans. But the spirit of termination was unscathed. Eisenhower replaced Dillon Myer with New Mexico banker Glenn L. Emmons as Commissioner of Indian Affairs; and, much to the delight of Senator Watkins and Representative Berry, Emmons promptly praised House Concurrent Resolution 108 as "one of the most valuable and salutary congressional measures we have had in Indian affairs for a great many years."* Emmons then suggested a much broader list of tribes ready for termination, including the Blackfeet, Catawbas, Spokanes, Nez Perces, Coeur d'Alenes, Yankton and Sisseton Sioux, Caddos, Fort Sill Apaches, Sacs and Foxes, Poncas, Ottawas, Wyandots, Peorias, Paiutes, and Uintah and Ouray Utes. Eventually, between 1953 and 1962, Congress passed laws terminating federal services to more than sixty separate Native American groups. Although Dillon Myer had identified the Osages as likely candidates, they escaped termination, even though they were hardly a drain on BIA resources, paid state and local taxes, and were highly assimilated. Tribal lands had been allotted in 1906, but the Osage Guardianship Act in 1925 had given them federal trust protection over tribal mineral rights. In 1953 tribal oil leases were valued at $131 million. With tribal unity, money, good attorneys, and legal protection of their lands, the Osages were able to put off all congressional attempts at termination. But weaker, poorer tribes were victims. In 1953, Public Law 280 transferred civil and criminal jurisdiction over tribal lands in California, Minnesota, Nebraska, Oregon, and Wisconsin to state and local governments; and in August 1954 President Eisenhower transferred all BIA health programs to the United States Public Health Service. Specific termination laws in 1954 affected the California tribes; the Alabamas and Coushattas in Texas; the Klamaths in Oregon; the Menominees in Wisconsin; the Ottawas, Wyandots, and Peorias in Oklahoma; the Paiutes in Utah; and the mixed-blood Uintah and Ouray Utes in Utah. Congress terminated the Catawbas of South Carolina in 1959 and the Poncas of Nebraska in 1962.

Once the laws had been passed, the only obstacle blocking termination was the "consultation" requirement. For years, BIA policy had required consultation with tribal leaders before implementing new programs, even though this stipulation had been interpreted quite

---

*Quoted in Frederick J. Stefon, "The Irony of Termination: 1943–1958," *Indian Historian* 11 (Summer 1978):9.

loosely. Soon after President Eisenhower signed the first termination
bills, the National Congress of American Indians demanded an
amendment providing, in addition to consultation, that the consent of
the tribes involved be secured. Emmons, Watkins, and Berry would
have none of it. Still, for obvious political reasons they did not want
termination to proceed against the vocal opposition of Native
Americans. Though they strongly opposed being legally required to
obtain consent, they hoped to secure it voluntarily—a tall order, considering the fact that most full-bloods opposed termination. Earl Old
Person, a Blackfeet leader, said:

It is important to note that in our Indian language the only translation for
termination is to "wipe out" or "kill off" . . . how can we plan our future when
the Indian Bureau threatens to wipe us out as a race? It is like trying to cook a
meal in your tipi when someone is standing outside trying to burn the tipi
down.*

Terminationists turned to a traditional weapon—exploiting the cultural divisions within the Native American community. Most full-
bloods living on the reservations hated the very concept of termination, but assimilated mixed-bloods and tribal members living in the
cities were usually not so adamant. Assimilated urban Native
Americans could be enticed by the promise of cash. One technique
was to get Congress to hold up appropriations for tribal claims. In
1951, for example, the United States Court of Claims had awarded the
Menominees a settlement of $8.5 million, but Congress delayed pay-
ment until the tribe agreed to accept termination. In 1963 the Indian
Claims Commission awarded the Kalispels $3 million, but in 1964
Senator Frank Church of Idaho blocked appropriation of the money,
arguing that the Kalispels were ready for termination. Another method the BIA employed was to hold out the possibility of enormous per
capita cash payments as a result of termination. Since mixed-bloods
outnumbered full-bloods in some cases, such promises helped secure
tribal consent. The Klamaths, for example, owned a million-acre reservation in the middle of Oregon's prime timber country. Since major
timber corporations estimated their land value at more than $120 mil-
lion and since there were only 2,000 full- and mixed-blood Klamaths,
each member could receive more than $50,000 if Congress terminated
the tribe and liquidated its assets. Mixed-blood Klamaths living off
the reservation, led by Wade Crawford, found the prospects of $50,000
each overwhelming, and they approved termination. Full-bloods, led
by Boyd Jackson, opposed it—unsuccessfully. As another example, in
1959 the Catawba Tribal Council approved termination by a vote of

---

*Quoted in Angie Debo, *A History of the Indians of the United States* (Norman:
University of Oklahoma Press, 1977), 371.

forty to seventeen. Tribal assets were then divided up, with 345 people accepting title to approximately five acres each and 286 people accepting cash payments of $296 each. Congress then revoked the constitution of the Catawba tribe.

The fact that termination was disastrous in specific instances is dramatically illustrated by the experience of the Menominees. When the United States Court of Claims awarded them their $8.5 million in 1951, the Menominees looked forward to a substantial distribution of the money in per capita payments. But Senator Arthur Watkins refused to distribute their money until they had agreed to termination. Afraid of losing the award, tribal leaders consented; and in June 1954 Congress passed Public Law 399 providing for a per capita distribution of $1,500 and termination of all federal services by 1958. The law coldly intoned that

the statutes of the United States . . . or any State, Territory, or the District of Columbia, applicable to Indians because of their status as Indians shall no longer be applicable to the members of the tribe.*

The Menominees had more than three years at first to prepare for termination, and eventually Congress extended the deadline to 1961. In 1953 the value of Menominee property was estimated at $34,431,126, owned in common by 3,270 members of the tribe. That year the reservation produced $115,189 in revenue from its wildlife resources, $1,321,797 from tribal businesses, and $1,551,635 from stumpage payments, agriculture, tourism, and cedar-bough and fern sales. In order to protect these tribal assets, the Menominees decided not to be incorporated into any existing Wisconsin counties but to create Menominee County, a separate jurisdiction encompassing the reservation. Except for public education and criminal justice services, which would be handled by neighboring Shawano County, Menominee County would provide normal health, welfare, and transportation services to tribal members. The tribe also created Menominee Enterprises, Incorporated (MEI), as the owner of tribal lands, forests, and the lumber mill and gave each Menominee a 4 percent negotiable bond worth $3,000 and one hundred shares of stock in the new corporation. MEI intended to manage tribal resources profitably and distribute the proceeds to the shareholders in the corporation. Confident that Menominee County and Menominee Enterprises, Incorporated, were capable of sustaining the tribe, the Bureau of Indian Affairs ended its relationship with the Menominee people on April 30, 1961.

---

*Quoted in Patricia K. Ourada, *The Menominee Indians: A History* (Norman: University of Oklahoma Press, 1979), 193.

Termination immediately resulted in a host of problems. Menominee County ranked last among Wisconsin's seventy-two counties in total population, family income, employment, adequate housing, high school graduates, and land in farms. With more than $380,000 in expenses for welfare, utilities, health services, and transportation, the county levied the bulk of its taxes on the only property owner in the county—Menominee Enterprises, Incorporated. Burdened with a fifty-year-old lumber mill, the end of guaranteed timber contracts from the federal government, and slumping housing starts nationwide in 1961, MEI had to raise money by forcing members of the tribe to purchase individually the property they were living on. The only way most Menominee families could pay for the property was to trade their $3,000 negotiable bonds with MEI, a practice which became quite common and the source of great resentment in the community. Upon purchasing their own homes, many Menominee families became cash destitute. For the first time in their lives they had to pay rent, utility bills, and health costs, and the added burden of property taxes was often too much. Tax auctions of homes and farms became all too common. The unemployment rate rose to "depression levels" of 25 percent in 1968, and county welfare costs doubled between 1963 and 1968. In order to apply for welfare payments, Menominee families had to prove financial destitution, which often required them to sell their $3,000 bonds. Unable to meet state licensing requirements because of inadequate funds, the reservation-turned-county hospital had to close. By 1965 nearly one-third of the Menominees registered positive in tuberculosis tests and the infant mortality rate was three times the national average. Termination had reduced the Menominees to a state of desperate poverty and ill health.

Termination was also a failure politically, for both the federal government and the Menominees. The original hope that termination would cut federal expenses was completely wrong. In 1960—the last year before termination—the federal government had spent only $144,000 on the Menominees, but the high costs of unemployment compensation and welfare forced the government to channel nearly $3 million into the reservation between 1961 and 1968. Nor did termination give the Menominees the individual freedom Senator Watkins had spoken of so eloquently. Now subject to Wisconsin fish and game laws, the Menominees could no longer hunt and fish for food at will, and many of them frequently spent time in jail for hunting and fishing out of season. Forced to buy their land and homes at market value, Menominee families could not sell their property without approval from MEI, which retained ultimate control of assets to prevent their sale outside the tribe. In 1956 Congress required a permanent sustained yield management of Menominee timber lands, limiting the amount of lumber the MEI could harvest and reducing the market value of the Menominee forest by 60 percent. The Wisconsin legislature then imposed a thirty-year restrictive covenant on the forest, prohibiting the sale or mortgage of tribal or MEI property without state approval. Even control of MEI was out of tribal hands, because the one hundred shares in MEI stock given the Menominee minors was placed in trust at the First Wisconsin Trust Company of Milwaukee, a bank owned by non–Native Americans. With more than 40 percent of MEI stock, the First Wisconsin Trust Company had effective control. The rapid ruin of the Menominees was the direct result of the government's program of termination.

The third major concern of the assimilationists after World War II was the commitment to relocate Native Americans from economically marginal reservations or small allotments to jobs and housing in the cities. The idea was a logical product of European American values.

The great irony of allotment had been that no sooner had Native Americans been placed on small family farms than the United States had begun its rapid transformation into a highly centralized and technologically advanced industrial economy. The small, labor-intensive, allotted farms were unable to compete with large, capital-intensive, commercial farms. Throughout the United States between 1917 and 1945, a large population shift to the cities was underway, inspired primarily by sharp cycles in agricultural profits and by millions of new industrial jobs in the cities, particularly during World Wars I and II. During those years, nearly one hundred thousand Native Americans left the reservations to look for new ways to support themselves economically. As Stan Steiner has written, they made their way to the "Cement Prairies." When Glenn L. Emmons became Commissioner of Indian Affairs in 1953, he seized upon that trend as a possible solution to the chronic (and increasing) problem of reservation poverty. Out of the liberals' concern for Native American welfare, the plans of assimilationists, and the demands of developers interested in reservation land he constructed two proposals, one designed to bring industrial jobs to the reservations and the other to relocate Native Americans to the cities. Both programs were to be achieved within the larger framework of termination, for only as Native Americans became more self-sufficient economically could the federal government hope to ultimately withdraw its services.

Another irony was the simultaneous existence of a vast supply of labor and undeveloped timber, oil, coal, gas, and mineral resources on the reservations. Commissioner Emmons was convinced that the reservations—as markets for mass-produced goods and sources of cheap labor and raw materials—could easily attract corporate investment and increase employment opportunities. In 1954 Emmons established the American Indian Research Fund, a private nonprofit organization designed to seek grant funds to survey reservation economic potential.

When the AIRF proved unsuccessful in raising much money, Emmons reluctantly decided to involve the BIA directly in the attempt to attract businesses to the reservations. In a series of nationwide speaking engagements to business audiences and advertisements in trade journals, Emmons sold the idea of "factories on the reservations," always focusing on the need to "free" Native Americans from their dependence on the federal government through jobs in such labor-intensive industries as electronics, textiles, woodworking, and metal fabrication. Like state and local governments, the tribes would have to offer financial inducements to businesses relocating. Emmons specifically authorized the tribes to accept loans from private banks and put up reservation land as collateral, and he permitted individuals to sell their allotments without tribal permission. He was unwilling to let Native Americans borrow from a traditional source—the BIA Revolving Credit Fund—as further access would have been unacceptable under termination philosophy. Banks and real estate buyers thus began looking at tribal lands with great enthusiasm. Finally, Emmons promised private businessmen that corporations, not the tribes, would have title to any factory on a reservation, thus freeing them from any tribal direction.

During the 1950s the attempt to bring jobs to reservations was largely unsuccessful, but some tribes with substantial incomes were able to make attractive offers. In 1955, for example, the Navajo Tribal Council appropriated three hundred thousand dollars for plant construction and job training, and in 1956 the Baby Line Furniture Corporation of Los Angeles placed a factory at Gamerco, New Mexico. Poorer tribes did not have the capital to make such offers, however, and the BIA would not extend them further credit. Additionally, the trust status of reservation land made leasing arrangements very complicated, and businessmen were often cautious about reservation investment. Inadequate roads and, often, limited utility services discouraged investment, as did the inadequate markets for mass-produced goods on thinly populated, isolated reservations. Finally, Native American workers were often ill prepared for industrial labor, and businessmen worried about high training costs and low productivity. As a result, few businesses made the move to the reservations and those that did had limited success. For instance, the Baby Line Furniture Corporation only employed ten Navajos in 1957. Expecting to employ 125 Pima and Papago Indians, the Parsons and Baker Manufacturing Company opened a garment factory at Casa Grande, Arizona; but in 1958 the firm employed seventy-four non–Native Americans there and only one Pima. For all the BIA's efforts, fewer than a thousand Native Americans found new jobs in reservation factories during the 1950s—clear indication that the program was a dismal failure.

To assimilationists like Dillon Myer and Glenn Emmons, relocating Native Americans was just as important as developing the reservation economies. Myer considered reservations little more than "prison camps"; and as long as Native Americans remained isolated there, even under favorable economic conditions, they would never join the mainstream of American life. In 1947 Congress appropriated money for a Labor Recruitment and Welfare Program on the Navajo and Hopi reservations to train people for work in Denver, Los Angeles, Phoenix, and Salt Lake City. The Hoover Commission called for an ambitious relocation program to drain surplus labor off the reservations, and in 1949–50 the BIA established urban job bureaus for Native Americans. In April 1950, after a disastrous blizzard struck the Navajo and Hopi reservations, Congress passed the Navajo-Hopi Rehabilitation Act, appropriating $88.5 million over a ten-year period to construct roads, schools, and irrigation systems; attract industry to the reservations; and relocate thousands of Navajos and Hopis to urban centers where they could secure jobs and housing among non–Native Americans. Myer made relocation a part of the general termination program when the Bureau of Indian Affairs established the Voluntary Relocation Program to provide job training, travel and moving expenses, assistance in locating jobs and housing in the cities, free medical care for one year, and a thirty-day subsistence allowance. Most full-bloods were suspicious. A BIA official on the Colville Reservation reported:

They seem to feel that the program is a government means to move the Indians from the reservation in order to allow white operators to exploit the reservation and eventually force all Indians from the reservation areas.*

Still, the BIA persisted, and the Adult Vocational Training Program expanded relocation in 1957, placing Native Americans in Denver, Phoenix, Albuquerque, San Francisco, Dallas, Los Angeles, Oklahoma City, Tulsa, and Chicago. Between 1952 and 1960 the BIA managed to send more than thirty-five thousand Native Americans to those urban areas.

Urban life proved a difficult challenge. Although Native Americans brought to the city a wide variety of tribal backgrounds, they did share a common heritage of small communities, rural folk cultures, and a history of dependence on the BIA. Insulated from the mainstream culture by strong aboriginal traditions, they were often ill prepared for city life, especially full-bloods, illiterates, and non-veterans. The anonymity of the city contrasted sharply with the personalisms so characteristic of the reservation, and their collective

---

*Quoted in Hasse, "Termination and Assimilation," 259.

identity was at odds with the individualistic materialism of city life. For example, Navajos, whose experience was that of a people thinly scattered over a vast, enchantingly beautiful wilderness, were staggered by an environment that was in most respects totally opposite. They had a hard time dealing with police, traffic, pace of life, lack of privacy, and the utter dearth of space and land.

Native Americans in the cities also encountered serious economic problems. Accustomed to free medical care, low rent, low utility bills, and limited transportation costs, they were inundated with bills and debts. Limited to low-paying, unskilled, and often seasonal jobs, they were vulnerable to layoffs; they rarely had the financial resources to meet their obligations. During the early 1950s only three thousand of the thirty-five thousand relocated Native Americans found jobs in "permanent" industries, and even those jobs were closely related to Korean War production. The entire culture of middle-class European Americans—personal acquisitiveness, long-range planning, and saving for the future—so necessary to success in the cities, was alien to many Native Americans. Raised in noncompetitive, noncapitalistic cultures, they often had little concept of budgeting or saving, preferring to share their money or material goods with others as a way of surviving. Valuing agreement and consensus, most Native Americans had great difficulty accepting or understanding their role in a social setting dominated by majority rule and adversary legal procedures. Too often Native Americans were badly exploited simply because they would not speak out, complain, or demand their rights. Native American cultures were often the opposite of competitive capitalism, and as a result urban life often became a world of poverty, unemployment, inadequate medical care, poor housing, and frequent moves from one rented place of residence to another. Of the more than thirty-five thousand people relocated between 1952 and 1960, about 30 percent returned to the reservation.

By 1960, after more than fifteen years of dedicated political maneuvering, the advocates of compensation, termination, and relocation were no closer to integrating Native Americans into the larger society than before. The compensation program had been delayed by Justice Department stalling and Native American bickering; the termination program in many cases created destitution rather than self-sufficiency; and the relocation program in most cases created the same result by sending thousands of Native Americans into alien cities to fend unsuccessfully for themselves. The compensation, termination, and relocation programs from 1946 to 1960 joined the allotment, education, and citizenship programs from 1887 to 1934 among the bankrupt efforts of the assimilationists to solve the "Indian problem."

Suggested Readings

Ablon, Joan. "American Indian Relocation: Problems of Dependency and Management in the City." *Phylon* 26 (Winter 1965).

Barker, Robert W. "The Indian Claims Commission—the Conscience of the Nation in Its Dealings with the Original American." *Federal Bar Journal* 20 (Summer 1960).

Bearking, Leonard. "Indian Education under Federal Domination." *Indian Historian* 2 (Spring 1969).

Bodine, John J. "Blue Lake: A Struggle for Indian Rights." *American Indian Law Review* 1 (Winter 1973).

Boender, Debra R. "Termination and the Administration of Glenn Emmons as Commissioner of Indian Affairs, 1953–1961." *New Mexico Historical Review* 54 (October 1979).

Brown, Mrs. Douglas Summers. *The Catawba Indians: The People of the River.* Columbia: University of South Carolina Press, 1966.

Burt, Larry W. "Factories on the Reservations: The Industrial Development Programs of Commissioner Glenn Emmons, 1953–1960." *Arizona and the West* 19 (Winter 1977).

———. *Tribalism in Crisis: Federal Indian Policy, 1953–1961.* Albuquerque: University of New Mexico Press, 1982.

Butler, Raymond V. "The Bureau of Indian Affairs: Activities since 1945." *Annals of the American Academy of Political and Social Science* 436 (March 1978).

Carriker, Robert C. "The Kalispel Tribe and the Indian Claims Commission Experience." *Western Historical Quarterly* 9 (January 1978).

Clemmer, Richard O. "Land Use Patterns and Aboriginal Rights: Northern and Eastern Nevada, 1858–1971." *Indian Historian* 7 (Winter 1974).

Clifton, James A. *The Prairie People: Continuity and Change in Potawatomi Indian Culture, 1665–1965.* Lawrence: Regents Press of Kansas, 1977.

Clow, Richmond L. "State Jurisdiction on Sioux Reservations: Indian and Non-Indian Responses, 1952–1964." *South Dakota History* 11 (Summer 1981).

Corbett, William P. "The Red Pipestone Quarry: The Yanktons Defend a Sacred Tradition, 1858–1929." *South Dakota History* 8 (Spring 1978).

Danforth, Sandra C. "Repaying Historical Debts: The Indian Claims Commission." *North Dakota Law Review* 49 (Winter 1973).

Debo, Angie. *A History of the Indians of the United States.* Norman: University of Oklahoma Press, 1977.

Forbes, Jack D., ed. *The Indian in America's Past.* Englewood Cliffs, N.J.: Prentice-Hall, 1964.

Gibson, Arrell Morgan. *The American Indian: Prehistory to the Present.* Lexington, Mass.: D. C. Heath, 1980.

Guillemin, Jeanne. *Urban Renegades: The Cultural Strategy of the American Indians.* New York: Columbia University Press, 1975.

Hasse, Larry J. "Termination and Assimilation: Federal Indian Policy, 1943 to 1961." Ph.D. diss., Washington State University, 1974.

Herzberg, Stephen J. "The Menominee Indians: From Treaty to Termination." *Wisconsin Magazine of History* 60 (Summer 1977).

Hood, Susan. "Termination of the Klamath Tribe in Oregon." *Ethnohistory* 19 (Fall 1972).

The Hoover Commission Report on Organization of the Executive Branch of the Government. New York: McGraw Hill, 1949.

Hoover, Herbert T. "Yankton Sioux Tribal Claims against the United States, 1917–1975." *Western Historical Quarterly* 7 (April 1976).

Jackson, Curtis E., and Marcia J. Galli. *A History of the Bureau of Indian Affairs and Its Activities among Indians.* San Francisco: R and R Research, 1977.

Johnson, N. B. "The National Congress of American Indians." *Chronicles of Oklahoma* 30 (Summer 1952).

Jorgensen, Joseph G. "A Century of Political and Economic Effects on American Indian Study, 1880–1980." *Journal of Ethnic Studies* 6 (Fall 1978).

Kersey, Harry A., Jr. "Federal Schools and Acculturation among the Florida Seminoles, 1927–1954." *Florida Historical Quarterly* 59 (October 1980).

Kickingbird, Kirke, and Karen Ducheneaux. *One Hundred Million Acres.* New York: Macmillan, 1973.

Koppes, Clayton R. "From New Deal to Termination: Liberalism and Indian Policy, 1933–1953." *Pacific Historical Review* 46 (November 1977).

Lawson, Michael L. *Dammed Indians: The Pick-Sloan Plan and the Missouri River Sioux, 1944–1980.* Norman: University of Oklahoma Press, 1982.

Lurie, Nancy O. "The Indian Claims Commission." *Annals of the American Academy of Political and Social Science* 436 (March 1978).

Margon, Arthur. "Indians and Immigrants: A Comparison of Groups New to the City." *Journal of Ethnic Studies* 4 (Winter 1977).

McNickle, D'Arcy. *Native American Tribalism: Indian Survivals and Renewals.* New York: Oxford University Press, 1973.

Meriam, Lewis, et al. *The Problem of Indian Administration.* Baltimore: Johns Hopkins Press, 1928.

Moquin, Wayne, and Charles Van Doren, eds. *Great Documents in American Indian History.* New York: Praeger, 1973.

Orfield, Gary. *A Study of the Termination Policy.* Denver: National Congress of American Indians, 1965.

Ourada, Patricia K. *The Menominee Indians: A History.* Norman: University of Oklahoma Press, 1979.

Peroff, Nicholas C. *Menominee Drums: Tribal Termination and Restoration, 1954–1974.* Norman: University of Oklahoma Press, 1982.

Philp, Kenneth R. *John Collier's Crusade for Indian Reform, 1920–1954.* Tucson: University of Arizona Press, 1977.

————. "Termination: A Legacy of the Indian New Deal." *Western Historical Quarterly* 14 (April 1983).

Robbins, William G. "Extinguishing Indian Land Title in Western Oregon." *Indian Historian* 7 (Spring 1974).

Shames, Deborah, ed. *Freedom with Reservation: The Menominee Struggle to Save Their Land and People.* Madison, Wis.: National Committee to Save the Menominee People and Forests, 1972.

Shanahan, Donald G. "Compensation for the Loss of the Aboriginal Lands of the California Indians." *Southern California Quarterly* 57 (Fall 1975).

Sorkin, Alan L. "The Economic and Social Status of the American Indian, 1940–1970." *Journal of Negro Education* 45 (Fall 1976).

————. *The Urban American Indian.* Lexington, Mass.: D. C. Heath, 1978.

Stefon, Frederick J. "The Irony of Termination: 1943–1958." *Indian Historian* 11 (Summer 1978).

Steiner, Stan. *The New Indians.* New York: Harper and Row, 1968.

Tyler, S. Lyman. *Indian Affairs: A Work Paper on Termination, with an Attempt to Show Its Antecedents.* Provo, Utah: Institute of American Indian Studies, 1964.

Vance, John T. "The Congressional Mandate and the Indian Claims Commission." *North Dakota Law Review* 45 (Spring 1969).

Vernon, Howard A. "The Cayuga Claims: A Background Study." *American Indian Culture and Research Journal* 4 (1980).

Waddell, Jack O., and O. Michael Watson, eds. *The American Indian in Urban Society.* Boston: Little, Brown. 1971.

Washburn, Wilcomb E. *The Indian in America.* New York: Harper and Row, 1975.

Watkins, Arthur V. "Termination of Federal Supervision: The Removal of Restrictions over Indian Property and Person." *Annals of the American Academy of Political and Social Science* 311 (May 1957).

Wise, Jennings C. *The Red Man in the New World Drama: A Politico-Legal Study with a Pageantry of American Indian History.* New York: Macmillan, 1971.

Chapter Seven

The Rise of
Native American Militancy

When a small group of Native Americans came ashore at Alcatraz Island in San Francisco Bay in November 1969, demanding return of the land to its native owners, non–Native Americans throughout the United States realized that the days of submission and acquiescence were over. Like African and Hispanic Americans before them, Native Americans had begun a campaign of demand and protest. But the occupation of Alcatraz only seemed like the beginning because the media focused so much attention on the event. Native Americans had never really been passive; individual tribes like the Pueblos in the 1920s and pan-Indian groups like the Society of American Indians or the Native American Church had been demanding fairness and equity, as well as respect for tribal integrity, for many years. The modern age of Native American protest—marked by pan-Indian organizations, interest-group lobbying, political activism, and finally militancy— began during the last years of World War II, when attacks on the "Indian New Deal" intensified and grew to maturity during the struggle against termination in the 1950s.

By 1943 John Collier realized that the mood of Congress was changing, that Native American affairs were no longer commanding much attention because people were too preoccupied with the war. To prevent any shift back toward assimilation as the goal of public policy, Collier urged tribal leaders to form a pan-Indian organization to lobby for and against particular legislation. Members of the organization would be the elected leaders of all tribes participating in the Indian Reorganization Act of 1934. In November 1944 more than one hundred Native Americans from all over the country gathered in Denver, Colorado, to form a national organization. Calling themselves the National Congress of American Indians (NCAI), they dedicated themselves to lobbying on behalf of specific tribes and working for voting rights and civil equality.

For several years the NCAI worked in support of the Indian Claims Commission and the Navajo-Hopi Rehabilitation Act, but it was the termination program of the early 1950s that really galvanized the NCAI into action. When Senator Arthur Watkins's termination policies went into effect in 1954, the NCAI met in Washington, D.C., for eight weeks to protest the abrogation of tribal trusteeship. When thousands of Native Americans from all over the country descended on Capitol Hill, it quickly became apparent to most congressmen that termination was a politically explosive issue. At their 1954 convention in Omaha, Nebraska, the NCAI bitterly denounced termination and for the next five years led the fight for the survival of tribal trust status. Other groups like the Indian Rights Association and the Association on American Indian Affairs joined the NCAI in opposing termination, as did liberal organizations such as the National Council of Churches, and several Quaker relief groups. Ralph Nader denounced termination while he was editor of the *Harvard Law School Record* in 1957, and such liberal journals of opinion as *Christian Century, Harper's,* and *Nation* regularly criticized government Native American policy. Dozens of tribes sent delegations to Washington, D.C., between 1954 and 1970 protesting attempts to terminate them.

By 1956 politicians were no longer so enthusiastic about termination, and President Eisenhower announced that in the future no tribes would be terminated unless they specifically requested it. Still, throughout the late 1950s and into the 1960s the Bureau of Indian Affairs and Congress tried unsuccessfully to negotiate several tribes into termination. For example, late in the 1950s the U.S. Army Corps of Engineers decided to implement plans to construct Kinzua Dam and flood thousands of acres of Seneca land in western New York. Seneca leaders opposed the plan and demanded compensation, but Congress offered compensation only if they agreed to develop a termination plan. With assistance from the NCAI, the Senecas successfully repulsed congressional demands; but the NCAI had to be on guard against termination attempts even after the federal government had vocally ended the policy.

A more formal, visible shift toward activism came in 1961 with the American Indian Chicago Conference. Late in the 1950s a series of intertribal rivalries between Oklahoma and Great Plains tribes divided the NCAI, as did a number of disputes between the more traditional tribal leaders who dominated the NCAI and an impatient generation of younger, mostly urban Native Americans. Raised and educated in the cities, less willing to defer to tribal customs, and very conscious of pan-Indian values, they believed that most tribal leaders had capitulated to European American control through the Bureau of Indian Affairs. The Chicago conference served to expose their discontent.

Sol Tax, an anthropology professor at the University of Chicago, worked with the NCAI in organizing the conference. More than five hundred Native Americans from sixty-seven tribes came to the meetings, hoping to impress the new Kennedy administration with their unity as they demanded cultural survival and preservation of their land base. In their "Declaration of Indian Purpose," they said:

We believe in the inherent rights of all people to retain spiritual and cultural values and that the free exercise of these values is necessary to the normal development of any people. Indians exercised this inherent right to live their own lives for thousands of years before the white man came and took their lands. . . . When Indians speak of the continent they yielded, they are not referring only to the loss of some millions of acres in real estate. They have in mind that the land supported a universe of things they knew, valued, and loved. With that continent gone, except for the few parcels they still retain, the basis of life is precariously held, but they mean to hold the scraps and parcels as earnestly as any small nation or ethnic group was ever determined to hold to identity and survival.*

They also declared their intention to secure "Indian involvement in the decision-making process for all programs that would affect them." But younger Native Americans such as Clyde Warrior, an Oklahoma Ponca; Melvin Thom, a Nevada Paiute; and Herbert Blatchford, a New Mexico Navajo, were skeptical of their elders' resolve. Too much time, they believed, had been wasted on patience, caution, and cooperation; they were ready for a more aggressive policy. Several months after the Chicago meeting they met at the Gallup Indian Community Center in Gallup, New Mexico, and formed the National Indian Youth Council (NIYC).

At the Gallup meeting, the leaders of the NIYC denounced the racism, ethnocentrism, and paternalism so characteristic of traditional European American policies and demanded a new role for Native Americans in determining the policies affecting their lives. In their "Statement of Policy," they argued that the

weapons employed by the dominant society have become subtler and more dangerous than guns—these, in the form of educational, religious, and social reform, have attacked the very centers of Indian life by attempting to replace native institutions with those of the white man. . . .

The major problem in Indian affairs is that the Indian has been neglected in determining the direction of progress and monies to Indian communities. It has always been white people or white-oriented institutions determining what Indian problems are and how to correct them. The Establishment viewpoint has neglected the fact that there are tribal people within these tribal situations who realize the problems and that these people need only the proper social and economic opportunities to establish and govern policies affecting themselves. Our viewpoint, based in a tribal perspective, realizes, literally, that the Indian problem is the white man, and, further, realizes that poverty, educational drop-out, unemployment, etc., reflect only symptoms of a social-contact situation that is directed at unilateral cultural extinction.†

---

*Quoted in Shirley Hill Witt and Stan Steiner, eds., *The Way: An Anthology of American Indian Literature* (New York: Alfred A. Knopf, 1972), 216–19.

†Quoted in ibid., 221.

In addition to condemning Native American conservatives as "Uncle Tomahawks" who too willingly accepted BIA policies, the NIYC sounded the call for self-determination.

In 1964 the NIYC, in part motivated by the then-rising activism of Afro-American civil rights leaders, made a dramatic jump from rhetorical protest to open activism by staging a number of "fish-ins" in the Pacific Northwest. For a thousand years Native Americans living around Puget Sound in Washington had fished to feed and sustain their families and had retained earlier treaty rights to fish along the several rivers in that region. In 1954 Congress had recognized those treaty rights and exempted them from state fishing and hunting regulations. Many Native Americans refused to purchase state fishing licenses or comply with boat, line, and net regulations because of the exemptions. State game wardens, under the political pressure of commercial fishermen who denied the existence of any special "Indian rights," began harassing Native American fishermen along the Nisqually, Green, and Puyallup rivers, often seizing their boats, cutting their nets, and even beating them up. State courts in Washington also fined and jailed Native Americans for breaking state game laws. Under the direction of the NIYC, hundreds of Native Americans from many tribes descended on Puget Sound to fish in open defiance of state game laws. Movie star Marlon Brando and African American activist Dick Gregory joined the NIYC in a protest demonstration at the state capitol. Between 1964 and 1966 many "fish-ins" took place in Washington, and also in Oregon, Idaho, and Montana; and in 1966 the Department of Justice intervened in the cases of several arrested and indicted demonstrators and restored their treaty rights. The news media picked up on the story, and millions of non–Native Americans realized for the first time that a younger generation of Native Americans was insisting on controlling the state and federal policies affecting their tribes.

In the mid-1960s a number of other Native American groups appeared, all of which followed the lead of the NIYC in actively demanding federal acceptance of the policy of self-determination. Several tribal leaders among the Sioux formed the American Indian Civil Rights Council, which, as its name implied, dedicated itself to equal opportunities and equal treatment for all Native Americans. Another organization, the Indian Land Rights Association, was committed to a restoration of traditional tribal lands, condemning the idea behind the Indian Claims Commission that monetary settlements could ultimately satisfy all Native American grievances. Still another such group, the Alaskan Federation of Natives, was formed in 1966 to regain tribal lands lost to the federal government and to prevent wholesale exploitation of state resources.

More groups organized. As the struggle against termination became more successful in the 1960s, the NCAI directed much of its attention to the problems of urban Native Americans. As if in response, and in order to make sure that their own interests would still be represented, tribal leaders on the reservations formed the National Tribal Chairman's Association in 1971. In 1968 Lehman Brightman, a Sioux and director of Indian Studies at the University of California, formed the United Native Americans, a group of 5,000 Native American young people and college students committed to pan-Indian values, self-determination, and civil equality. Wallace "Mad Bear" Anderson convened a series of "North American Indian Unity Conventions" with the same objectives in mind. Regional organizations also appeared in the 1960s. Robert Hunter formed the Nevada Intertribal Council, representing many tribes in the Great Basin. Gerald One Feather, Frank LaPointe, and Ray Briggs established the American Indian Leadership Conference, an activist organization of Sioux youth in South Dakota. Ernie Stevens, a Wisconsin Oneida, played an important role in the California Intertribal Council, an organization of 130,000 Native Americans in California. All demanded changes in public policy.

The major objective for the new pan-Indian activists was tribal self-determination. To be sure, self-determination usually meant different things to different people; but there were several controlling principles to the philosophy which most Native Americans accepted. Since the 1880s European American assimilationists had worked to absorb Native Americans into the mainstream of the dominant society, in the process eliminating tribal codes in favor of Anglo-American legal values. The cessation by federal law of tribal sovereignty in 1871, the citizenship campaigns of the late nineteenth and early twentieth centuries, and the termination program of the 1950s all looked to the ultimate disappearance of tribal values. Periodically, when assimilationists saw the need to slow down or even halt such programs, they still operated under the paternalistic assumption that Native Americans, for obvious cultural reasons, were not capable of running their own affairs. Certain that Native Americans, if left to their own devices, would lose their land or fail to use it effectively, would dissipate their resources, and would remain culturally unprepared for life in European American society, the Bureau of Indian Affairs had taken over tribal government; restricted property disposal; and taken control of the schools, hospitals, and jobs on the reservations. Even the Indian Reorganization Act, for all its commitment to self-determination, required approval of the Secretary of the Interior for all newly written tribal constitutions. Each constitution also had to delegate significant veto powers over tribal affairs to the Secretary of the Interior. After years of feeling like pawns of federal politicians and bureaucrats, Native American leaders in the 1970s were determined to gain control over the medical, educational, and economic programs affecting them, as well as restoring tribal government to some semblance of real power.

Self-determination also involved a new respect for tribal cultures and a commitment to their survival. Assimilation, by definition a celebration of non–Native American values, became a bad word in the 1970s, a reminder of three centuries of cultural imperialism. Allotment, citizenship, education, termination, and relocation—all designed to transform Native Americans into farmers and workers living (and thinking) just like European Americans—came under attack as militants demanded programs to sustain rather than obliterate tribal cultures. They also wanted the freedom to adopt whatever non–Native American institutions were compatible with Native American values, and yet to do so at their own pace in order to prevent the social instability often accompanying rapid changes in society.

A third, more important, element to self-determination was maintaining the trust status of the tribes with the federal government. Although President Nixon announced the end of termination in 1970, most Native Americans remained vulnerable to legal assimilationists bent on breaking up the reservations, distributing the land among tribal members, and absorbing Native American families into the mainstream of American life. To many non–Native Americans, the demands for self-determination and a continued trust status seemed contradictory—an attempt for independence and paternalism at the same time. But most Native American militants believed that they would be better able to achieve self-determination by dealing with federal officials than with state and local officials, upon whom the influence of economic interest groups was much more powerful. Self-determinationists argued that the special legal relationship between the tribes and the federal government should continue indefinitely and that tribal separateness should be protected. The idea of turning the tribes over to state and local authorities was a guarantee of discrimination and exploitation as far as Native American activists were concerned—a repugnant possibility to be opposed at all costs.

And yet, even then the self-determinationists did not want Native American tribes to be dependent wards of the federal government forever. Perhaps more than anyone else in the country, they realized that permanent dependence on the federal government for economic assistance inevitably meant some type of bureaucratic controls and a continuing vulnerability to the winds of political change. If Native Americans were certain of anything, it was that the philosophy of assimilation would live on, exerting itself in other assaults on tribalism as it had done so many times in the past.

Economic development of reservation resources—both human and natural—was the ultimate key to self-determination. As long as reservation jobs were inadequate, tribal survival would be threatened by the migration of Native Americans to the cities. Reservation development would permit members of the tribes to stay on the reservation rather than move to the cities in search of work. If the reservations could become economically self-sustaining while retaining their special legal status with the federal government, they would have the best of both worlds—protection from state and local interference by federal statute and freedom from the controls that federal economic dependence would certainly involve. An additional benefit of economic development under tribal direction was protection of the environment. Native American leaders wanted very much to preserve their traditional respect for land and animal life; and if tribal leaders determined the pace and extent of economic development, they could prevent any unacceptable changes in the reservation environment.

Those favoring self-determination received a major boost in the 1960s when the numbers of Native Americans moving to the cities rose dramatically. Indeed, the single greatest change in the structure of the Native American community in the 1960s and 1970s was the mass migration of young people to major urban centers. Ironically, out of that migration came a new interest in tribal values, a drive for pan-Indian unity, an emphasis on self-determination as the panacea for Native American problems, and a stronger sense of urgency and militancy in the Native American community—an outcome precisely opposite of what the relocation program was intended to accomplish.

Throughout their history most Native Americans had lived in small rural villages or as nomadic wanderers, and as late as 1900 less than 1 percent were living in urban areas. Between 1900 and 1940, even though the pace of urbanization had quickened throughout the country, the number of Native Americans living in cities had risen to only 24,000, barely more than 7 percent of the total. Between 1940 and 1980, however, because of World War II, federal government programs, and the economic development of metropolitan areas, a remarkable demographic change occurred. More than 25,000 Native Americans served in active military duty during World War II. They traveled widely throughout the United States and the world, and upon their discharge many decided to stay in the cities with their families. Thousands of other Native Americans moved to the cities during the war to work in defense industries. Under the BIA relocation program between 1953 and 1972, more than 100,000 Native Americans moved to metropolitan areas. Finally, thousands of Native Americans moved to the cities on their own, searching for better jobs and better housing. The results were extraordinary. Since 1940, when about

24,000 Native Americans (only 13 percent of the total) lived in urban-ized areas, urban Native Americans have at least doubled each dec-ade, and in 1980 over 740,000 Native Americans—more than half of the national total—lived in urbanized areas.

By far the largest urban Native American community is in the vi-cinity of Los Angeles and Long Beach, which community numbered 60,893 in 1980. Many more Native Americans have also settled in Cal-ifornia urbanized areas; in fact, of the 201,369 Native Americans in that state in 1980, 82 percent were urban. This contrasts markedly with the Native American population of North Carolina, which was 78 percent rural in 1980, and those of Arizona, New Mexico, and Alaska, which were about 70 percent rural. Interestingly, Oklahoma Native Americans were half urban and half rural in 1980—roughly the national average. Other large urban Native American communities are, in decreasing order: New York City-Jersey City-Newark, San Francisco-Oakland, Seattle-Tacoma-Everett, Tulsa, Oklahoma City, Phoenix, Minneapolis-St. Paul, San Diego, Detroit, and Chicago.*

Despite serious economic problems in the cities, Native Americans were usually better off there—at least in strictly economic and statisti-cal terms—than on the reservations or rural areas. In terms of income, occupation level, education, employment, and housing they ranked higher than rural Native Americans. In 1970 the median income for Native American males living in the cities was over $4,700 as com-pared to only $2,800 for reservation residents. Nearly 48 percent of Native American men living in the cities worked as professionals, tech-nicians, business managers, white-collar workers, craftsmen, and fore-men, while only 35 percent of their rural counterparts were similarly employed. For urban men the median number of completed school years was 11.2, but it stood at only 8.7 for rural men. In 1975 the aver-age unemployment rate for urban men was 11 percent, while 40 per-cent of reservation Native American men were out of work. By the early 1980s, because of the severe recession in the economy, urban unemployment had risen to 16 percent and more than 50 percent for reservation residents. Unemployment exceeded 90 percent on some reservations. Finally, more than half of all Native Americans lived in substandard housing with inadequate plumbing facilities and with

---

*Native American communities in the urbanized areas named all exceeded 10,000 in 1980. Urbanized areas with 5,000 to 10,000 Native Americans in 1980 were, in decreasing order: Dallas-Ft. Worth, San Jose, Sacramento, An-chorage, Albuquerque, Denver, San Bernardino-Riverside, Portland (Ore-gon), Tucson, Washington, D.C., and Houston. U.S. Bureau of the Census, *1980 Census of Population,* vol. 1, *General Population Characteristics* (Washington, D.C.: U.S. Government Printing Office, 1983), 1:212–24.

insufficient living space. A 1981 housing inventory by the Bureau of Indian Affairs indicated that for 176,400 Indian families there were some 84,200 existing dwellings in standard condition and some 92,200 in substandard condition. Of the substandard homes, only 32,000 were even worth renovating. Among urban Native Americans, perhaps 20 percent lived in overcrowded homes and 8 percent in houses with inadequate plumbing.

To deal with life in the cities—the faster pace, pollution, crowding, discrimination, and poverty—Native Americans developed a number of urban institutions. As was the case with previous generations of Irish and East European immigrants, a bar or saloon culture appeared in the Native American ghettos. For recently arrived immigrants to the city, the bar provided recreation; social contact with old friends from the reservation; assistance in finding jobs, housing, and medical care; and help in successfully adjusting to the culture shock of city life. As the new arrivals adjusted to their jobs and found nicer houses or apartments outside the immediate ghetto, the Indian Center became far more important than the bar in providing necessary services. Indian Centers provided employment assistance, financial counseling, tutoring, legal advice, athletic programs, day-care centers, emotional treatment, alcoholic rehabilitation, and health care. In 1974 Congress passed the Native American Program Act, providing permanent funding for these centers.

The migration of tens of thousands of Native Americans to the cities had enormous political ramifications. On the reservations, where individuals were largely confined socially to members of their own tribes, political interests were narrow and insular, focusing usually on local issues and concerns. Social and cultural life—religion, family, marriage, and personal activities—were also confined to the reservation community. Not surprisingly, it was difficult and sometimes impossible to generate any political movements transcending the tribal level. The Society of American Indians, the Native American Church, and the National Congress of American Indians were exceptions. By the mid-1960s, however, thousands of young Native Americans raised in the cities were reaching adulthood. Better educated than any earlier generation of Native Americans, they observed with interest the rising activism of African and Hispanic Americans and decided that dramatic, media-capturing events intrigued European Americans and focused their attention on minority issues. More important, they also acquired a pan-Indian perspective. In the neighborhoods, schools, and Indian Centers they interacted with people from many tribes, frequently marrying exogamously. Being Native American in the city was an important ingredient to personal identity, often as important as membership in any particular tribe.

The increase in pan-Indianism in turn led to increased political activity. Tribal differences had always weakened Native American political movements in the past and would continue to be a problem in the future, but the dramatic increase of urban Native Americans proved a watershed in Native American politics. In their statement of policy in 1968, the United Native Americans recognized the problems of the past and the potential for the future. Their purpose in coming together was

(1) To bring together all people of Indian identity and Indian descent everywhere . . .
(2) To bring together all who can identify with the Native American liberation struggle without getting involved in full-blood vs. mixed-blood infighting or intertribal squabbles . . .
(3) To foster a spirit of unity and brotherhood among all Native Americans and to avoid vicious attacks on each other . . . to bring every Native American "home" to his people, to not waste one precious Indian life (the white man has already destroyed enough Indians—why should we destroy each other?)*

The emerging political activism of young urban Native Americans in groups like the United Native Americans, the American Indian Movement, and the National Indian Youth Council also helped inspire a resurgent nationalism on the reservations. Traditionalists and full-bloods there had for years resented BIA paternalism and manipulation, but in the 1960s they too began to demand a new respect for the ways of the past. Tribal leaders such as Thomas Banyacya of the Hopi, Mad Bear Anderson of the Tuscaroras, Clifton Hill of the Creeks, and Rolling Thunder of the Shoshones openly called for a return to traditional customs, including revival of ancient tribal religions, the use of tribal chiefs and open councils selected by traditional means (unsupervised by the BIA), and the abandonment of majority rule and elections in favor of consensus politics. The National Traditionalist Movement of the Iroquois League was a prominent reservation group advocating the old ways. Only by separating themselves from European American culture and even from other tribal cultures could particular Native American identities survive. Although these resurgent tribal values contradicted pan-Indian goals—as well as the goals of the civil rights movement—and introduced more conflict between various Native American groups, the demands of tribal traditionalists still helped forestall the assimilation process and sent a powerful message to European Americans. Not only were national pan-Indian groups lobbying and demonstrating for self-determination, but individual reservation tribes were also resisting BIA control.

---

*Quoted in Witt and Steiner, eds., *The Way*, 228-29.

The most radical of all the new Native American organizations was the American Indian Movement (AIM). By the late 1960s more than ten thousand Native Americans were living in Minneapolis—a third of the Minnesota total and more than any single reservation in the state. Confined to substandard housing, low incomes, and high rates of welfare dependence, they were going through many of the problems suffered earlier by other urban ethnic groups. They also complained of harassment and brutality at the hands of the overwhelmingly European American police force of Minneapolis. Most of these Native Americans were Chippewas, and in 1968 a group of Chippewas formed an "Indian patrol" to watch and follow the police on weekend nights as they traveled through Native American neighborhoods. Acting as witnesses whenever police arrested a Native American, they usually demanded his release; and during the nine-month existence of the patrol, arrest rates for Native Americans in Minneapolis declined back to general city averages. George Mitchell and Dennis Banks, who had emerged as leaders of the patrol, decided to organize formally to protect migrating Native Americans from ethnically selective law enforcement policies. They called themselves the American Indian Movement.

During the late 1960s the new Native American organizations attempted to monitor the legislative activities of the federal government and of the individual states, watching for any talk of termination or attempts at restricting tribal liberties. In 1967, for example, the Committee on Interior and Insular Affairs in the House of Representatives reported on the Indian Resources Development Act, which would allow Native Americans more liberty in selling, leasing, or mortgaging their land by applying individually to the BIA for permission. Both the new pan-Indian organizations and traditionalists opposed the measure bitterly. Johnson Holy Rock, chairman of the Oglala Sioux Tribal Council on the Pine Ridge Reservation, was certain "we'd lose more than we'd gain and we've lost too much already."* More than 40 percent of reservation land had already passed to European American control on Pine Ridge, and on the wheat-farming eastern reaches of the reservation 99 percent of the land was held by non–Native Americans. Fearing the transfer of even more property, the Oglala Tribal Council denounced the measure and successfully opposed it. Two years later, activist groups banded together to oppose the new Secretary of the Interior, Walter Hickel. At the Western Governors' Conference in Seattle in July 1969, Hickel had remarked that the federal government had been too protective of the tribes, rendering them dependent on the "crutch" of government largesse. Fears of termination developed immediately, and such groups as the United

---

*New York Times, October 15, 1967.

Native Americans, the National Traditionalist Movement, and AIM began demanding his removal—even his impeachment. Their instantly negative response to Hickel's public attitude played a major role in President Nixon's announcement in 1970 that the BIA would no longer pursue termination as a national policy.

Activist organizations also rallied around the public efforts of individual tribes to assert their rights. During the mid-1960s, for example, they vocally supported the series of "sit-ins" in the Pacific Northwest and the Upper Midwest, and in 1968 they supported a Mohawk protest against both the United States and Canada. Earlier in the 1960s Canada began restricting the free movement of Mohawks across the Seaway International Bridge between Canada and the United States. Arguing that Canada was bound to uphold the 1794 Jay's Treaty guaranteeing easy access for Mohawks to both sides of the border, a group of Mohawks blocked the bridge connecting Canada and New York. Canadian officials arrested them but later refused to prosecute because of political pressures. The *Akwesasne Notes,* the Mohawk newspaper with a national following of 50,000 readers, described the militant blockade in detail and editorialized on the merits of direct action against infringement of tribal privileges by European American authorities.

Motivated by the struggle against termination and the isolated acts of individual tribes, Native American activism was transformed into militancy in 1969 at Alcatraz. A military and then federal penitentiary since 1868, Alcatraz was closed in 1963, and federal officials promptly declared the island to be surplus government property. Originally, the island had been part of the tribal land of the Ohlone Indians and was a familiar place to the Coast Miwoks, Pomos, Wintuns, Maidus, and Northern Yokuts. When the federal government vacated Alcatraz, some local Native Americans considered taking it over but eventually declined because of prevailing legends that the island was not a place for humans but only for animal life. They even suggested to the Department of the Interior that the island be declared a national wildlife refuge.

But other Native Americans living in San Francisco came from non-California tribes and thus had no knowledge of the local legends. In 1964 a small group of Sioux landed on the island, claiming settlement rights on public land. Federal authorities removed them the next day, but the Native American settlers then sued in the courts, demanding government recognition of their claim. They argued that the Fort Laramie Treaty of 1868, ending the Red Cloud War, promised that any man who was a member of the Sioux tribes and a

resident or occupant of any reservation or Territory not included in the tract of country designated and described in this treaty for the permanent home of the Indians, which is not mineral land, nor reserved by the United States for special purposes other than Indian occupation, and who shall have made improvements thereon of the value of $200 or more, and continuously occupied the same as a homestead for the term of three years, shall be entitled to receive from the United States at patent for 160 acres of land. . . .*

The Sioux argued that their treaty rights had been violated when federal marshals forcibly removed them from the twelve-acre island before they could establish their occupancy claim. After four years of litigation, a federal court dismissed their case.

Native American students at San Francisco State College and the University of California at Berkeley, inspired by the militant activism of African and Hispanic American students, decided to reoccupy Alcatraz. On November 9, 1969, a small group of Native American students sailed out to the island. Federal marshals removed them the next day, but the wire services and local media picked up the story and for a few days the landing captured a good deal of national press coverage. The leaders of the occupation came from several tribes. Earl Livermore was a Blackfoot, Dennis Hastings an Omaha, Richard Oakes a Mohawk, and John Trudell a Sioux. Seeing a dramatic opportunity to focus even more attention on Native American affairs, other Native American students in the Bay Area organized the Indians of All Tribes; and on November 20, 1969, seventy-eight of them returned to Alcatraz to stay.

This time, federal officials were reluctant to remove them. President Nixon worried about the political consequences of sending federal marshals or soldiers and risking a military confrontation. After the initial arrival of the students on November 20, reporters from all over the country descended on San Francisco to chronicle the "invasion." Day after day more Native Americans arrived at the island until 150 were living there. Church and philanthropic groups in San Francisco shipped food and medical supplies to the island, as did sympathetic students at area colleges. Tourists by the thousands sailed out to the island, and thousands of messages of support poured in from around the world. Seeing the need for discretion in the face of such support, the federal government let them stay, hoping that time and boredom would end the "crisis."

The students' objective was twofold: first, to gain title to Alcatraz and build a Native American cultural center there, and second, to use the occupation as a psychological-political basis for launching a major pan-Indian movement known as the Confederation of American Indian Nations (CAIN). In a message issued on December 16, the leaders declared:

---

*Quoted in Rupert Costo, "Alcatraz," *Indian Historian* 3 (Winter 1970): 7.

While it was a small group which moved onto the island, we want all Indian people to join with us. . . . We are issuing this call in an attempt to unify all our Indian Brothers behind a common cause. . . . We realize . . . that we are not getting anywhere fast by working alone as individual tribes. If we can gather together as brothers and come to a common agreement, we feel that we can be much more effective, doing things for ourselves, instead of having someone else doing it, telling us what is good for us.*

From their pan-Indian base they hoped to create a ground swell of support for self-determination, confidently assuming that they could resolve the basic ideological problem between the concepts of tribal self-determination and pan-Indian unity.

Their hopes were only partly realized. Although one young woman claimed that there was "absolute unity for Alcatraz among every single tribe in this land,"† factionalism and a lack of leadership plagued Indians of All Tribes from the beginning. Those on Alcatraz elected a central council to "suggest, not to govern"; but bickering, boredom, and intertribal rivalries weakened the organization. Every few weeks another "spokesman" emerged to make a case with the press, only to fade away. After two years, as public interest in the occupation waned, federal marshals removed the remaining protestors. The seizure of Alcatraz failed to achieve its aims of securing title to the island and building a cultural center; but the students succeeded, as no one had before, in dramatizing the Native American demand for self-determination, tribal lands, and tribal identities.

Militant activism and new factionalism flared up again in 1972 and 1973. At a Cass Lake, Minnesota, convention in the spring of 1972, AIM leaders openly condemned the tribal councils for letting European Americans and BIA officials exploit tribal resources, especially the fishing rights on the Chippewa lakes. For a few days, with guns bared and roads into the convention center blocked, AIM leaders demanded that the Chippewa Tribal Council take a militant stand on fishing rights—militant enough to scare surrounding non–Native Americans into accepting absolute tribal control. At the same time, AIM led one thousand Native Americans into Gordon, Nebraska, to protest the beating and killing of Raymond Yellow Thunder, an elderly Pine Ridge Sioux, by five European Americans. They also protested the murders of other Native Americans in Arizona and California, as well as the shooting death of Richard Oakes, an early leader of Indians of All Tribes, by a prison guard in California. Throughout 1972 at tribal meetings, gatherings in urban Indian Centers, Sun Dance ceremonies, and organizational meetings, Native

---

*Quoted in Alvin M. Josephy, Jr., *Red Power: The American Indians' Fight for Freedom* (New York: McGraw-Hill, 1971), 187–88.

†Quoted in Costo, "Alcatraz," 10.

American militants debated goals and tactics while generally agreeing that 1972, because of the presidential election, would be an opportune time to focus national attention on Native American demands.

In the summer of 1972, activist leaders like Hank Adams of the "fish-ins" in Washington and Dennis Banks of the AIM met in Denver to plan the "Trail of Broken Treaties" caravan. Their hope was to generate media support for self-determination by moving thousands of Native Americans from the West Coast to Washington, D.C., during the last month of the presidential election. In cars, buses, and vans, they left in October, stopping at reservations across the country to pick up more protesters. At Minneapolis, where many Chippewas joined them, the caravan leaders issued their Twenty Points, a series of demands for a complete revival of tribal sovereignty by repeal of the 1871 ban on future treaties, restoration of treaty-making status to individual tribes, the granting of full government services to the unrecognized eastern tribes, a review of all past treaty violations, complete restitution for those violations, formal recognition of all executive order reservations, and admission of the tribal right to interpret all past treaties. They also demanded elimination of all state court jurisdiction over Native American affairs.

From Minneapolis the Trail of Broken Treaties moved on to Washington, where they discovered that their advance people had not made enough room arrangements. Most of the caravan went over to the BIA building, where they demonstrated for several hours. When federal guards in the building tried to push some of the demonstrators outside, the affair quickly became violent—the Native Americans seized the BIA building, blockading all the doors and windows with office furniture. For six days they occupied the building, demanding amnesty and a return to tribal sovereignty. Files were seized and some BIA property was damaged. Caravan leaders claimed that federal agents had infiltrated the movement and had done most of the damage. One week later, on November 8, federal authorities offered the Native American protesters immunity from prosecution and $66,000 for return transportation. The offer was accepted and the crisis was over.

The strength of such groups as AIM, Indians of All Tribes, and United Native Americans (UNA)—and the Trail of Broken Treaties—dramatically illustrated a new sense of independence and political aggressiveness, particularly among young urban Native Americans. However, the militant philosophies of the new pan-Indian leaders exposed more strains and factionalism within Native America. Questioning the legitimacy of tribal governments established under the Indian Reorganization Act was a case in point. Melvin Thom, a Nevada Paiute and leader of the NIYC, had long believed that many tribal leaders and most tribal representatives on the NCAI were simply pawns of the BIA, unwilling to protest government policies vigorously for fear of losing their privileged positions. Lehman Brightman, a Sioux-Creek and president of the UNA, bitterly protested the condition of most Native American schools and the willingness of tribal leaders to acquiesce to the substandard conditions and anti–Native American curricula. Dennis Banks and Russell Means of the AIM were convinced that many mixed-blood tribal leaders were hopelessly corrupt, lining their own pockets with federal government money at the expense of entire tribes. Most of the militant, pan-Indian organizations opposed both the appointment of tribal leaders by the BIA as well as elections of tribal leaders through majority rule. Too often, tribal rolls contained mostly those of mixed ancestry who were little interested in the survival of tribal culture and tribal sovereignty. They voted for people who would promote their individual economic interests rather than the tribal welfare. The very concepts of representative government, interest group politics, and majority rule were often alien to tribal traditions of consensus, unanimity, and inherited authority. Finally, they argued that most tribal leaders were assimilated mixed-bloods attuned to European American culture and willing pawns of the BIA.

The militant attitude, of course, opened a wide breach between such groups as AIM, UNA, and NIYC and such groups as the NCAI or the National Tribal Chairman's Association (NTCA). Ever since the "Indian New Deal" the BIA had dealt directly with elected tribal leaders, and both the NCAI and the NTCA were simply national unions of those elected officials. Militants found them to be conservative and subservient, representative only of rural mixed-bloods and not full-bloods and urban Native Americans. Not surprisingly, both the NCAI and the NIYC condemned the occupation of Alcatraz in 1969 and the Trail of Broken Treaties caravan in 1972, claiming that the militants were fanatics who would only bring a devastating backlash.

The differences between elected tribal leaders and the militants of the new pan-Indian organizations reached a peak in 1973 with the controversy at the village of Wounded Knee, South Dakota. Wounded Knee had become a familiar term to millions of Americans because of Dee Brown's bestselling *Bury My Heart at Wounded Knee* (1969); and Russell Means and Dennis Banks of AIM saw in it an opportunity to dramatize their hatred of the BIA and their demand for self-determination and a return of tribal sovereignty. For two months in the spring of 1973, a confrontation took place on the Pine Ridge Reservation that became a major media event which more than anything else imprinted on non–Native American minds the image of Native American militancy.

In 1972 Russell Means, a Sioux raised in midwestern and western cities, returned to the Pine Ridge Reservation and announced that he would soon run for tribal chairman. In an earlier election, Richard Wilson had defeated Gerald One Feather, a full-blood and traditionalist from the village of Oglala, with the support of mixed-bloods and assimilated Native Americans dependent upon tribal jobs and government assistance. Wilson despised the American Indian Movement, condemned the Trail of Broken Treaties caravan and other AIM demonstrations, and prohibited all AIM activities on the Pine Ridge Reservation. In February 1973, when AIM members were demonstrating at Rapid City, South Dakota, Wilson offered to send tribal police to assist city police officers. When Russell Means and Dennis Banks returned to the reservation at the end of the month, tribal police followed them around; tensions between the two factions became so strong that federal marshals requested by the BIA were stationed at Pine Ridge. On February 28, 1973, Banks and Means took control of the trading post at Wounded Knee village and AIM members, moving into the village immediately, declared their independence.

A number of discontented tribal factions rallied to AIM's support. Full-bloods moved into the village to demonstrate their own opposition to the leadership of Richard Wilson and to the "brutality" of tribal police. Another group wanted AIM to help them terminate all "unit leasing" rules which kept them from combining individual allotments into tribal or community grazing and farming lands. During the next ten days negotiations went on between AIM leaders and the FBI, usually with Senators George McGovern and James Abourezk of South Dakota or representatives of the National Council of Churches acting as intermediaries. On two occasions federal authorities actually considered an open assault on the village, a move which surely would have ended in violence and death. But no assault was ordered; and on March 11, AIM leaders announced the creation of the Oglala Sioux Nation, declared independence from the United States, and defined their national boundaries according to the Fort Laramie Treaty of 1868.

The occupation continued for two months, with periodic gunfire and threats coming from both sides. Veterans of other movements, including Angela Davis and William Kunstler, visited Pine Ridge and proclaimed their support for AIM, and Russell Means and Dennis Banks vowed to hold out at Wounded Knee until the Senate Foreign Relations Committee had reviewed all broken treaties, Richard Wilson had been removed as Oglala tribal chairman, and BIA corruption had been exposed to the entire world. After seventy days, the siege ended when AIM leaders agreed to leave the trading post and immediate village if the federal government would send a team of lawyers and investigators to meet with Oglala full-bloods and traditionalists to discuss the problems of broken treaties. The government team arrived at Pine Ridge in May, where they met with the Oglala full-bloods and finally admitted that only Congress had the power to act on treaty violations.

The end of the occupation did not end the violence at Pine Ridge, however. Russell Means shortly thereafter announced his candidacy for tribal chairman in the next Oglala elections, and for the remainder of the year bitterness and violence were constant on the reservation. The rivalry between Richard Wilson's mixed-blood "BIA faction" and Russell Means's full-blood "revolutionary faction" had turned to hatred. Arson, beatings, and murder became commonplace. In October BIA police shot and killed Peter Bissonette, an AIM leader and president of the Oglala Sioux Civil Rights Organization; the subsequent tepee funeral and procession became another AIM event designed to demonstrate hatred for Richard Wilson and the BIA. In the end the mixed-bloods prevailed, and Wilson defeated Means by 1,709 votes to 1,530, a slim margin of victory that guaranteed future conflict on the Pine Ridge Reservation.

Although the occupation of Alcatraz in 1969, the Trail of Broken Treaties caravan in 1972, and the occupation of Wounded Knee in 1973 were the most dramatic and well-publicized acts of Native American militancy, they were not the only ones. In 1970, after refusing an Indian Claims Commission offer of forty-seven cents per acre for the 3,368,000 acres they had lost, more than 150 Pit River tribesmen claimed and occupied portions of the Lassen National Park and Pacific Gas & Electric Company land in northern California. Several dozen other demonstrators took over Ellis Island briefly that same year to protest the loss of Native American land. In Littleton, Colorado, Native Americans occupied a BIA office to protest discrimination and corruption, and several Sioux camped on top of Mount Rushmore to claim it as a tribal heritage. More than 250 Chippewas occupied a lighthouse on Lake Superior in Michigan in 1975, and several dozen Menominees took over the Alexis Brothers Roman Catholic monastery in Wisconsin. AIM militants that year also invaded an electronics factory on the Navajo Reservation in New Mexico. In the mid-1970s 50 Mohawks occupied old cabins on state land in the Adirondack Mountains in New York, claiming that the land was stolen from their ancestors. In 1978, 25 Chumash tribesmen invaded the site at Point Conception, California, where a liquid natural gas terminal was to be constructed. Also in 1978, more than 200 Native Americans, led by Clyde Bellecourt of AIM, marched on the "Longest Walk"—from Alcatraz to Washington, D.C.—to protest BIA attempts to exploit Native American land. In 1980 a Miwok Indian, Swift Turtle, had himself nailed to a cross for several hours in San Leandro, California, to protest the construction of a condominium development on what once had been Native American land. And in 1981 a group of Crow tribesmen blocked the roads into their reservation to prevent non–Native American hunters and fishermen from taking their game.

No longer could European Americans or the BIA confidently expect Native Americans to acquiesce—Native American militancy made sure of that.

Suggested Readings

Bahr, Howard M., Bruce A. Chadwick, and Robert C. Day, eds. *Native Americans Today: Sociological Perspectives.* New York: Harper and Row, 1972.

Barsh, R. L. "The Omen: *Three Affiliated Tribes v. Moe* and the Future of Tribal Self-Government." *American Indian Law Review* 5 (1977).

Barsh, R. L., and R. L. Trosper. "Title I of the Indian Self-Determination and Education Assistance Act of 1975." *American Indian Law Review* 3 (1975).

Barsh, Russel Lawrence, and James Youngblood Henderson. *The Road: Indian Tribes and Political Liberty.* Berkeley: University of California Press, 1980.

———. "Tribal Administration of Natural Resource Development." *North Dakota Law Review* 52 (Winter 1975).

Burnett, Donald L., Jr. "An Historical Analysis of the 1968 'Indian Civil Rights Act'." *Harvard Journal of Legislation* 9 (1972).

Burnette, Robert, and John Koster. *The Road to Wounded Knee.* New York: Bantam Books, 1974.

Butler, Raymond V. "The Bureau of Indian Affairs: Activities since 1945." *Annals of the American Academy of Political and Social Science* 436 (March 1978).

Cahn, Edgar S., ed. *Our Brother's Keeper: The Indian in White America.* New York: World Publishing Co., 1969.

Costo, Rupert. "Alcatraz." *Indian Historian* 3 (Winter 1970).

Debo, Angie. *A History of the Indians of the United States.* Norman: University of Oklahoma Press, 1977.

Deloria, Vine, Jr. *Custer Died for Your Sins: An Indian Manifesto.* New York: Macmillan, 1969.

———. *God Is Red.* New York: Grosset and Dunlap, 1973.

———. *We Talk, You Listen: New Tribes, New Turf.* New York: Macmillan, 1970.

Dollar, Clyde D. "Renaissance on the Reservation." *American West* 11 (January 1974).

———. "The Second Tragedy at Wounded Knee: A 1970s Confrontation and Its Historical Roots." *American West* 10 (September 1973).

Fey, Harold E., and D'Arcy McNickle. *Indians and Other Americans: Two Ways of Life Meet.* New York: Harper and Row, 1970.

Gibson, Arrell Morgan. *The American Indian: Prehistory to the Present.* Lexington, Mass.: D. C. Heath, 1980.

Hertzberg, Hazel W. *The Search for an American Indian Identity: Modern Pan-Indian Movements.* Syracuse, N.Y.: Syracuse University Press, 1971.

Jackson, Curtis E., and Marcia J. Galli. *A History of the Bureau of Indian Affairs and Its Activities among Indians.* San Francisco: R and R Research, 1977.

Josephy, Alvin M., Jr. *Red Power: The American Indians' Fight for Freedom.* New York: McGraw-Hill, 1971.

Levitan, Sar A., and Barbara Hetrick. *Big Brother's Indian Programs, with Reservations.* New York: McGraw-Hill, 1971.

Levitan, Sar A., and William B. Johnson. *Indian Giving: Federal Programs for Native Americans.* Baltimore: Johns Hopkins University Press, 1979.

Margon, Arthur. "Indians and Immigrants: A Comparison of Groups New to the City." *Journal of Ethnic Studies* 4 (Winter 1977).

McNickle, D'Arcy. *Native American Tribalism: Indian Survivals and Renewals.* New York: Oxford University Press, 1973.

Meyer, William. *Native Americans: The New Indian Resistance.* New York: International Publishers, 1971.

Murdock, Donald B. "The Case for Native American Tribal Citizenship." *Indian Historian* 8 (Fall 1975).

Nolen, Curtis L. "The Okmulgee Constitution: A Step towards Indian Self-Determination." *Chronicles of Oklahoma* 58 (Fall 1980).

Ortiz, Roxanne Dunbar. "Wounded Knee 1890 to Wounded Knee 1973: A Study in United States Colonialism." *Journal of Ethnic Studies* 8 (Summer 1980).

Roos, Philip D., Dowell H. Smith, Stephen Langley, and James McDonald. "The Impact of the American Indian Movement on the Pine Ridge Indian Reservation." *Phylon* 41 (March 1980).

Sorkin, Alan L. *American Indians and Federal Aid.* Washington, D.C.: Brookings Institution, 1971.

————. *The Urban American Indian.* Lexington, Mass.: D. C. Heath, 1978.

Trosper, Ronald L. "Native American Boundary Maintenance: The Flathead Indian Reservation, Montana—1860–1970." *Ethnicity* 3 (September 1976).

Waddell, Jack O., and O. Michael Watson, eds. *The American Indian in Urban Society.* Boston: Little, Brown, 1971.

Washburn, Wilcomb E. *Red Man's Land/White Man's Law: A Study of the Past and Present Status of the American Indian.* New York: Charles Scribner's Sons, 1971.

Wise, Jennings C. *The Red Man in the New World Drama: A Politico-Legal Study with a Pageantry of American Indian History.* New York: Macmillan, 1971.

Witt, Shirley Hill, and Stan Steiner, eds. *The Way: An Anthology of American Indian Literature.* New York: Alfred A. Knopf, 1972.

Chapter Eight

Change and Continuity
in Modern America

For more than 370 years Native American history, buffeted by a series of political, economic, social, and cultural forces emerging from both European American and Native American society, has been complex in the extreme. From the beginning of their contact, neither has adequately understood the other. The dominant society has exalted the Protestant ethic to a theological level, figuratively worshipping at the intricately related altars of individualism, materialism, progress, and technology. To Native Americans, European American society has seemed obsessed with the temporal rather than the spiritual, the individual rather than the community, change rather than stability, and chaos rather than peace and harmony. For their part, non–Native Americans have viewed Native American life as hopelessly stagnant and inefficient, retarded by communal values, subsistence economies, and cultural ecologies. In these mutual misunderstandings, the twentieth century has been no different from the seventeenth, eighteenth, and nineteenth centuries.

Cultural hostility has inevitably led to political and economic conflict. From the dominant society, coalitions of reformers and developers have generated an overpowering political and economic movement which has scattered farmers, miners, and railroads across the continent and has gradually alienated Native American land. Various religious and philanthropic groups—intent on protecting, "saving," or transforming Native American society—have supported a long series of removal, reservation, education, allotment, and termination programs, always in the name of Native American welfare. Economic interest groups, realizing that such policies would surely separate Native Americans from their land, have enthusiastically thrown support behind the reformers' demands; and, decade after decade, the Native American land base has shriveled amid a torrent of economic development and liberal rhetoric. Public policy on the national and local levels throughout most of American history has reflected that coalition of European American economic and reform groups.

But unlike so many other ethnic groups facing political and economic pressures, Native Americans have too often been unable to harness the resources necessary to protect their ways of life. Throughout the nineteenth and early twentieth centuries, their population declined as disease, economic decay, and cultural change decimated them. In 1890 there were only about 250,000 Native Americans in a general population of nearly 63 million and by 1980 only 1.4 million in a general population of 226 million. In the early and middle decades of the twentieth century, while African and Hispanic Americans could muster considerable political strength by virtue of their larger numbers, Native Americans were few in number and scattered—factors that assured that they would be insignificant as a voting bloc either locally or nationally and would remain dependent upon the sympathies of non–Native American liberals rather than on their own power. During these years, political and cultural conflict within and between various tribes weakened Native Americans even further. Long before Europeans came to the New World, the cultural diversity of Native America had combined with frequent tribal migrations to create strong rivalries between important tribes, and those divisions continued into the twentieth century. Within individual tribes, inter-marriage and varying rates of assimilation into the mainstream society created new divisions, with mixed-bloods and assimilated Native Americans more willing to consider and even accept European ways than full-bloods. Intertribal and intratribal hostilities left Native Americans tragically vulnerable to the cultural, political, and economic pressures constantly exerted by European American society.

In many ways, the legacy of the past continues to exert pressure on Native American tribalism—particularly on their culture, standard of living, and land base. Problems with the federal government persist, especially complaints about the insensitivity of the Bureau of Indian Affairs and the bureaucratic delays associated with so many of its social and educational programs. In 1978, for example, Congress authorized the Acknowledgment Project, a special program administered by the BIA to evaluate the claims of Native American groups unrecognized by the federal government as legitimate tribes. In 1981 the federal government formally recognized 283 tribes, entitling them to both federal and state aid programs. But nearly 175 Native American groups, especially those east of the Mississippi River, remained unrecognized.

The Traditional Kickapoo Tribe, a group of 600 people living under the International Bridge at Eagle Pass, Texas, are descendents of Kickapoos expelled from Wisconsin and Michigan in the 1830s. Desperately poor and afflicted with epidemic levels of tuberculosis, these people cannot secure low-cost medical assistance—nor can the Eagle Pass School District receive Johnson O'Malley funds to help fund the education of their children, because the BIA does not recognize the Traditional Kickapoos as a legitimate tribe. Along with 70 other groups, the Traditional Kickapoos have applied for such recognition under the Acknowledgment Project; but the BIA argues that evaluation of these claims, which requires elaborate documentation of tribal histories, may take twenty-five years to complete. Kurt Blue Dog, a Sioux and lawyer for the Native American Rights Fund, argued before the Senate in 1980 that such delays were immoral and unconscionable and that the very survival of Native American people like the Traditional Kickapoo Tribe would depend upon rapid acceleration of the Acknowledgment Project. In another instance, the Native American Rights Fund, after years of lobbying, won recognition for the Cow Creek Band of the Oregon Umpquas in 1982. For Native American activists like Kurt Blue Dog, such "stonewalling" has been clear, undeniable proof of BIA insensitivity to the needs of Native American communities.

Throughout American history, Native Americans have been repeatedly consigned to "worthless" reservations—land which European settlers and private corporations had at the time deemed without economic value. But time and again, westward expansion and technological change have enhanced the value of reservation land, making it a target for further exploitation. A recent example of the threat to Native American land due to increased value came in the wake of the Arab oil boycott of 1973 with its resulting geometric rise in petroleum prices and subsequent search for alternate energy sources. Western reservations in particular—in North Dakota, Montana, Idaho, Washington, Oklahoma, New Mexico, Utah, and Arizona—possessed vast amounts of coal, oil, shale oil, natural gas, timber, and uranium. As world oil prices skyrocketed in the 1970s, the economic value of reservation resources rose dramatically, and for the first time those resources could be developed profitably. More than 40 percent of the national reserves of low sulphur, strippable coal, 80 percent of the nation's uranium reserves, and billions of barrels of shale oil exist on reservation land. On the 15-million-acre Navajo Reservation, there are approximately 100 million barrels of oil, 25 trillion cubic feet of natural gas, 80 million pounds of uranium, and 50 billion tons of coal. The 440,000-acre Northern Cheyenne Reservation in Montana sits atop a 60-foot-thick layer of coal. In New Mexico, geologists estimate that the Jicarilla Apache Reservation possesses 2 trillion cubic feet of natural gas and as much as 154 million barrels of oil. American and multinational corporations are clamoring after these resources, arguing once again that progress, destiny, and now national security make "economic development" of Native American land imperative. Reflecting that point of view, the American Farm Bureau Federation passed Resolution 621 at its January 1983 convention:

We support legislation to establish the rule that all people have equal rights and responsibilities under the law. All citizens should be required to obey the laws of local, state and national governments. The "nation unto a nation" treatment of native Americans should be abolished.

We favor abolition of the Bureau of Indian Affairs and termination of special treaty rights to purchase or negotiate for fair compensation.

These steps will end special treatment of native Americans and bring everyone to full equality under the law.

Also resolved: that we oppose the granting of power of eminent domain to Indian tribes.*

Legal pressures to incorporate Native Americans into the polity persist as well. Still committed to the "melting pot" ideology, many liberal reformers are uncomfortable with the special legal status allowed tribal entities, such status appearing to be much like the unacceptable, second-class, "separate-but-equal" status which has been the lot of Afro-Americans for so many decades. They argue that if Native Americans are to be fully accepted in the United States, with the privileges and responsibilities of citizenship, the law should be color-blind, subjecting everyone to the same benefits and obligations.

Disputes over fishing and hunting rights, which burst on the public consciousness with the National Indian Youth Council "fish-ins" in 1964, continue to create controversy. Fish and game wardens argue that Native Americans should be subject to the same laws as non–Native Americans in order to preserve game supplies, while Native Americans respond that only European Americans have over-killed and overfished.

On the White Earth Reservation of the Chippewas in northern Minnesota, the dispute over hunting and fishing rights intensified in 1979. In August the state supreme court ruled that Minnesota had no jurisdiction over hunting and fishing by Chippewas on the White Earth Reservation, but that others living there were still subject to existing game laws. The non–Native Americans, who outnumber the Chippewas and own more than 40 percent of reservation land, bitterly protested the court decision, arguing that it would lower property values and destroy the resort industry there. A similar dispute developed on the Bay Mills Reservation in northern Michigan, where federal courts have nullified all state regulations on Chippewa hunting and fishing practices. Many Chippewas have become commercial fishermen, but non–Native American sportsmen argue that Chippewa fishing will destroy recreational fishing in Michigan waters. In August 1981 some members of the Crow tribe barricaded the highway bridge over the Bighorn River in Hardin, Montana, to keep non–Native American fishermen off that part of the river running through the reservation. Finally, in December 1982, a federal district court awarded the Klamaths the right to hunt, fish, and trap on 617,000 acres of former reservation land in southeastern Oregon.

Wassaja: A National Newspaper of Indian America 9 (January/February 1983):1.

Another threat to tribal sovereignty came in the form of the Indian Civil Rights Act of 1968, which extended full civil rights to all Native Americans and required tribal consent before any state could assume civil and criminal jurisdiction over any reservation. On the surface, the Indian Civil Rights Act seems a benignly positive law—one that non–Native American liberals and conservatives can support as well as Native Americans—but many activists look on the law not as a victory for individual rights but as a violation of tribal prerogatives.

A dispute between the federal government and the Navajo tribe illustrates this perceived threat to tribal sovereignty. The Economic Opportunity Act of 1964 provided for legal aid services in poor communities, and in 1967 an elaborate legal aid program was established for members of the Navajo nation. Government lawyers, calling their local organization the "Navajo DNA," assisted individual Navajos with problems involving welfare services, VA benefits, Social Security, local police, and creditors. Although they were able to be of significant service, by so doing the DNA lawyers posed a threat to the standing of traditional tribal leaders accustomed to assisting tribesmen with such difficulties. Tribal leaders asked the DNA to work only under supervision of the Navajo Tribal Council; the lawyers refused, and in 1968 Raymond Nakai, chairman of the Navajo Tribal Council, excluded DNA leader Theodore Mitchell from the reservation. Mitchell sued in the federal courts, and in 1969 a federal district court found in Mitchell's favor, arguing that tribal leaders had violated his individual civil rights by banning him from the reservation. Chairman Nakai and others replied that the Navajo Treaty of 1868 specifically empowered the tribe to exclude anyone from the reservation except legal representatives of the United States. Navajo leaders felt that the decision compromised tribal authority. The legal services program was in itself a non–Native American program because it concentrated on securing individual rights outside the tribal setting, and for most tribes individual rights had always been subservient to community needs. So the Indian Civil Rights Act—with its exaltation of private property and individual rights—seems to many Native Americans to be another triumph of Anglo-American jurisprudence.

Pressures for assimilation have come in other ways as well. Although many non–Native Americans became increasingly curious in the 1960s and 1970s about Native American values, they still have a difficult time taking them seriously. Ethnocentrism is very powerful. In 1977, for example, several hundred Navajo employees of the Peabody Coal Company demanded that United Mine Worker and company medical benefits cover the fees charged by tribal healers as well as those of certified physicians. When both Peabody and the UMW claimed inadequate resources, Navajo militants argued that that in itself was proof of a biased perspective reflecting a belief in the superiority of European American medicine, because in spite of these limited resources the certified physicians still got paid. Even civil rights workers among other ethnic groups do not understand, and some Native American leaders look on the civil rights movement itself as an assault on tribalism. With its commitment to individual rights, integration, and middle-class morality, the civil rights movement epitomizes non–Native American values and not communal tribalism. Therefore, many Native American activists have resisted the overtures of "Third World" leaders for a united campaign against white racism, since tribal sovereignty and self-determination, and not integration and assimilation, are their goals.

Finally, Native Americans still face the pressure of assimilation in their educational programs. Although many tribes were able to gain control of their own schools in the 1960s and 1970s and teach tribal history and culture for the first time, they have had to face the intense hostility of local school boards, state education authorities, and teacher association members who remain convinced that the new curriculum will not prepare Native American children for successful economic life in the dominant society. This, of course, is why many tribal leaders resent BIA and local public schools in the first place, since by emphasizing education for life in the mainstream society the schools are helping alienate Native American children from tribal values. Activists, demanding the tribal over the traditional curriculum, have raised the ire of many traditional non–Native American groups committed to assimilation.

The economic conditions of Native American tribes, with few exceptions, remained dismal in the 1980s—another nagging remnant of the past. Despite decades of federal manpower development—John Collier's "Indian New Deal" of the 1930s, Glenn Emmons's economic development program of the 1950s, and Lyndon Johnson's "Great Society" of the 1960s—Native Americans still suffered severe problems in the areas of employment, education, income, and health.

Unemployment was an especially severe problem. Because of the geographical isolation of many reservations, poor transportation facilities, lack of skilled labor, and an absence of capital, few industrial jobs appeared on the reservations. Although more than 120 firms had established industrial plants on reservations by 1975, only 12,000 jobs had been thereby created. White Mountain Apaches and Mescalero Apaches were successfully operating hunting, fishing, and skiing resorts in the mountains of Arizona and New Mexico; the Navajos were enjoying some income from coal and oil leases; and the Osages were well-to-do from their oil leases in Oklahoma; but these were the exceptions. Most reservations were not self-sustaining, and many Native Americans employed there had only seasonal agricultural jobs.

Off the reservations, racism and lack of education often handicapped Native Americans in securing employment. Perhaps most important, major changes occurred in agricultural employment after World War II. The application of capital, technology, and economies of scale to agriculture brought dramatic increases in production, driving small farmers and marginal producers—including tens of thousands of Native Americans—out of agricultural labor altogether. In 1940 more than 68 percent of Native American workers were employed in agricultural pursuits, but by 1978 that figure had dropped to less than 15 percent. Industrial jobs were not available to fill the vacuum.

Unemployment rates, although they varied widely from reservation to reservation, averaged 40 percent for Native Americans in the 1970s—the highest rate for all ethnic groups in the nation and far more severe than anything experienced by European Americans during the Great Depression. For instance, during the winter, unemployment among the Oglala Sioux at Pine Ridge, South Dakota, and the Mississippi Choctaws often reached 90 percent; the San Carlos Apaches in Arizona, the Fort Berthold Mandans in North Dakota, and the Pueblos and Hopis in New Mexico averaged 75 percent unemployment at this season, while the Standing Rock and Rosebud Sioux in South Dakota and the Blackfeet in Montana experienced 60 percent.

Educational problems have exacerbated the unemployment problem. For a number of reasons, Native American children and their parents were and are frustrated with the public schools, which nearly 65 percent of Native American students attended in the 1970s. Cultural alienation, especially among full-bloods or those who speak a native language at home, has been extensive. The biased, assimilationist curricula of most religious, BIA, and local public schools have often failed to meet the needs of many Native American children, and tribal culture has often militated against the Anglo-American education process. Among the Lakota-speaking Oglala Sioux, young boys are raised to be physically aggressive, independent, and impetuous from the time they reach school age. Unaccustomed to such behavior, teachers have often reacted harshly, suspending many boys or so alienating them that they have dropped out. Long bus rides over poor roads have posed another obstacle to regular attendance, particularly when students and parents have a difficult time identifying with the school in the first place. Racism among non–Native American teachers and students has also alienated Native American students. Finally, the circumstances of poverty—poor housing, lack of electricity, sickness, and malnutrition—have worked against good study habits and educational achievement in a viciously reinforcing cycle. By 1982 there were 40,774 students in BIA schools and 165,988 students in twenty-six states receiving assistance from Johnson-O'Malley funds. But school enrollment and educational success varied from tribe to tribe. Among the Pimas and Papagos in Arizona, more than 95 percent of children were enrolled in school, but only 35 percent of Alaskan Eskimos were enrolled. Native Americans in the early 1980s had the lowest school enrollment figures of any ethnic group in the United States. More than 40 percent of Native American students entering high school dropped out before graduation. Among the Klamaths in Oregon the drop-out rate was about the same as for European Americans, but among the Sioux in South Dakota the number reached nearly 60 percent, and nearly 70 percent for the White Mountain Apaches.

When employment could be found, the lack of education led inevitably to low-paying jobs and limited family income. By the early 1980s, nearly 40 percent of all Native American men worked in unskilled or semiskilled factory, service, or farm occupations compared to a national average of less than 15 percent. And because of the surplus of reservation workers over reservation jobs, wage rates there were quite low. On the Pine Ridge Reservation, for example, typists averaged only $400 per month in 1976, compared to salaries of nearly twice that amount for typists working in metropolitan areas of the north central states. Reservation laborers and truck drivers received only 60 percent of the wages normally paid to non–Native American laborers and truck drivers in the Midwest.

In 1970 the median income for Native American men over the age of sixteen was barely more than $3,500, compared to an average for European Americans of nearly $9,000, and $5,400 for Afro-Americans. Average annual earnings for Native American women in 1970 were $1,700, compared to $6,823 for European American and $5,258 for Afro-American women. On reservations it was even worse, with annual per capita income for Native Americans averaging less than $1,000 in 1980. In 1983 only 25 percent of reservation workers were earning more than $1,000 per year.

Unemployment and low incomes have meant poverty, with its attendant poor housing, malnutrition, poor community sanitation, and health problems. By the mid-1970s more than a third of all Native American families were living in houses with fewer than three rooms and 63,000 reservation families were without plumbing facilities, often having to carry water from wells more than a mile from home. Those on reservations suffered from a number of serious diseases. Poor nutrition and housing generated a tuberculosis rate more than six times the national average in 1980, and frequently contaminated water supplies made Native Americans seventy times more likely than European Americans to suffer from dysentery. Their influenza and pneumonia rates are three times the national average; and they are ten times more likely than European Americans to fall ill of strep throat, eight times more likely to get hepatitis, and three to four times more likely to catch mumps, chicken pox, and whooping cough. The Native American suicide rate in the early 1980s is six times greater than for any other ethnic group in the United States. And because alcoholism rates among Native Americans are the highest in the nation, their death rate from cirrhosis of the liver is also the highest—five times the national average. Because of all these health problems and an infant death rate almost twice the national average, the Native American life expectancy in the 1970s was 63 to 64 years compared to 71 years for European Americans. Taken together, Native American employment, education, income, and health problems make them the poorest people in the United States.

Nor has discrimination been put to rest. A number of state and national studies done by public civil rights commissions in the 1970s has revealed continuing patterns of prejudice and discrimination against Native Americans, from the mildest forms of stereotyping to vigilante violence. In school textbooks and television programs, the most common image of Native Americans has remained that of the nineteenth-century pony-riding, arrow-shooting enemies of European and American settlers, a stereotype bearing no resemblance to reality. Most Native American children are attending public schools where Native American customs, languages, and history have little or no part in the curriculum and where the pressures to assimilate into the dominant culture are powerful. In towns located close to the reservations, Native American arrest and incarceration rates in 1980 were thirty times higher than for non–Native Americans. Police harassment of Native American men has been common. In these same towns, employment discrimination against them has been similarly common.

Finally, the problems of intratribal factionalism and intertribal rivalries have continued to affect Native American society. Disagreements over tribalism—between full-bloods and mixed-bloods, traditionalists and progressives, and reservation and nonreservation Native Americans—continue to give European American policymakers a powerful political advantage. It has not been difficult for reformers to find a tribal faction, or individual leader, to provide "Indian support" to any intended reform. The rise of the peyote cult and the process of assimilation, for example, has inspired intense religious factionalism in many tribes. The Navajo Tribal Council has resisted peyotism throughout the twentieth century, since Navajo Christians find it sacrilegious and followers of the native religion view it as a threat to tribalism. In 1940, the tribal council even imposed a one-hundred-dollar fine and nine-month jail sentence for any Navajo found importing, selling, or using peyote on the reservation. When a group of Navajo tribal police, without search or arrest warrants, raided a peyote ceremony in 1957, the Native American Church sued, claiming gross violation of their First and Fourteenth amendment rights. Two years later, the Tenth Circuit Court decided *Native American Church v. Navajo Tribal Council,* upholding the tribe's right to outlaw peyote.

A similar case divided the Pueblo tribe. Six residents of the Jemez Pueblo in New Mexico who were faithful Protestants claimed that the tribal leaders, who were Roman Catholics, would not allow them to build a chapel, bury their dead in the tribal cemetery, hold church services in their homes, or permit Protestant missionaries to visit the reservation. They sued, but in *Toledo et al. v. Pueblo de Jemez et al.* (1954), the federal district court in New Mexico in effect found in favor of the tribe by refusing to hear the case. Both cases cited above were part of a larger dispute involving individual civil rights and tribal sovereignty. Did individual Native Americans have the right to worship freely in nontribal religions, or could tribal leaders absolutely determine the religious atmosphere on the reservation? Throughout the 1960s the controversy divided many tribes, bringing on the Indian Civil Rights Act of 1968, which limited tribal sovereignty by guaranteeing all individual rights.

On the St. Regis Reservation in upstate New York, two groups of Mohawks today remain bitterly divided. There are more than ten thousand Mohawks on the reservation, and for more than a century a dispute has raged between the "traditionalist" minority and the "tribal" majority. The traditionalists adhere to ancient customs of matriarchy: their society is divided into clans and their male chiefs are selected by nine "clan mothers." They view the tribal faction as grossly acculturated to non-Mohawk values and hence a threat to traditional society. Because of their loyalty to ancient customs, the traditionalists claim the legitimate right to rule the reservation and administer the $5 million in annual BIA grants. In 1979, after traditionalist Leonard Garrow was arrested by tribal police for stealing the tools tribal Mohawks had used to cut down trees belonging to traditionalists, the angry traditionalists raided the tribal police headquarters and held people hostage there for several hours. Further violence erupted periodically in 1980 and 1981, occasionally requiring the intervention of state police.

Use of tribal assets—from oil, gas, timber, and land leases; from tribal enterprises; and from government grants and awards—is also a source of tribal contention. Some tribes, particularly those still concentrated on traditional reservations, speaking the native tongue, and supporting tribal leaders, have managed to plan carefully the disposal of tribal income. By the mid-1970s the Navajos were enjoying an income of more than $100 million a year—a substantial amount of money but an amount rendered less significant by the fact that the

Navajo Nation had also increased dramatically to 150,000 people. They used the money to build a lumber mill, a tribal utility system and transmission line, natural gas lines, several motels, water and sewage systems, improved roads, the Navajo Training Farm, and the Navajo Agricultural Products Industries. Even then, economic issues on the Navajo Reservation triggered bitter factionalism resulting in the ousting of Peter MacDonald as tribal chairman in January 1983. Peterson Zah, who became the new Navajo Tribal Council chairman, charged MacDonald with becoming too involved with his job as head of the Council of Energy Resource Tribes (CERT) to focus on Navajo problems. The tribal budget was running an annual deficit of $25 million; the Navajo Agricultural Products Industries had run up a $14 million debt; the federal government was demanding the return of $7.3 million in misappropriated CETA grants; and the tribe had leased its oil and gas reserves at unfavorable rates to multinational corporations. Campaigning on all those themes, Zah defeated MacDonald in a close election.

Among the Nez Perces, bitter controversy surrounded the use of tribal income. During the 1950s and 1960s the tribal governing committee had used the tribe's money for the construction of community centers, horse breeding programs, and several tribal businesses; but a large number of Nez Perces, primarily mixed-bloods and those living off the reservation, wanted tribal income distributed in per capita payments. When this demand was refused, they asked—again unsuccessfully—that the blood quanta requirement used for determining tribal membership be lowered to less than one-quarter, giving mixed-bloods a majority interest of the tribe. Mixed-bloods and non-reservation Nez Perces had little to gain from reservation development, while full-bloods living on the reservation had an extraordinary interest. A similar division of opinion prevailed on other reservations throughout the country.

Intertribal rivalries are still playing important roles in reservation politics, as they have for centuries in all Native American relations. Three tribes—the Wascos, Warm Springs, and Paiutes—share the Warm Springs Reservation in Oregon, but the Paiutes constantly argue with the Wascos, claiming that the Wascos are too interested in attracting tourism and not concerned enough about preserving tribal values. Tourism, the Paiutes believe, is accelerating assimilation at the expense of tribal culture. In California, where the federal government agreed to a distribution of $37 million to sixty-five thousand California Native Americans for wrongs committed in the past, the Pit River tribe refused the money, arguing they wanted their land around Pyramid Lake, not the government's dollars. Other tribes favored the settlement and resented Pit River "obstructionism."

In Arizona, the Hopis and Navajos have continued to dispute Navajo occupation of Hopi land. In 1882 President Chester A. Arthur granted 2.5 million acres of land inside the huge Navajo Reservation to the Hopis. At that time only three hundred Navajos were living in the area, but by 1970 more than ten thousand Navajos were there and the Hopis were demanding their removal. The BIA concurred in 1974 and ordered the Navajos to move, offering them cash bonuses and new houses for relocating. But many refused. After years of negotiations, Congress settled the issue officially in 1981 by creating the Federal Navajo and Hopi Indian Relocation Commission and giving it $200 million to use in dividing the land between the two groups and compensating those who had to be relocated. In 1981 and 1982, when some Navajos still refused to move, the BIA began seizing their livestock and forcing them to go. The whole issue merely added to the feelings of stress and rivalry between Hopis and Navajos.

Competition for federal funds has become another source of contention in the Native American community. By 1975 there were twelve major Native American organizations in Los Angeles, twenty-four in Minneapolis, and eleven in Chicago. Serving the needs of urban Native Americans, these organizations were often dependent upon federal funding, and the competition for those funds created much disputation. The Chicago Indian Center, for example, had purchased a Masonic hall in 1967 and from it offered a wide variety of services. But late in 1970, in support of the Indians of All Tribes on Alcatraz, a faction split off from the Chicago Indian Center, called itself the Native American Committee, and began duplicating the work of the Chicago Indian Center. Of course, both groups were in competition for the same private and public funding. In 1977 the Los Angeles Indian Center lost a $1 million CETA grant for job training to the Tribal American Corporation, a federal decision which led to an enormous amount of anger and protest.

Native Americans also continue to disagree over matters of tribal identity and pan-Indian values. The rise of pan-Indian groups such as the National Congress of American Indians, the National Indian Youth Council, the National Tribal Chairman's Association, the American Indian Movement, and the Council of Energy Resource Tribes at least initially organized Native Americans into interest groups which provided some national perspective to Native American demands and a measure of combined political power. But the very essence of the pan-Indian spirit—that tribes suppress narrow, parochial customs and goals in favor of broader "Indian values"—has offended some and is distrusted by others. The movement seems particularly to be a threat to tribes such as the Wisconsin Winnebagos, the Hopis, or the Navajos, who jealously guard traditional values. Many of them have refused to participate in pan-Indian activities, or they have participated only in part. Traditionalists, such as most reservation full-bloods, have branded pan-Indianism as primarily the work of mixed-bloods and assimilated Native Americans who have surrendered much of their tribal identities. In South Dakota, for example, members of the American Indian Movement occupied Yellow Thunder Camp in 1981 in the Black Hills, hoping to convert the area into a religious-based community. The Oglala Sioux Tribal Council, however, opposed the occupation on the grounds that the controversy might jeopardize some of the tribe's land claims. In 1982 the Council of Energy Resource Tribes (CERT) accepted a BIA assignment to draft, in cooperation with major oil and gas trade associations, a series of regulations governing tribal severance taxes on mineral deposits. Since the Supreme Court had already decided in *Merrion v. Jicarilla Apache Tribe* that tribes could indeed charge such taxes, many Native Americans are worried that CERT will become an agent of multinational corporations, giving away rights that individual tribes have already won.

Finally, Native Americans have continued to argue about the nature of tribal government and the powers of the Bureau of Indian Affairs. Although most full-bloods favor self-determination and fear termination, they often disagree about the merits of the BIA and its role in tribal government. Dennis Banks and Russell Means, leaders of the American Indian Movement, have called for the destruction of the Bureau of Indian Affairs and a resurrection of pure tribal sovereignty. They expect the federal government to honor existing treaties and negotiate with individual tribes as sovereign nations—a return to pre-1871 legal conditions. In their confrontation at Wounded Knee in 1973, they called for removal of Oglala Sioux leader Richard Wilson because he was an elected rather than hereditary chief in power; that is, his leadership was imposed by the BIA when it imposed an electoral process on the tribe. On the other hand, Wilson found AIM leaders presumptuous—first, because he believed that, since most of them were Chippewas, they had no business dictating policy to the Oglala Sioux, and second, because he felt that their tactics and goals were counterproductive.

Less radical leaders want to combine tribal self-determination with the continued existence of the Bureau of Indian Affairs. Only then, they feel, can Native Americans stave off termination and assimilation, institutionalize their tax-exempt land base, and maintain even the semiautonomous tribal authority they now enjoy.

But if the legacy of the past has survived, the winds of change have blown as well; and out of the general civil rights movement and the demands of pan-Indian activists during the 1960s and 1970s has come an important change in the climate of opinion in the United States. Beginning with the Montgomery bus boycott in 1955, the African American civil rights movement captured national attention with sit-ins across the country; freedom rides in the South; mass marches in such places as Selma, Birmingham, Cicero, and Washington, D.C.; racial rebellions in Watts, Newark, and Detroit; and the "Black Power" movement led by people like Stokely Carmichael, Bobby Seale, H. Rap Brown, and Eldridge Cleaver. The assassinations of Malcolm X, Martin Luther King, Jr., and Medgar Evers only intensified that attention. Depending upon their points of view, white Americans might have been alternately thrilled by the vision of Martin Luther King, Jr., and terrified by the flaming rhetoric of Stokely Carmichael; but in each instance they have become more conscious of the problems of racism and discrimination in the United States. The antipoverty crusade, following so closely in the wake of the civil rights movement, has also confronted millions of middle-class Americans of European descent with the economic plight of, as Michael Harrington wrote, "the other Americans."

While the black civil rights movement first raised the conscience of white America, the demands and proposals of pan-Indian activists in the 1960s and 1970s focused national attention on the special situation of Native Americans. Though sympathetic with the goals of Black Power, Brown Power, and Yellow Power, Native Americans usually considered themselves as different from African, Hispanic, and Asiatic Americans as they were from European Americans and consequently felt the need to define clearly their position in the larger society.

The rise of pan-Indian activism triggered an extraordinary national interest with all things "Indian." Since there were so few Native Americans in the total population and because they were often isolated in rural reservations or urban ghettos, European Americans did not feel so threatened by Native American militancy; without those visceral fears raised by the Black Power and Brown Power movements, they could afford to be more generous in spirit with the demands of Native Americans. And because of a preoccupation with the frontier past as well as a curiosity about Native American values, millions of European Americans nursed feelings of guilt for the historical plight of Native Americans—poverty, disease, death, and the loss of tribal lands. To be sure, they were more interested in the Native Americans of yesterday than with those of contemporary America—as Vine Deloria, Jr., has written in *God Is Red*:

Indians are unable to get non-Indians to accept them as contemporary beings. Non-Indians either cannot or will not respond to the problems of contemporary Indians. They insist on remaining in the last century with old Chief Red Fox, whoever he may really be, reciting a past that is basically mythological, thrilling, and comforting.*

---

*Vine Deloria, Jr., *God Is Red* (New York: Grosset and Dunlap, 1973), 56.

But even if non–Native Americans then were more interested in the past than in the present—more caught up with myths and stereotypes than with reality—their growing interest in Native American life has nevertheless created a more favorable political climate for the appearance of Native American activism.

Recent public curiosity about Native Americans surfaced in a series of public and private investigations in the 1960s. To be sure, liberals have often commissioned studies of national problems when political reality would not permit more radical action; but like the Meriam Report of the 1920s, the studies did serve to publicize some of the more troubling problems faced by Native Americans. The Department of the Interior, the Fund for the Republic, and the United States Commission on Civil Rights all released reports in 1961 describing urban and reservation life; and in 1966 the Coleman Report and the White House Task Force on Indian Health surveyed educational, medical, and sanitation conditions among Native Americans. Senator Robert Kennedy of New York and, later, Senator Edward Kennedy of Massachusetts conducted extensive investigations into the quality of Native American education during the late 1960s and 1970s. In each instance, these reports generated significant press coverage—and some political pressure for a solution to the "Indian problem." Few had any idea of what that solution should be, and such demands were hardly new to American history; but, when combined with pan-Indian activism, the assimilationist cant of earlier years was not nearly so compelling.

In addition to spawning professional investigations, pan-Indian activism also helped change the popular Native American cultural image in the United States. Although some of the "noble savage" stereotypes survived, as in the Advertising Council's antipollution commercials of the late 1970s or the Mazola Corn Oil commercials of 1980, public promotion of "heathen" images became less frequent. Universities such as Stanford and Dartmouth abandoned the name "Indians" as titles for their sports teams. Stereotypical frontier stories in which European American successes were always "victories" and Native American successes always "massacres" appeared less frequently in the media. Films like *Little Big Man* (1970) or *A Man Called Horse* (1972) showed Native Americans in a sympathetic, if stereotypical, light, as did some television shows such as "The Waltons," "Little House on the Prairie," and "Lou Grant." Books critical of European American attitudes and views of history, including Dee Brown's *Bury My Heart at Wounded Knee* (1970) and Vine Deloria's *Custer Died for Your Sins* (1969) became best-sellers. In 1969, Kiowa-Cherokee writer N. Scott Momaday won the Pulitzer Prize for his novel *House Made of Dawn*, a poignant portrayal of a Native American's confrontations with and acceptance of his Indianness.

The combination of pan-Indian activism and growing interest in Native American affairs affected Congress in a number of ways during the 1970s. Assaulted for more than two decades by such groups as the National Congress of American Indians and the National Indian Youth Council, the termination program finally expired in 1970 when President Richard Nixon announced his support for an indefinite continuation of the federal government's trust relationship with Native American tribes. Since its origins in the late 1940s, termination had victimized most Native Americans to some degree, convincing them that the end of federal supervision would only lead to more exploitation by state and local interest groups. The troubled history of the Menominees in Wisconsin and the Klamaths in Oregon only confirmed those fears. Not surprisingly, Native Americans celebrated openly when Congress restored the Menominees to federal trust status in 1973; extended federal benefits to the Passamaquoddies and Penobscots of Maine in 1976; and returned federal protection to the Modocs, Wyandots, Peorias, and Ottawas in 1978, and to the Paiutes in 1980.

Congress also accelerated the compensation program in the 1970s, overcoming the legal entanglements and bureaucratic delays so common in earlier years. Between 1946 and 1960 the Indian Claims Commission had denied 88 claims and awarded only $20 million in 17 other cases; but in the next ten years the commission picked up the pace, dismissing only 66 new cases and granting $285 million in 133 other tribal claims. And between 1970 and 1978, when the Indian Claims Commission expired and all outstanding cases were transferred to the United States Court of Claims, the commission granted nearly $500 million more to various tribes in 180 cases. To satisfy the demands of Alaskan tribes, Congress passed the Alaska Native Claims Settlement Act in 1971, which assigned $1 billion to the tribal corporations of the Alaskan Federation of Natives. Although the cash awards of the Indian Claims Commission by no means settled all the wrongs of the past, as reformers and developers had hoped in 1946, Native Americans were still pleased to see a more concerted effort in resolving the hundreds of claims against the federal government.

In the end, the awards of the Indian Claims Commission had an unexpected result. Designed initially to speed assimilation and end the Native Americans' status of wardship with the federal government, the money actually stimulated tribalism because the benefits of tribal membership became much more tangible, particularly to mixed-bloods and assimilated Native Americans no longer living on the reservation. Federal funding accomplished the same thing. In 1960 the BIA administered all programs with a budget of $120 million, but in 1980 the BIA budget had increased to approximately $1 billion. At the same time, the antipoverty program of the Great Society and the other programs of the welfare state were channeling another $1 billion to Native Americans by 1980. Many tribes became like universities or private foundations in their ability to secure federal grants. The seven tribes of South Dakota, for example, received grants totaling $185 million in 1979. Since 1980 the flow of federal funds has become so extensive that, despite talk of sovereignty and tribal independence, Native Americans are more dependent on federal largesse than ever before. Ed Driving Hawk, 1980 president of the National Congress of American Indians, said that "tribal governments have become more administrators of federal programs than tribal governments."* And more so than ever before, Native American groups are resisting any mention of terminating their relationship with the federal government. Early in 1983, when Secretary of the Interior James Watt suggested that Native American economic and social problems are the natural consequences of federal government "socialism" on the reservations, a storm of protest arose from Native Americans who were convinced that he was in fact calling for termination.

In addition to expediting the bureaucratic and legal procedures for handling claims, the new mood of the late 1960s and 1970s brought about a significant change in the original goals of the Indian Claims Commission Act. Although the 1946 law specifically stated that tribes "with valid claims would be paid in money" and that no "lands would be returned to the tribe," a number of tribes rejected financial offers from Congress, insisting on the restoration of tribal lands rather than the appropriation of government money. One example of government willingness to bend to such demands has involved the Taos tribe which had refused an offer of $10 million to compensate them for the incorporation of Blue Lake into the Kit Carson National Forest in New Mexico in 1906. The offer was refused because the lake was a religious shrine for them, the source of life, and a final resting place for the spirits of the dead. At a 1961 meeting of the Association on American Indian Affairs a Taos spokesman said:

We don't have gold temples in this lake, but we have a sign of a living God to whom we pray—the living trees, the evergreen and spruce and the beautiful flowers and the beautiful rocks and the lake itself. . . . We are taking that water to give us strength so we can gain in knowledge and wisdom. . . . That is the reason this Blue Lake is so important to us.†

They demanded return of Blue Lake through the 1960s, but the Department of Agriculture, fearing the implications of returning land

---

*Quoted in William T. Hagan, "Tribalism Rejuvenated: The Native American since the Era of Termination," *Western Historical Quarterly* 12 (January 1981): 11.

†Quoted in Angie Debo, *A History of the Indians of the United States* (Norman: University of Oklahoma Press, 1977), 419.

to Native American tribes, persistently offered a cash settlement through the Indian Claims Commission. Finally, President Nixon supported the Taos position and in 1970 Congress returned the lake and 48,000 acres of land to the tribe.

There were other successes. In addition to the appropriation of $1 billion in compensation, the Alaska Native Claims Settlement Act in 1971 awarded 40 million acres of state land to the Alaskan Federation of Natives, much to the dismay of mining, energy development, and hunting and fishing groups. In western Nevada, the Paiutes wanted the restoration of control of Pyramid Lake and the land surrounding it—their traditional tribal homeland. The land had been guaranteed to them in 1859, long before any European Americans had seen any economic use for it. In 1969 California negotiated an agreement with Nevada to divert the Truckee River, which would have destroyed Pyramid Lake—a completely unacceptable proposal as far as the Paiutes were concerned. Tribal representatives fought the agreement, and in 1972 and 1973 court orders required stabilization of Pyramid Lake at a size large enough to sustain tribal fishing needs. Paiute militance had succeeded. In addition, the Havasupais have received trust title to 185,000 acres in the Grand Canyon, along with permanent access to another 95,000 acres adjacent to their land. The Yakimas of Washington have regained title to 21,000 acres of land placed in the Mt. Rainier Forest Reserve in 1908. And the Warm Springs tribe of Oregon has managed to win back tribal land taken in the nineteenth century.

To a large extent, the militant occupations of the late 1960s and 1970s were aimed at the return of tribal lands. The Passamaquoddy tribe claimed much of the state of Maine; the Wampanoags much of central Massachusetts; the Narragansets a large part of Charlestown, Massachusetts; the Pequots and Mohegans several thousand acres in Connecticut; the Oneidas, Senecas, and Mohawks a large portion of upstate New York; and the Eklutnas of Alaska more than 378,000 acres in that state. These claims at least communicated to the nation at large that tribal lands are priceless; monetary settlement is therefore not a totally acceptable solution.

Two recent cases further illustrate the problems inherent in Native American land claims. Point Conception, California, a beautiful headland thirty miles north of Santa Barbara, for centuries has been *Tolakwe* to thousands of California Native Americans, the place where all new life enters the world and where the souls of the dead leave the earth. The decision by California state officials and the board of directors of the Western Liquid Natural Gas Company to build a huge storage facility at Point Concepción enraged Native Americans across the country in 1977 and 1978, especially after the company dug two large trenches that desecrated a Chumash burial site. In May 1978 a group of Chumashes invaded the site and prevented further work on the project while other Native Americans blocked it in federal court.

Sioux demands in South Dakota are even more problematic. In the Fort Laramie Treaty of 1868, the Sioux had been guaranteed eternal sovereignty over the Black Hills; but the Black Hills gold rush and then the defeat of Custer at the Little Big Horn in 1876 gave Congress an excuse to abrogate the treaty. On July 1, 1980, after years of litigation, the U.S. Supreme Court awarded the Sioux $122 million for 7.3 million acres in the Black Hills illegally taken from them in 1876. But the settlement money cannot be distributed until eight Sioux tribes accept the court order, and the Oglala Sioux are demanding return of the land, not the money. Two activist groups there—the Lakota Treaty Council and the Black Hills Sioux Nation Treaty Council—are working to prevent settlement of the case by cash award. At the same time, other tribes are demanding distribution of the award as the only way of developing reservation resources and easing the pressures of poverty. Such attachments to the land and intertribal rivalries will undoubtedly further postpone settlement of the claim.

In addition to achieving some gains in cash settlements and land restorations, Native Americans have recently made major gains in income, education, employment, occupational levels, and health. Between 1950 and 1970 the median income for adult Native American males rose 220 percent, compared to 103 percent for Afro-Americans and 105 percent for European Americans. Between 1960 and 1970 the median income for Native American families increased fivefold to nearly $6,000. In 1940, only 5.6 percent of adult Native American males were engaged in white-collar jobs, but by 1970 that number had increased to 22.3 percent, compared to 18.5 percent for Afro-American and 42.1 percent for European American men. The median number of years of school completed by Native Americans was only 5.5 in 1940, but that figure rose to 9.8 by 1970. And between 1955 and 1971 Native Americans enjoyed an 80 pecent decline in the incidence of tuberculosis, a 75 percent decline in syphilis, a 60 percent decline in dysentery, a 90 percent decline in whooping cough, and a 35 percent decline in influenza. Infant mortality dropped from 62.5 per 1,000 in 1955 to 15.5 in 1979, while the European American rate dropped from 26.4 to 13.8.

Late in the 1960s and throughout the 1970s, Native American activists also made notable gains in self-determination. Although the Snyder Act gave citizenship to all Native Americans in 1924, state restrictions continued to disfranchise many Native Americans into the 1960s. In 1948 the Arizona Supreme Court declared unconstitutional the state law against Native American suffrage, and Maine and New Mexico followed suit in 1954 and 1962 respectively. In some areas, particularly in Oklahoma and the "four corners" area of Utah,

Arizona, New Mexico, and Colorado, Native Americans became a political force that politicians had to accept.

The appearance of pan-Indian militant organizations also gave politicians a greater inclination to listen to tribal moderates, and some tribal governments thereby gained in power. Since 1906, for example, the Bureau of Indian Affairs had selected tribal chiefs and governors for the Five Civilized Tribes in Oklahoma as a means of guaranteeing compliance with federal policy; but in 1970 tribal citizens regained the right to elect their own leaders without BIA interference. That was unacceptable to militant groups like the American Indian Movement, who considered elections to be a European American imposition on older Native American beliefs in consensus and hereditary right; but, again, some tribes gained power from the BIA. As another example, the Office of Economic Opportunity offered to establish a legal services program, similar to the Navajo DNA legal services unit, on the Pueblo reservations. The Pueblos were very skeptical, finally agreeing to the program only if the OEO contractually agreed not to initiate any litigation against Pueblo tribal organizations, as they had done against the Navajos. The federal government had not surrendered total power to tribal authorities, but important changes in their relationship were nevertheless underway in the 1970s.

Central to tribal self-determination was the question of religion. Throughout much of the twentieth century, Native American activists have struggled to preserve traditional values and beliefs, not only against federal and state laws restricting them but against the forces of acculturation as well. The Ghost Dance, Sun Dance, Dream Dance, peyotism, and other Native American religions had been outlawed on reservations late in the nineteenth century and early in the twentieth century, and not until the 1930s did the federal government significantly relax the pressure. But in the 1960s, as European American attitudes changed somewhat under the impact of pan-Indian activism, the climate of opinion in the United States became more conducive to freedom of religion for Native Americans, even in the case of peyotism.

The 1964 decision of the California Supreme Court in *People v. Woody* epitomized the evolution of non–Native American opinion. On April 28, 1962, John Woody and a group of Navajos met in a hogan near Needles, California, for a peyote ceremony. Local police arrested them on charges of possessing a controlled substance, and a superior court in San Bernardino County convicted them. Woody appealed the conviction to the California Supreme Court, and in August 1964 the court held that the state could not constitutionally apply the statute prohibiting consumption of peyote when used as a sacrament similar to the bread and wine used in many Christian churches. Native Americans, particularly those loyal to the Native American Church, hailed the decision as a turning point in the general struggle for self-determination.

President Carter's support of and signature on the American Indian Religious Freedom Act in 1978 was another victory. The Chumash fear that the liquid natural gas facility at Point Conception, California, would prevent dead souls from leaving the earth, condemning them to endless wandering, helped precipitate the law which directed federal agencies to evaluate regulations which either deprive Native Americans of access to sacred places on government land or prevent them from performing traditional ceremonies. Examples of how Native Americans have benefited from the new law are nearly as numerous as the various native religions. A Wintu medicine woman was able to keep her healing tent in Trinity National Forest in California. Customs agents must now permit Blackfeet, Crees, and Mohawks to cross the United States–Canada border without having their sacred medicine bundles searched. The Navy now permits Paiutes and Shoshones to visit healing springs on the China Lake Naval Weapons Center in the Mojave Desert. Nebraska and South Dakota state prisons now allow Native American convicts to build sweat lodges for purification rites, and inmates at several federal penitentiaries are suing for similar privileges.

Additionally, the law serves as the basis for ongoing litigation for further decisions favoring Native American demands on religious grounds. For instance, Navajo and Hopi leaders are now resisting a National Forest Service decision to permit the Arizona Snow Bowl ski resort to build more ski lifts and a new lodge at the San Francisco Peaks near Flagstaff, Arizona. Hopis believe that their gods dwell on these peaks, and for Navajos they are a holy site marking the border of the ancient tribal homeland.

Equally important to the advocates of self-determination is control of Native American economic resources. The skyrocketing prices of oil, coal, uranium, and natural gas after 1973 have placed a new premium on the value of much reservation land, as well as putting new pressures on water supplies needed to develop those resources. Peter MacDonald, chairman of the Navajo Tribal Council until 1983, concerned about the economic colonization of reservations by private energy corporations and the federal government, played a key role in organizing in 1975 the Council of Energy Resource Tribes (CERT), a consortium of twenty-three western tribes representing more than six hundred thousand Native Americans. Modeled after OPEC, CERT was designed to prevent environmental damage to reservation land, preserve water supplies, protect energy resources from non–Native American exploitation, maximize tribal profits by controlling individual leases, and guarantee a fair return on assets and certainty that revenues from energy resources will be used to convert the reservations into self-sustaining economic communities.

In the West, water is the foundation for all economic development, especially in terms of energy resources. Although five multimegawatt coal-burning plants now generate electricity on the Navajo Reservation, the government and corporate planners hope to build massive plants that together will generate as much as 36,000 megawatts of power in the Colorado River Basin in the next few years, some of these plants possibly on reservation land. Planners also look to build seven coal-gasification plants and several deep, high-grade uranium mines on reservation land. But such ambitious plans will require more than a trillion acre-feet of water—nearly ten percent of the Colorado River's annual flow. Such large amounts would require tapping Navajo and Apache water resources, and the Navajos and Apaches are already arguing that previous development programs have desperately weakened their water reserves. For example, early in the 1960s the federal government diverted much of the San Juan River's flow—which served much of the water needs of Navajos, Apaches, and Utes—into the Rio Grande for development purposes. The tribes affected bitterly protested the government project, and CERT has vowed never again to permit the BIA and the Army Corps of Engineers to tamper so cavalierly with Native American water resources.

CERT has also assisted the Crows in Montana in renegotiating their coal leases with the Westmoreland Resources Company, raising the tribal royalty from 17½ cents to 40 cents per ton, and it is continuing to assist the Crows in invalidating older leasing agreements for 30,248 acres held by the Shell Oil Company; 14,237 acres held by the Amax Coal company; 86,122 acres held by the Peabody Coal Company; and 73,293 acres held by the Gulf Oil Corporation. In each instance the Crows feel that the leases are anachronistic because world oil and coal prices have risen so dramatically since 1973. Tribes on the Fort Berthold Reservation in North Dakota and the Northern Cheyenne Reservation in Montana are making similar demands.

Finally, CERT is concerned with maintaining the environmental quality of reservation life. In 1977, for example, the Northern Cheyennes blocked construction of a large coal-fired power plant because they were convinced that local air quality would deteriorate. Although Patrick Stands Over Bull, the tribal chairman on the adjoining Crow Reservation, joined with the power company in favoring the plant as an economic boon for his people, the Northern Cheyennes held strong to their conviction that the strip-mining of coal would change their tribal homeland irrevocably. For CERT, development had to be compatible with tribal cultural values; therefore, they legally assisted the Northern Cheyennes.

Advocates of self-determination have also been concerned about the problem of education, particularly since the survival of tribal values is so inextricably linked to childhood and acculturation. Throughout the twentieth century Native American education has been subject to the capricious whim of Congress as expressed through the Bureau of Indian Affairs. From Richard Henry Pratt's nonreservation boarding school in the 1880s through John Collier's temporary restoration of tribal culture to reservation curricula in the 1930s to Hildegard Thompson's commitment to preparing Native American children for life in an urban, technological world during the termination and relocation programs of the 1950s, Native American education has been controlled by non–Native Americans with Native Americans the objects of political change rather than active participants in the institutions affecting their lives. As late as 1966, Secretary of the Interior Stewart Udall excluded Native American leaders from a BIA conference planning changes in Native American education programs. Not until Vine Deloria, Jr., and the National Congress of American Indians protested vehemently and publicly did the federal government open the sessions to pan-Indian leaders.

Such paternalism and discrimination have been anathema to those espousing self-determination, and pan-Indian activists have continually called for Native American control of their own education. Despite significant bureaucratic resistance within the BIA, Native Americans made some progress late in the 1960s and early in the 1970s. In 1968 President Johnson appointed the National Council on Indian Opportunity, and various tribal leaders appearing before the council repeatedly made the case for self-determination. The Kennedy Report of 1969, entitled *Indian Education: A National Tragedy— A National Challenge,* echoed in many ways the Meriam Report of forty years earlier. Indeed, the Kennedy Report gained wide attention precisely because educational conditions for Native Americans had changed so little since the 1920s. Racism, poverty, discrimination, absenteeism, and academic underachievement still plagued Native American education, and Native Americans still viewed federal and public schools as "alien institutions." In addition to condemning termination and BIA education policy, the report called for the addition of Native American history, culture, and language to school curricula and the direct involvement of parents and tribal leaders in the local education process. In 1971 the NAACP Legal Defense and Education Fund released *An Even Chance,* which confirmed the findings of the Kennedy Report.

A controversy between the Bureau of Indian Affairs and the Tamas clearly revealed the importance of self-determination and the significance of the Kennedy Report. A division of the larger Fox group, the Tamas were the last Native American tribe living in Iowa; and since 1938 they had enjoyed an elementary school on their three-thousand-acre settlement. In 1968, however, without advance notice, the BIA closed the school and assigned the fifty-six children to nearby public schools. Tribal leaders and parents were outraged and frightened. They resented the arrogance of the BIA's lack of consultation. They were deeply concerned over the discrimination their children would inevitably face in the public schools, and they feared that the closure would ultimately seriously undermine their culture. As Don Wanatee, a Tama leader, expressed it: "If you take away our language, you take away our religion. If you take away our religion, you take away our tribe. The three go together."* To protect their children from racism, to preserve their heritage, and to prevent arbitrary actions by the Bureau of Indian Affairs, the Tamas soon came to advocate the need for tribal self-determination. They needed to have and control their own schools. However, they failed in their efforts to keep the school opened; it is no longer listed among the day schools operated by the BIA.

Perhaps the precedent for Native American–controlled schools was set in 1966 in Rough Rock, a small community on the Navajo Reservation. Tribal members served on the school board and parents worked frequently as dormitory attendants. They were also free to visit the Rough Rock Demonstration School at any time, and they were invited to participate in summer adult education classes. The Navajo Curriculum Center there specialized in Navajo history and culture, and the tribe identified so closely with the school that they began calling it "Diné bi 'olta,"† meaning "Navajos' school." For the first time the Navajos had a school with which they could proudly identify.

The Rough Rock Demonstration School became a model for other Native American–controlled schools. New Native American groups demanding self-determination became more and more visible. In 1969 the National Indian Education Advisory Commission, the Americans for Indian Opportunity, and the National Indian Education Association began calling for "Indian involvement and Indian control" of schools teaching Native American children. The Navajo Education Association, the National Indian Leadership Training Program, the National Tribal Chairman's Association, and the Coalition of Indian Controlled School Boards were all formed in 1970 and 1971. Drawing on the experience of the Rough Rock Demonstration School, they helped the drive for self-determination gain momentum.

---

*P. Boyd Mather, "Tama Indians Fight for Their Own Schools," *The Christian Century* 85 (October 2, 1968): 1252.

†In contrast, they refer to public schools as "Bilagaana Yazhi bi 'olta" (white children's school), BIA schools as "Washington bi 'olta" (school of the federal government), and church schools as "ee'neeshoodii bi 'olta" (long coats' school). Margaret Connell Szasz, *Education and the American Indian: The Road to Self-Determination since 1928* (Albuquerque: University of New Mexico Press, 1977), 172.

In 1969, with grants from the Office of Economic Opportunity (OEO), the Navajo tribe, and several private foundations, the Navajo Community College opened for classes. A Board of Regents composed of tribal leaders governed the college, and central to the curriculum was the Navajo Studies Program. Regardless of occupational preferences, all students participated in the Navajo Studies Program, but the college offered a more traditional curriculum for students planning to transfer later to four-year colleges or technical schools. Congress passed the Navajo Community College Act in 1971, providing permanent funding for the college.

With a grant from OEO, the Navajos in Ramah, New Mexico, opened their own school in 1970, despite the concerted opposition of the state department of public instruction. Only the growing awareness of Navajo political power in New Mexico and the efforts of Senator Joseph Montoya overcame that hostility. A few months later the Chippewas and Crees gained control of the Rocky Boy School District on the Rocky Boy Reservation in northern Montana. Still bent on assimilation, the Bureau of Indian Affairs opposed these Native American–controlled schools on the grounds that the curriculum did not really prepare Native American children for life in the dominant society. That attitude, of course, was exactly why more and more Native Americans came to support self-determination. Hundreds of thousands of Native Americans simply did not want to live in the larger society. So great was the momentum for self-determination that by 1974 the Coalition of Indian Controlled School Boards served nearly one hundred school boards and education groups throughout the United States.

Complete Native American control of their education was impossible, however, because most Native American children attended public schools, where they were an ethnic minority. In 1980 the Office of Indian Education Programs of the BIA supported 209 schools and 15 dormitories. More than 43,000 Native American students attended these facilities. However, some 176,000 students attended nonfederal schools, most of which were public schools, in 1980. For parents with children in federal schools, the idea of tribal control and self-determination was at least feasible, but it was less realistic in the public schools. Non–Native American parents there were not about to surrender control to tribal leaders. Self-determination required other approaches. Four laws passed previously—the Johnson-O'Malley Act of 1934, Public Law 874 of 1950, Public Law 815 of 1950, and the Elementary and Secondary Act of 1965—all provided special appropriations to public school districts enrolling Native American children. But instead of using the money on special programs for Native American students, most school districts placed the funds into the general budget to benefit the entire student population. In the 1960s advocates of self-determination focused their attention on the budgets of school districts receiving such appropriations specifically intended to support Native American needs.

Young Native American activists demanded wider participation of parents and tribal leaders in the budget review process in school districts, insisting that federal funds targeted for Native American children be spent specifically for Native American children. Under the auspices of the National Indian Leadership Training Program, parents were instructed on budget procedures; and in Nebraska, North Dakota, and South Dakota, pan-Indian groups gained the authority to review federal allocations before school districts could spend the money. Special Native American programs in public schools, financed with federal resources, became the goal for self-determinists. The Yakimas, for instance, were successful in their effort to include a series of Yakima history and culture classes in summer school curricula in central Washington, and the Shoshone-Bannocks and Blackfeet were similarly successful in the introduction of tribal history and culture courses at local high schools in Idaho and Montana.

From the Kennedy Report, campaigns of pan-Indian and tribal groups, and growing non–Native American interest in Native American affairs came the Indian Education Act of 1972, a major step toward self-determination. Tribal leaders applauded the legislation. The act mandated parental and tribal participation in all federal impact-aid programs to public schools; allocated funds to encourage the establishment of community-run schools; provided funds to state and local education agencies, colleges and universities, and tribes for new Native American history, culture, and bilingual curricula; appropriated money for tribal use in adult-education projects; established an Office of Indian Education, controlled by the National Advisory Council on Indian Education (entirely staffed by Native Americans), to administer the programs of the Indian Education Act; and allocated funds for teacher training for BIA schools. Herschel Sahmaunt, a Kiowa and president of the National Indian Education Association, described the Indian Education Act as "the first piece of legislation enacted into law that gives Indian people on reservations, in rural settings, and in the cities control over their own education."* Although funding disputes with the Nixon administration and problems over appointments to the National Advisory Council on Indian Education disappointed many Native American activists, the Indian Education Act was still a major victory.

The greatest victory for pan-Indian activists in American history came in 1975 when the Indian Self-Determination and Education Assistance Act went into effect. The act has once again swung the great pendulum of relations between Native Americans and European

---

*Quoted in Margaret Connell Szasz, *Education and the American Indian: The Road to Self-Determination since 1928* (Albuquerque: University of New Mexico Press, 1977), 199–200.

Americans away from overt assimilationist policies toward tribalism and Native American sovereignty. The Indian Self-Determination Act states in part:

The Congress hereby recognizes the obligation of the United States to respond to the strong expression of the Indian people for self-determination by assuring maximum Indian participation in the direction of educational as well as other Federal services to Indian communities so as to render such services more responsive to the needs and desires of those communities.

The Congress declares its commitment to the maintenance of the Federal Government's unique and continuing relationship with and responsibility to the Indian people through the establishment of a meaningful Indian self-determination policy which will permit an orderly transition from Federal domination of programs for and services to Indians to effective and meaningful participation by the Indian people in the planning, conduct, and administration of those programs and services.*

In particular, the act has established a new relationship between federal agencies and tribal authorities. By permitting tribal governments to negotiate and contract directly with the Bureau of Indian Affairs and the Department of Health, Education, and Welfare for social welfare services, the act restores tribalism in an important legal sense and gives to Native Americans a greater measure of control over federal programs. Tribal governments can set goals, priorities, and administrative procedures for social and educational programs, and tribal governments can restructure and even reject those programs when they conclude that tribal needs are not being met. The act also permits the federal government to make direct cash grants to tribal governments for training programs in financial management, administrative control, and personnel supervision; for the acquisition of any land needed to fulfill social services programs; and for the construction and operation of health facilities. Tribal leaders are to be in direct control of the programs. Finally, the Indian Self-Determination and Education Assistance Act makes a number of changes in education programs. All school districts enjoying contracts under the Johnson-O'Malley Act of 1934 have been required to guarantee that funds received for Native American students are to be used only for Native American students; and, where Native Americans do not control school boards, an Indian Parents Committee must be consulted on all decisions affecting Native American children.

Congress also approved several other measures supporting the basic concept of self-determination. The Indian Finance Act of 1974 provided new assistance to enterprises and development projects by enlarging revolving loan funds, creating a new loan guaranty and insurance

---

*U.S. Congress, House, *Indian Self-Determination and Education Assistance Act*, 93rd Cong., 2d sess., H. Rep. 93-1600, p. 2.

fund, partially subsidizing loan costs, and providing grants for businesses. The Education Amendments Act of 1978 made major changes in the administration of education programs by giving controlling authority to local communities. Policy setting and program guidance became the responsibility of local school boards. Finally, the Indian Child Welfare Act of 1978 was designed to restrict the placement of children by non-Native American social agencies in non-Native American homes and environments. The act declared the federal government's intention to promote the stability of tribes and families by establishing minimum standards for any removal of children from the family and for placement, when needed, in homes reflecting the values of Native American culture. The law also made it clear that tribal courts had jurisdiction over children living on reservations.

Given the general course of Native American tribalism, however, the entire thrust of self-determination has not pleased all. Many militants continue to be concerned about self-determination because non–Native Americans might interpret it as dominance by *elected* tribal leaders; people in groups like AIM, of course, refuse to recognize the legitimacy of any decisions made by BIA-approved leaders or leaders selected in BIA-supervised elections. They favor self-determination as long as their own organizations enjoy enough power to dictate the planning and implementation of government Native American programs. Other tribes fear that legislation supporting self-determination has been just another subterfuge, a subtle way of removing the federal government from Native American affairs in one more move toward assimilation. But if current self-determination is not a panacea to all Native Americans, it is nevertheless a major change in Native American history, considering the probability that for the first time officials of the federal government are dealing correctly with Native American concerns and demands.

The overwhelming and most visible development in Native American affairs in the 1970s has been the resurgence of Native American tribalism and the willingness of tribal leaders to state their concerns openly. The Red Power movement has intensified the awareness of being "Indian" and at the same time has stimulated tribal consciousness. The changing mood of the general American public and its increasing willingness at least to address major Native American concerns has also contributed to a changing climate of opinion which has forced the government away from its course of termination toward one of self-determination. Finally, the financial awards coming from the Indian Claims Commission and federal grants have increased the economic rewards of tribal membership. And more than at any time in the twentieth century, Native Americans have committed themselves collectively to survival in the dominant society.

Native American Tribal Areas

Dr. Charles A. Eastman, Santee Sioux, 1897. Eastman was a founder of the Society of American Indians. He wrote several books and lectured on Native-American life.

Dr. Carlos Montezuma, Yavapai, 1896. Montezuma was an important pan-Indian leader in the early 1900s.

Henry L. Dawes, sponsor of the General Allotment (Dawes Severalty) Act, 1887.

John Collier, Commissioner of Indian Affairs, 1933–1945.

These photographs are of the same group of Navajo children taken six months apart, Carlisle Indian Industrial School, Pennsylvania, late 1880s. Reformers used such "before and after" photographs to show how successfully such schools had "civilized" the children, as if the haircuts and uniforms were proof of conversion to non-Native American culture. Richard H. Pratt, superintendent of Carlisle School, is seated on the porch in the earlier photograph.

These photographs indicate the effect of non-Native American culture on Native American lifestyles. Above is Geronimo, Bedonkohe Apache (at the wheel of the automobile), 1905. Although officially a prisoner of war, nonetheless he was considered a celebrity. Below is Jack Wilson (Wovoka), Paiute, *left*, leader of the Ghost Dance Religion, with motion picture actor T. J. McCoy, *right*, near Walker Lake, Nevada, 1926.

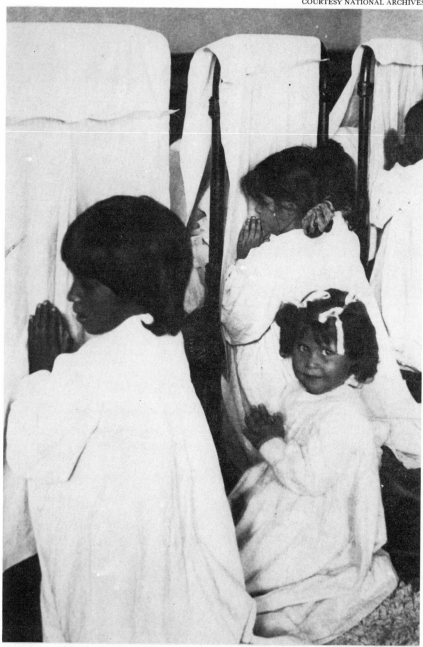

Resident students at prayer before bed, Phoenix Indian School, 1900. The attempt by non-Native Americans to transform and assimilate Native American children became a crusade in the late nineteenth and early twentieth centuries. Kneeling in prayer, white dresses, and ribbons in the hair were artifacts of non-Native American culture.

Relocated Native American children, ca. 1950s. The BIA legend for this photograph stated: "Children of a relocated Indian family differ little from their contemporaries." The legend perfectly indicates the continuing inability of BIA personnel to understand the depth and tenacity of Native American tribalism.

Children at a federal Headstart Program activity, Phoenix, Arizona, late 1960s. Ignoring Native American tribalism, many civil-rights activists thought that Native Americans, like African and Hispanic Americans, would agree that integration was the best solution to discrimination and poverty.

Ishi, the last living member of the Yana tribal group, California, 1916. His life became symbolic to many Native Americans of the struggle to maintain tribal identity and independence.

Arapahos in a prayer ceremony of the Ghost Dance, late 1880s.

Catawbas displaying pottery, Catawba Reservation, South Carolina, 1932.

Will Jim, Choctaw, and his family, near Philadelphia, Mississippi, 1925. The half century preceding World War II was a desperate time for large numbers of Native Americans as they tried to cope with the combination of severe poverty and assimilationist attacks on their tribal values.

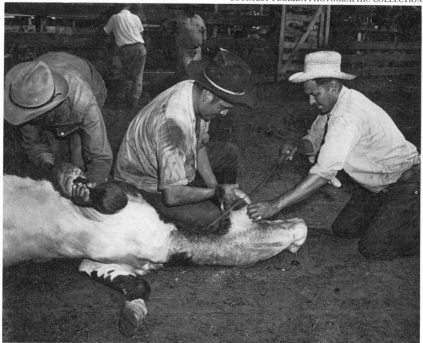

Seminoles dehorning cattle at the Brighton Reservation, Florida, ca. 1950.

Vocational students at Navajo Community College, Shiprock, New Mexico, early 1970s.

Chief Dan George, Suquamish and Sushwap, as he appeared in the motion picture *Little Big Man*. Enormously popular, Dan George was the most visible Native American in the United States during the 1960s and 1970s.

Peter MacDonald, longtime chairman of the Navajo Tribal Council, 1972. As a tribal leader and chairman of the Council of Energy Resource Tribes, MacDonald was a symbol of a new generation of Native Americans committed to self-determination.

David Long (Crazy Horse), vice-president of the Oglala Sioux Tribe, Pine Ridge Reservation, South Dakota, reading a statement before the Indian Claims Commission, ca. 1957.

Protesters in Washington, D.C., with the Trail of Broken Treaties Caravan, 1972. Their occupation and ransacking of the Bureau of Indian Affairs building became a symbol of Native American militancy and frustration with federal policy.

Dennis Banks, Chippewa, American Indian Movement leader, Minneapolis, 1974.

Russell Means, Oglala Sioux, American Indian Movement activist, 1978.

N. Scott Momaday, Kiowa-Cherokee, Pulitzer Prize winning author of *House Made of Dawn.*

Native American scholar and best-selling author Vine Deloria, Jr., Hunkpapa Sioux, *right,* speaking with activist Vernon Bellecourt, Chippewa, *left,* Cedar Rapids, Iowa, 1976.

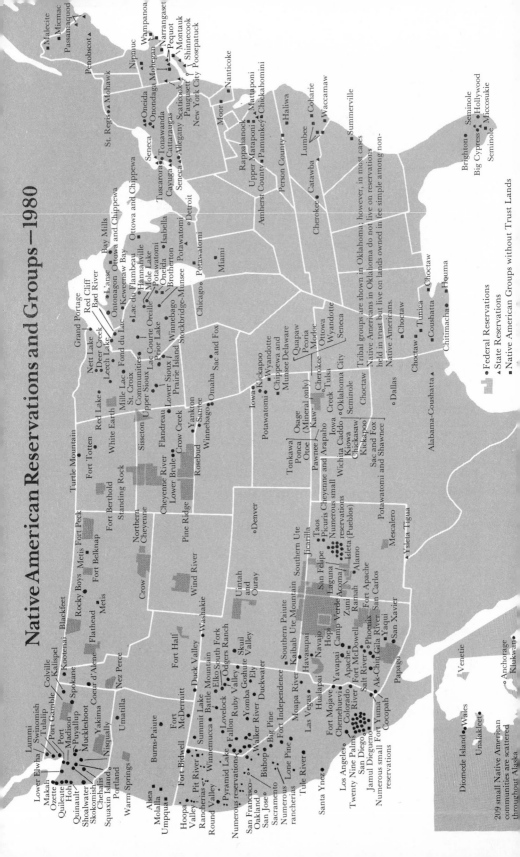

Native American Reservations and Groups—1980

Tribal groups are shown in Oklahoma; however, in most cases Native Americans in Oklahoma do not live on reservations held in trust but live on lands owned in fee simple among non-Native Americans.

- Federal Reservations
- ▲ State Reservations
- ■ Native American Groups without Trust Lands

209 small Native American communities are scattered throughout Alaska

Suggested Readings

Barsh, R. L., and R. L. Trosper. "Title I of the Indian Self-Determination and Education Assistance Act of 1975." *American Indian Law Review* 3 (1975).

Barsh, Russel Lawrence, and James Youngblood Henderson. *The Road: Indian Tribes and Political Liberty.* Berkeley: University of California Press, 1980.

————. "Tribal Administration of Natural Resource Development." *North Dakota Law Review* 52 (Winter 1975).

Burnett, Donald L., Jr. "An Historical Analysis of the 1968 'Indian Civil Rights Act.'" *Harvard Journal of Legislation* 9 (1972).

Butler, Raymond V. "The Bureau of Indian Affairs: Activities since 1945." *Annals of the American Academy of Political and Social Science* 436 (March 1978).

Deloria, Vine, Jr. *Custer Died for Your Sins: An Indian Manifesto.* New York: Macmillan, 1969.

————. "Legislation and Litigation Concerning American Indians." *Annals of the American Academy of Political and Social Science* 436 (March 1978).

Gibson, Arrell Morgan. *The American Indian: Prehistory to the Present.* Lexington, Mass.: D. C. Heath, 1980.

Hagan, William T. "Tribalism Rejuvenated: The Native American since the Era of Termination." *Western Historical Quarterly* 12 (January 1981).

Hertzberg, Hazel W. *The Search for an American Indian Identity: Modern Pan-Indian Movements.* Syracuse, N.Y.: Syracuse University Press, 1971.

Jackson, Curtis E., and Marcia J. Galli. *A History of the Bureau of Indian Affairs and Its Activities among Indians.* San Francisco: R and R Research, 1977.

Josephy, Alvin M., Jr. *Now That the Buffalo's Gone: A Study of Today's American Indians.* New York: Alfred A. Knopf, 1982.

Levitan, Sar A., and Barbara Hetrick. *Big Brother's Indian Programs, with Reservations.* New York: McGraw-Hill, 1971.

Mather, P. Boyd. "Tama Indians Fight for Their Own Schools." *The Christian Century* 85 (October 2, 1968).

Murdock, Donald B. "The Case for Native American Tribal Citizenship." *Indian Historian* 8 (Fall 1975).

Smith, Michael. "Tribal Sovereignty and the 1968 Indian Bill of Rights." *Civil Rights Digest* 3 (Summer 1970).

Sorkin, Alan L. *American Indians and Federal Aid.* Washington, D.C.: Brookings Institution, 1971.

Szasz, Margaret Connell. *Education and the American Indian: The Road to Self-Determination since 1928.* Albuquerque: University of New Mexico Press, 1977.

Tallchief, A. "Money v. Sovereignty: An Analysis of the Maine Settlement." *American Indian Journal* 6 (May 1980).

Trosper, Ronald L. "Native American Boundary Maintenance: The Flathead Indian Reservation, Montana—1860–1970." *Ethnicity* 3 (September 1976).

U.S. Congress. House. *Indian Self-Determination and Education Assistance Act.* 93d Cong., 2d sess., 1975. H. Rept. 93-1600.

Veeder, William H. "Water Rights: Life or Death for the American Indian." *Indian Historian* 5 (Summer 1972).

Washburn, Wilcomb E. *Red Man's Land/White Man's Law: A Study of the Past and Present Status of the American Indian.* New York: Charles Scribner's Sons, 1971.

Wise, Jennings C. *The Red Man in the New World Drama: A Politico-Legal Study with a Pageantry of American Indian History.* New York: Macmillan, 1971.

Epilogue

In 1980 there were just over 1.4 million Native Americans living in the United States. Because of the relentless migration of settlers and the periodic removals of Native Americans from their tribal homelands between 1640 and 1900, the majority live west of the Mississippi River, with the five states of California, Oklahoma, Arizona, New Mexico, and Washington alone containing more than 40 percent. Still, there are thousands of Native Americans—descendents of those who either avoided removal or returned home later—living east of the Mississippi River, including Eastern Cherokees in North Carolina; Choctaws in Mississippi; Creeks in Alabama; Seminoles in Florida; Penobscots, Passamaquoddies, and Narragansets in New England; Rappahannocks and Chickahominies in Virginia; Oneidas, Onondagas, Tuscaroras, Mohawks, and Tonawandas in New York; and Menominees and Chippewas in Wisconsin. By 1980 over half of all Native Americans were living in cities, with concentrations over 10,000 in Los Angeles-Long Beach, New York City-Jersey City-Newark, San Francisco-Oakland, Tulsa, Oklahoma City, Phoenix, Minneapolis-St. Paul, Seattle-Everett, San Diego, Detroit, and Chicago. Rural Native Americans were living on farms acquired during the allotment period or on 250 reservations, ranging from the huge Navajo Reservation in Arizona, New Mexico, and Utah with over 104,000 Navajo residents to one of several tiny California rancherias with fewer than ten Native American residents. There were 283 Federally recognized tribes in 1980, and the federal government held in trust 52 million acres of Native American land. However, these lands were shared with non-Native Americans to a considerable extent. Nationwide, Native Americans accounted for only 49 percent of those living on reservation land in 1980.*

---

*U.S. Bureau of the Census, *1980 Census of Population,* vol. 1, *General Population Characteristics* (Washington, D.C.: U.S. Government Printing Office, 1983), 1:300–303. Percentages ranged widely with particular reservations. In Arizona 91 percent of the total individuals living on reservation land were Native Americans, whereas in Washington State 83 percent of those living on reservations were non-Native American.

After thousands of years in the New World, Native American tribalism remains complex and diverse, with different languages, religions, customs, economies, and political styles still creating hundreds of separate ethnic loyalties. In addition to all the original centrifugal forces that helped to create tribalism, the processes of acculturation in the twentieth century—the rise of pan-Indian organizations, the migration from the reservations to the cities, the increasing ratio of mixed-bloods to full-bloods, and the conscious and unconscious pressures to assimilate—have brought even more diversity to tribal communities. In the 1980s, no less than in 1492, Native America is characterized by extraordinary variety.

Linguistic diversity still survives in the 1980s, even though English continues to gain ground as the primary language of most Native Americans. Indeed, in 1978, 65 percent of Native Americans spoke English as their primary language, 4 percent spoke Spanish, and perhaps 30 percent spoke a tribal language. By the mid-1970s, there were still forty native languages with more than one thousand fluent adherents each. The Athapascan languages of the Navajos and Apaches were the strongest, with more than 125,000 adherents, while more than 45,000 Chippewas still spoke Ojibwa, 25,000 spoke Algonquian languages (Delawares, Cheyennes, Kickapoos, Blackfeet, and Shawnees); 20,000 spoke Iroquoian languages (Wyandots, Oneidas, Mohawks, Senecas, and Cherokees); 20,000 spoke Muskhogean languages (Choctaws, Chickasaws, Creeks, and Seminoles); 13,000 spoke Pueblo languages (Zuñis, Taos, Kiowas, San Juan Pueblos, and San Ildefonso Pueblos); 17,000 spoke Shoshonean languages (Shoshones and Bannocks); and 25,000 spoke Siouan languages (Sioux, Osages, Poncas, and Crows). On the other hand, only 600 people still spoke the Caddoan languages (Wichitas, Caddos, Pawnees, and Arikaras), and 1,200 the Shahaptian languages of tribes such as the Nez Perce. Hundreds of other languages, like those of the many California tribes, had become extinct by 1980, however.

Living patterns also vary from tribe to tribe, depending upon the extent of the allotment programs, the success of relocation programs, and the pull of tribal and reservation life. During the twentieth century some tribes have been able to resist allotment and relocation, sustain the tribal population, and remain on the reservation. Early in the 1970s, more than 70 percent of the Tanoans, Keresans, Palouses, and Crows still lived on their reservations, as did more than 60 percent of the Navajos, Apaches, Papagos, Pimas, Hopis, Zuñis, Utes, and Warm Springs. On the other hand, because of allotment and relocation, less than 10 percent of the Achomawis, Chimarikos, Pit Rivers, Shastas, Caddos, Catawbas, Cherokees, Chickasaws, Choctaws, Comanches, Creeks, Mohawks, Kickapoos, Kiowas, Klamaths, Modocs, Miwoks, Ottawas, Pawnees, Pomos, Potawatomis, Wintuns, and Yokuts lived on tribal reservations. Some tribes, like the Navajos or the Sioux, had large and growing populations, while others had dwindled to only a handful of people. In California, for example, there were only 41 Chumashes living on the 100-acre Santa Ynez Reservation and only another 118 living elsewhere. Only two Kumeyaays were left on the 15,000-acre Campo Reservation of the Mission Band people. Perhaps 50 of the Mission Band lived with them. The 850-acre Inaja-Cosmit Reservation was abandoned when the last two Ipais left there in 1975.

Among some tribes the pull of ethnic loyalties remains very strong in the 1980s, while other tribes have ceased to exist as conscious ethnic communities. Among the Navajos, for example, ethnic identity is powerful. Most Navajos are still familiar with the native tongue and either live on or return frequently to the reservation. Even in the cities the Navajos confine most of their social contacts to other Navajos, marry endogamously, and avoid contact with non–Navajo Native American and pan-Indian organizations as well as non–Native American organizations. Most Sioux, whether on the South Dakota reservations or in the cities, similarly confine their social lives to contacts with other Sioux. Among the Pueblo people of the Southwest, tribal identities are especially strong, as are loyalties to traditional customs. The western Pueblos—Hopis, Hanos, Zuñis, Acomas, and Lagunas—remain loyal to their matrilineal clan systems; native tongues; religious ceremonialism; and emphasis on sobriety, control, and inoffensiveness. The Hopis of the "Second Mesa" in Arizona rarely marry non-Hopis and are extraordinarily loyal to traditional values.

Other tribes have adjusted to European American ways while maintaining tribal customs and values as well. On the Blackfeet Reservation in northern Montana, where just over 5,000 Native Americans live, only ten percent are full-bloods. Two communities coexist there, one highly acculturated to European American values and the other more traditionally oriented and concerned with participating in Native American activities, continuing the Blackfeet tradition of unlimited generosity, and speaking the Blackfeet language. The other group tends to reflect the acquisitive individualism of European America. The Warm Springs tribe of Oregon, once hunters and fishermen in the Cascade Mountains and the Columbia River Basin, have lost their former way of life, but they have built prosperity around timber, plywood, and tourism industries while preserving a strong sense of tribal identity. And 800 Havasupais are living on the Hualapai Reservation in Arizona, a land along the Colorado River and Havasu Creek in the Grand Canyon. Although many tribal customs have been forgotten, the reservation still exerts a powerful pull on the Havasupai people.

Some tribes have either completely forgotten the old ways or assimilated almost completely into the dominant society. In the Hoopa
Valley of northern California, the Hupas are rapidly acquiring
European American ways. Instead of using all timber income for tribal enterprises, they distribute the money on a per capita basis to individuals. Automobiles and every other conceivable item of European
American material culture have appeared on the reservation, along
with businesses to serve the needs of that culture. The Hupa language
finally disappeared in the 1970s, as did traditional ceremonies and
hunting methods. Still, the Hupas maintain a sense of peoplehood. In
contrast, some tribes have lost contact with their ethnicity altogether.
Such California tribes as the Nomlakis, Patwins, Yukis, and Nisenans
have forgotten ancient customs, abandoned the native language, and
even look upon themselves more as extended families than as members
of any particular tribe.

The great variety of Native American tribalism can best be seen
today in the religious practices and beliefs of Native American peoples. For thousands of years theology and ceremonialism divided
them, playing the major role in defining the unique identity of individual tribes. Among some tribes these ancient beliefs still survive.
Many Sioux still take comfort in the image of Wakan Tanka, the spirit
of life emanating from the Black Hills of South Dakota. Thousands of
Hopis, participating in kiva ceremonies, look to the sacred hole in the
kiva chamber as the sacred symbol of the emergence of the ancestral
twins from whom all Hopis are descended. The Taos in New Mexico
still look to Blue Lake as the center of the universe, the source of all
life. The western Pueblos conduct elaborate ceremonies to bring rain,
while eastern Pueblos use their ceremonies primarily to cure illness.
For most Pueblos, the Katcina Cult remains a powerful vehicle for
bringing rain and curing sickness. Among many Plains tribes, including the Crows of Montana, Sun Dance ceremonies continue, and each
summer thousands seek out their place in the universe. The Yumas of
Arizona annually hold the karok ceremony in which the images, personal effects, and names of the recently dead are cremated. And the
ceremonies of the California Mojaves still aim at interpreting dreams
and relating them to the questions of life.

The fusion of traditional tribal religions with Christianity has also
created a unique variety of spiritual practices. At Our Lady of the
Sioux Catholic Church at Pine Ridge, Sioux images of the peace pipe,
buffalo, and thunderbird have been added to the statues of Jesus
Christ, the sacred pipe has been substituted for the wine and wafer of
the Eucharist, and the Sun Dance vision quests occur alongside
Christian meditation. On the Fort Apache Indian Reservation, the
same White Mountain Apaches who often attend Protestant and
Catholic churches still conduct such rites of passage as the Sunrise

Dance for adolescent women, still bury their dead with personal possessions to equip them for the next life, and still trek each year to the peak of White Mountain to thank the gods with spruce offerings for their beautiful land. To nurture tribal unity and lessen sectarian factionalism, many Sioux have revived the Brotherhood of Christian Unity, practicing Christian faith along with traditional tribal religion. Finally, tens of thousands are active in the Native American Church, which fuses Christian symbols with peyote-induced visions.

Hundreds of thousands of assimilated Native Americans, especially those living in the cities, are faithful to various Christian denominations. In Bell Gardens, California, the Indian Revival Center, run by the Assembly of God, is the most active Native American organization in the Los Angeles area, recruiting members of many different tribes. Thousands of Native Americans have joined The Church of Jesus Christ of Latter-day Saints (the Mormon Church), and Native American congregations of Latter-day Saints exist in most large western cities. In various parts of the Southwest, where Spanish priests proselytized and built missions, and in parts of the Pacific Northwest where French missionaries did the same, tribes such as the Pueblos or Flatheads combine loyalty to Roman Catholicism with their tribal faiths. The same is true where Episcopalians, Baptists, Methodists, Presbyterians, and those of other denominations have worked among Native Americans.

Just as Native American diversity survives, so too will other trends continue. And the Native American population will increase. Mortality and morbidity rates will continue to decline, as they have for thirty years, and Native American income, education, and occupation levels will continue to rise. Pressures to develop Native American land will multiply, as will pressures to assimilate; but Native American impulses for self-determination will also grow stronger.

But no less today than three hundred years ago, Native American values are distinct from those of middle-class European American society. Taken together and compared to those of the dominant society, Native American values are a clear alternative to much of the thrust of western civilization. Twentieth-century Native American literature— through the writings of Vine Deloria, Jr., N. Scott Momaday, James Welch, Luther Standing Bear, Charles Eastman, Simon Ortiz, Black Elk, Ray Young Bear, Wamblee Wicasa, Wallace (Mad Bear) Anderson, and others—clearly shows that Native American values still stand out in sharp contrast to the individualism, acquisitive materialism, and private capitalism of European America. Although in a state of rapid change, the core of Native American culture survives.

Amid the major impulses of twentieth-century European American society—interest-group politics, specialization of labor, the decline of family and community, rapid technological change, and the social anomie of impersonal relationships—Native American culture defies the trend toward such contention and disharmony. Native American values lean toward a cosmic identity, a harmony of the individual with the tribe, the tribe with the land, and the land with the spirit of life in the universe. Culturally and historically, the circle symbolizes that harmony—the constant, cyclical dependability of nature. Writing in 1931, the Oglala Sioux holy man Black Elk said,

> You have noticed that everything an Indian does is in a circle, and that is because the Power of the World always works in circles, and everything tries to be round. In the old days ... the east gave us peace and light, the south gave warmth, the west gave rain, and the north with its cold and mighty wind gave us strength and endurance.... The sky is round.... The earth is round like a ball.... The wind, in its greatest power, whirls.... The sun comes forth and goes down again in a full circle. The moon does the same and both are round. Even the seasons form a great circle in their changing, and always come back again to where they were.*

So compelling is this sense of unity that many Native American tribes attribute all forms of human pain—physical illness, psychological confusion, evil, or natural disaster—to individual or tribal disharmony with nature. James Welch, through Yellow Calf, an elderly man, explains that the deer "are not happy with the way things are. They know what a bad time it is. They can tell by the moon when the world is cockeyed."† Native American medicine and religion have always worked and continue so today to restore and preserve harmony, guaranteeing political consensus within the tribe and tribal unity with the universe.

Central to the Native American quest for harmony is the sense of constancy, the timelessness and predictability of nature as the foundation of existence. Without beginning or end, the circle symbolizes eternity. For Native Americans, there is only one reality, and it transcends everything in its absoluteness. In the Sun Dance ceremonies the warriors try to plug into that reality, to comprehend it totally—indeed, to fuse their personality with it. That quest continues today. In *House Made of Dawn*, N. Scott Momaday describes a European American woman's attempt to fathom the meaning of a Pueblo corn dance:

> The dancers ... looked straight ahead, to the exclusion of everything ... they had not smiled.... They were not merely sad or formal or devout ... they were grave, distant, intent upon something that she could not see. Their eyes were held upon some vision out of range, something away in the end of distance, some reality that she did not know, or even suspect.... To see

---

*John G. Neihardt, *Black Elk Speaks: Being the Life Story of a Holy Man of the Oglala Sioux* (Lincoln: University of Nebraska Press, 1961), 198–99.

†James Welch, *Winter in the Blood* (New York: Harper and Row, 1974), 68.

beyond the landscape, beyond every shape and shadow and color. . . . That was to be free and finished, complete, spiritual.*

Neither time nor circumstance can alter that absoluteness, a phenomenon which non–Native Americans, in their compulsion to change things, cannot readily understand. Among the Cherokees, for example, there is a vast difference between "thinking" and "knowing." There is a finality to "knowing" about reality, a certainty to it implying acceptance and peace; but "thinking" implies process and continuation, the persistence of doubt, the probability of change, and the guarantee of dissonance. European Americans, in the opinion of the Cherokees, "think" a great deal but really "know" very little. Or as Herbert Blatchford, Navajo and founder of the National Indian Youth Council, expresses it,

the Indian does not project his aims and aspirations far into the distant future, but rather he thinks in terms of the present and the past so as not to disrupt the blessedness of harmony. Time is more a proving factor than a controlling factor to the Indian way of living.†

For any Native American individual, the quest for harmony and certainty begins with the tribe, "the people." Whether in the past centuries or in the twentieth century, many Native Americans have viewed the tribe in terms of some unique peoplehood—a chosen community not unlike the ancient Hebrew nation, a people different from all others. This view of tribal destiny, however, does not imply a superiority over all other people—just a profound sense of being different, special, and unique. The Navajos call themselves "Dine," meaning "the people," and the Biloxis identify themselves as "tanek aya," or the "first people." "Pai" means "people" to the Havasupais of the Grand Canyon. The Miwoks of California call themselves "koca," meaning "the people"; and "anishinabe," the Chippewas' name for themselves, means "original people." Property for most tribes is communal, as is welfare and survival; Native Americans nurture a powerful sense of mutual dependence and responsibility, and they condemn theft, abandonment, and cowardice as almost unforgiveable transgressions. Describing the need to identify with the tribe, Black Elk wrote that in

the old days when we were a strong and happy people, all our power came to us from the sacred hoop of the nation, and so long as the hoop was unbroken, the people flourished.‡

---

*N. Scott Momaday, *House Made of Dawn* (New York: Harper and Row, 1968), 36–37.

†Quoted in Shirley Hill Witt and Stan Steiner, eds., *The Way: An Anthology of American Indian Literature* (New York: Alfred A. Knopf, 1972), 176.

‡Neihardt, *Black Elk Speaks*, 198.

The advent of European American civilization—with relocation, assimilation, and intermarriage—broke the sacred hoop for many tribes, introducing contention and factionalism and making tribal consensus and unity more difficult to achieve. But the vision of "the people," the tribe with communal rather than individual values, survives in the twentieth century, still representing the views of most full-blood Native Americans.

Beyond harmony with the community, Native Americans seek harmony with the land, the home in which they live, die, and are buried. As Vine Deloria, Jr., has written, Native American religion differs from Christianity in its spatial dimension. While the Judeo-Christian tradition interprets religion in terms of linear time—the gradual unfolding of God's will on earth over thousands of years—Native Americans interpret religion in terms of a place where divinity has initiated natural life. Just as most Native Americans view their tribe as unique and special, they also look upon the tribal homeland with reverent spirituality and respect for the place where sacred forces are at work. Whether it is Eagle Nest Mountain and Rabbit Hole Mountain for the Cupeños in California, the Black Hills in South Dakota for the Sioux, Ozil Ligai in Arizona for the White Mountain Apaches, Blue Lake in New Mexico for the Taos, Madeline Island in Lake Superior for the Chippewas, the Colorado River and Grand Canyon in Arizona for the Havasupais, or the Black Mesa in Arizona for the Hopis, Native Americans have a special attachment for their homeland; and removal to the Great Plains in the 1830s or relocation to urban centers in the 1950s, 1960s, and 1970s has been a particularly wrenching experience. Combined with the concept of community, the concept of place gives Native Americans a sense of roots and belonging, a security unknown to most non–Native Americans on the move from state to state, city to city, farm to city, city to suburb, apartment to apartment, and house to house. Luther Standing Bear, a Sioux, writing in 1933, said that the

white man does not understand the Indian for . . . he does not understand America. He is too far removed from its formative processes. The roots of the tree of his life have not yet grasped the rock and soil. . . . But in the Indian the spirit of the land is still vested; it will be until other men are able to divine and meet its rhythm. Men must be born and reborn to belong. Their bodies must be formed of the dust of their forefathers' bones.*

The Native American homeland was inalienable, the residence of the spirit of the universe. In *The Way to Rainy Mountain,* N. Scott Momaday

---

*Luther Standing Bear, *Land of the Spotted Eagle* (Boston: Houghton Mifflin, 1933), 248.

describes the meaning of Rainy Mountain, a knoll on the plains of Oklahoma, to the Kiowa people.

All things on the plains are isolate; there is no confusion of objects in the eye, but one hill or one tree or one man. To look upon that landscape in the early morning, with the sun at your back, is to lose the sense of proportion. Your imagination comes to life, and this, you think, is where Creation was begun.*

Because of the sanctity of the land, Native Americans have for centuries relinquished it only with reluctance and foreboding, with the fear that non–Native Americans, out of touch with nature, will develop and damage it, upsetting the general harmony of life. An old holy woman of the Wintuns in California has condemned European Americans for their assault on nature.

The white people never cared for land or deer or bear. . . . White people plow up the ground, pull up the trees, kill everything. The tree says, "Don't. I am sore. Don't hurt me." But they chop it down and cut it up. The spirit of the land hates them. . . . Everywhere the white man has touched it, it is sore.†

Since the 1970s Native American leaders have been interested in developing reservation resources, but they are also concerned about the costs—financial and spiritual—of changing the land. They do not possess, of course, the implicit faith in technology characteristic of European American society. In *House Made of Dawn,* N. Scott Momaday epitomizes European American technology in Abel's description of a tank in World War II:

. . . Through the falling leaves, he saw the machine. It rose up behind the hill, black and massive, looming there in front of the sun. He saw it swell, deepen, and take shape on the skyline, as if it were some upheaval of the earth, the eruption of stone and eclipse, and all about it the glare, the cold perimeter of light, throbbing with leaves. For a moment it seemed apart from the land. . . . Then it came crashing down to the grade, slow as a waterfall, thunderous, surpassing impact, nestling almost into the splash and boil of debris.‡

The Native American concern for land has survived the arrival of European civilization. The earth is still alive, and all living things— mankind included—fit neatly and quietly into the whole: people to the tribe, the tribe to the land, and the land to the universe.

---

*Quoted in Frederick W. Turner III, ed., *The Portable North American Indian Reader* (New York: Penguin Books, 1973), 580.

†Quoted in Dorothy Lee, *Freedom and Culture* (Englewood Cliffs, N.J.: Prentice-Hall, 1959), 163–64.

‡Momaday, *House Made of Dawn,* 25.

In 1970, when the Peabody Coal Company began strip-mining Hopi and Navajo land at Black Mesa, Arizona, many tradition-conscious Hopis eloquently expressed the Native American love for the land—how religion, individuality, tribalism, and the environment all fused into one harmonious whole. Writing to President Richard Nixon, Thomas Banyacya, a Hopi traditionalist, said:

We, the true and traditional religious leaders, recognized as such by the Hopi People, maintain full authority over all land and life contained within the Western Hemisphere. We are granted our stewardship by virtue of our instruction as to the meaning of Nature, Peace, and Harmony as spoken to our People by Him, known to us as Massau'u, the Great Spirit, who long ago provided for us the sacred stone tablets which we preserve to this day. For many generations before the coming of the white man, for many generations before the coming of the Navajo, the Hopi People have lived in the sacred place known to you as the Southwest and known to us to be the spiritual center of our continent. Those of us of the Hopi Nation who have followed the path of the Great Spirit without compromise have a message which we are committed, through our prophecy, to convey to you.

The white man, through his insensitivity to the way of Nature, has desecrated the face of Mother Earth. The white man's advanced technological capacity has occurred as a result of his lack of regard for the spiritual path and for the way of all living things. The white man's desire for material possessions and power has blinded him to the pain he has caused Mother Earth by his quest for what he calls natural resources. And the path of the Great Spirit has become difficult to see by almost all men, even by many Indians who have chosen instead to follow the path of the white man. . . .

Today the sacred lands where the Hopi live are being desecrated by men who seek coal and water from our soil that they may create more power for the white man's cities. This must not be allowed to continue for if it does, Mother Nature will react in such a way that almost all men will suffer the end of life as they now know it. The Great Spirit said not to allow this to happen even as it was prophesied to our ancestors. The Great Spirit said not to take from the Earth—not to destroy living things. The Great Spirit, Massau'u, said that man was to live in Harmony and maintain a good clean land for all children to come. All Hopi People and other Indian Brothers are standing on this religious principle and the Traditional Spiritual Unity Movement today is endeavoring to reawaken the spiritual nature in Indian people throughout this land. Your government has almost destroyed our basic religion which actually is a way of life for all our people in this land of the Great Spirit. We feel that to survive the coming Purification Day, we must return to the basic religious principles and to meet together on this basis as leaders of our people.

Today almost all the prophecies have come to pass. Great roads like rivers pass across the landscape; man talks to man through the cobwebs of telephone lines; man travels along the roads in the sky in his airplanes; two great wars have been waged by those bearing the swastika or the rising sun; man is tampering with the Moon and the stars. Most men have strayed from the path shown to us by the Great Spirit. For Massau'u alone is great enough to portray the way back to Him.

It is said by the Great Spirit that if a gourd of ashes is dropped upon the Earth, that many men will die and that the end of this way of life is near at hand. We interpret this as the dropping of atomic bombs on Hiroshima and Nagasaki. We do not want to see this happen to any place or any nation again, but instead we should turn all this energy for peaceful uses, not for war.

We, the religious leaders and rightful spokesmen for the Hopi Independent Nation, have been instructed by the Great Spirit to express the invitation to the President of the United States and all spiritual leaders everywhere to meet with us and discuss the welfare of mankind so that Peace, Unity, and Brotherhood will become part of all men everywhere.*

After hundreds of years of conflict and competition with the values of an alien way of life, Native America perseveres.

---

*Quoted in T. C. McLuhan, ed., *Touch the Earth: A Self-Portrait of Indian Existence* (New York: Pocket Books, 1972), 170–71.

Suggested Readings

Angulo, Jaime de. *Indian Tales.* New York: A. A. Wyn, 1953.

Bataille, Gretchen M., and Charles L. P. Silet. *The Pretend Indians: Images of Native Americans in the Movies.* Ames: Iowa State University Press, 1980.

Ball, Eve. *Indeh: An Apache Odyssey.* Provo, Utah: Brigham Young University Press, 1980.

Cash, Joseph H., and Herbert T. Hoover, eds. *To Be an Indian: An Oral History.* New York: Holt, Rinehart, and Winston, 1971.

Chapman, Abraham, ed. *Literature of the American Indians: Views and Interpretations.* New York: New American Library, 1975.

Coe, Ralph R. *Sacred Circles: Two Thousand Years of North American Indian Art.* Seattle: University of Washington Press, 1977.

Debo, Angie. *A History of the Indians of the United States.* Norman: University of Oklahoma Press, 1977.

Deloria, Vine, Jr. *Custer Died for Your Sins: An Indian Manifesto.* New York: Macmillan, 1969.

————. *God Is Red.* New York: Grosset and Dunlap, 1973.

————. *We Talk, You Listen: New Tribes, New Turf.* New York: Macmillan, 1970.

Eastman, Charles. *Indian Boyhood.* New York: McClure, Phillips, 1902.

————. *The Indian Today: The Past and Future of the First American.* Garden City, N.Y.: Doubleday, Page, 1915.

————. *The Soul of the Indian: An Interpretation.* Lincoln: University of Nebraska Press, 1980.

Gibson, Arrell Morgan. *The American Indian: Prehistory to the Present.* Lexington, Mass.: D. C. Heath, 1980.

Gill, Sam D. *Sacred Words: A Study of Navajo Religion and Prayer.* Westport, Conn.: Greenwood Press, 1981.

Hertzberg, Hazel W. *The Search for an American Indian Identity: Modern Pan-Indian Movements.* Syracuse, N.Y.: Syracuse University Press, 1971.

Hill, Ruth Beebe. *Hanta Yo.* New York: Doubleday, 1979.

Kilpatrick, Jack F., and Anna G. Kilpatrick. *Run Toward the Nightland: Magic of the Oklahoma Cherokee.* Dallas: Southern Methodist University Press, 1967.

Lee, Dorothy. *Freedom and Culture.* Englewood Cliffs, N.J.: Prentice-Hall, 1959.

Linden, George. "Dakota Philosophy." *American Studies* 18 (Fall 1977).

McLuhan, T. C., ed. *Touch the Earth: A Self-Portrait of Indian Existence.* New York: Pocket Books, 1972.

McNeley, James K. *Holy Wind in Navajo Philosophy.* Tucson: University of Arizona Press, 1981.

Momaday, N. Scott. *House Made of Dawn.* New York: Harper and Row, 1968.

————. *The Way to Rainy Mountain.* Albuquerque: University of New Mexico Press, 1969.

Neihardt, John G. *Black Elk Speaks: Being the Life Story of a Holy Man of the Oglala Sioux.* Lincoln: University of Nebraska Press, 1961.

Powell, Peter J. *Sweet Medicine: The Continuing Role of the Sacred Arrows, the Sun Dance, and the Sacred Buffalo Hat in Northern Cheyenne History.* Norman: University of Oklahoma Press, 1969.

Powers, William K. *Oglala Religion.* Lincoln: University of Nebraska Press, 1977.

Sanders, Thomas E., and Walter W. Peek. *Literature of the American Indian.* Beverly Hills, Calif.: Glencoe Press, 1976.

Spade, Watt, and Willard Walker. *Cherokee Stories.* Middletown, Conn.: Wesleyan University Press, 1966.

Spicer, Edward H., ed. *Perspectives in American Indian Culture Change.* Chicago: University of Chicago Press, 1961.

Standing Bear, Luther. *Land of the Spotted Eagle.* Boston: Houghton Mifflin, 1933.

————. *My People, the Sioux.* Lincoln: University of Nebraska Press, 1975.

Tedlock, Dennis, and Barbara Tedlock, eds. *Teachings from the American Earth: Indian Religion and Philosophy.* New York: Liveright, 1975.

Trimmer, Joseph F. "Native Americans and the American Mix: N. Scott Momaday's *House Made of Dawn.*" *Indiana Social Studies Quarterly* 28 (Autumn 1975).

Turner, Frederick W. III, ed. *The Portable North American Indian Reader.* New York: Penguin Books, 1973.

U.S. Department of Commerce. *Federal and State Indian Reservations: An EDA Handbook.* Washington, D.C.: U.S. Government Printing Office, 1971.

Vizenor, Gerald. *Anishinabe Nagamon.* Minneapolis: University of Minnesota Press, 1965.

Washburn, Wilcomb E. *The Indian in America.* New York: Harper and Row, 1975.

Wax, Murray L., and Rosalie H. Wax. "Religion among American Indians." *Annals of the American Academy of Political and Social Science* 436 (March 1978).

Welch, James. *Winter in the Blood.* New York: Harper and Row, 1974.

Wilson, Raymond. "The Writings of Ohiyesa—Charles Alexander Eastman, M.D., Santee Sioux." *South Dakota History* 6 (Winter 1975).

Witt, Shirley Hill, and Stan Steiner, eds. *The Way: An Anthology of American Indian Literature.* New York: Alfred A. Knopf, 1972.

Index